OXFORD WO

ROMAN

WACE (*b.* after 1100, *d.* 1174 × 83), historian and poet, was born in Jersey. Some have considered him to have been of noble birth, but this has not been substantiated nor has the misnomer Robert Wace, which dates back to the eighteenth century. According to autobiographical passages in his last work, the *Roman de Rou* (1160–*c.*1174), a history of the Norman dukes from the founding of the duchy to 1106, which drew on Latin sources, including the Norman histories of William of Jumièges, William of Poitiers, and Dudo of St Quentin, and the English histories of William of Malmesbury and Eadmer of Canterbury, as well as oral sources, Wace was taken to Caen as a young boy for religious training. He continued his studies in the Île-de-France, later returning to Caen to devote himself to a literary career; in the *Rou*, he refers to himself as a *clerc lisant* (a reading or teaching cleric). Although none of the lyric poems which Wace says he wrote appear to have survived, three hagiographical texts are extant from the earlier part of his career: the *Vie de sainte Marguerite* and the *Conception Nostre Dame* (both *c.*1130–40) and the *Vie de saint Nicolas* (*c.*1150). In 1155, Wace completed the *Roman de Brut*, the oldest extant Old French chronicle of the early kings of Britain. Based largely on the vulgate and First Variant versions of Geoffrey of Monmouth's *Historia regum Britanniae* (*c.*1138), it contains material from oral sources and possibly also other written sources, including the earliest extant reference to King Arthur's Round Table. In his Middle English adaptation of Wace's *Brut* (*c.*1200), Laȝamon reports that Wace offered the *Roman de Brut* to Eleanor of Aquitaine, consort of Henry II; however, no other evidence has yet been found to support Laȝamon's claim. Wace played an important role in the development of the French language through his use of an especially large and varied vocabulary and in the development of Old French narrative, primarily Arthurian romance.

GLYN S. BURGESS is Emeritus Professor of French at the University of Liverpool. He has translated *The Lais of Marie de France* (with Keith Busby), *The Song of Roland*, the three twelfth-century romances of antiquity, and the *Roman de Rou* of Wace (2002). In 1990 he was made a *Chevalier des Palmes Académiques* and he is an honorary President of the International Courtly Literature Society.

JEAN BLACKER is Professor Emerita of French, Kenyon College. Her recent publications include *Wace: The Hagiographical Works* (with Glyn Burgess and Amy Ogden) and *Court and Cloister: Essays in the Short Narrative in Honor of Glyn S. Burgess* (with Jane Taylor). Her current research is on the uses of King Arthur in French and Latin historical narrative of the twelfth and thirteenth centuries, foundation myths, origins, and identities in the legendary history of Britain.

OXFORD WORLD'S CLASSICS

For over 100 years Oxford World's Classics have brought readers closer to the world's great literature. Now with over 700 titles—from the 4,000-year-old myths of Mesopotamia to the twentieth century's greatest novels—the series makes available lesser-known as well as celebrated writing.

The pocket-sized hardbacks of the early years contained introductions by Virginia Woolf, T. S. Eliot, Graham Greene, and other literary figures which enriched the experience of reading. Today the series is recognized for its fine scholarship and reliability in texts that span world literature, drama and poetry, religion, philosophy, and politics. Each edition includes perceptive commentary and essential background information to meet the changing needs of readers.

OXFORD WORLD'S CLASSICS

WACE

Roman de Brut

Translated by

GLYN S. BURGESS

With an Introduction and Notes by

JEAN BLACKER

OXFORD
UNIVERSITY PRESS

Great Clarendon Street, Oxford, OX2 6DP,
United Kingdom

Oxford University Press is a department of the University of Oxford.
It furthers the University's objective of excellence in research, scholarship,
and education by publishing worldwide. Oxford is a registered trade mark of
Oxford University Press in the UK and in certain other countries

Published in the United States of America by Oxford University Press
198 Madison Avenue, New York, NY 10016, United States of America

British Library Cataloguing in Publication Data
Data available

Library of Congress Control Number: 2023932988

ISBN 978–0–19–287126–8

Printed and bound in the UK by
Clays Ltd, Elcograf S.p.A.

ACKNOWLEDGEMENTS

WE should like to express our gratitude to all those who have assisted us during the time we have been working on this volume. In addition to our sponsoring editor at Oxford University Press, Luciana O'Flaherty, the copy editor Rowena Anketell, Elizabeth Chadwick, Emma Varley, the proofreader Dorothy McCarthy, typesetters, and reviewers, special thanks go to Leslie Brook, Edwina Finefrock, Jack Finefrock, Janet McArthur, and Ian Short.

CONTENTS

INTRODUCTION

Life and Work

WACE'S *Roman de Brut* (1155) can be seen as the gateway to the history of the Britons for the vernacular worlds, both French and English—and thus to Arthurian history as seen in one of his extremely popular Latin sources, Geoffrey of Monmouth's *Historia Regum Britanniae* (late 1130s). For historical texts the *Brut* was a foundational work, an inspiration for a series of anonymous verse *Brut*s of the late twelfth and thirteenth centuries and for the Anglo-Norman Prose *Brut*—the most widely read French vernacular text on this material in medieval England—as well as a forerunner of the Middle English *Brut* tradition, including Laȝamon's English verse *Brut* (*c.*1200). Wace's poem thus inaugurates *Brut* traditions in verse and in prose, in historiography and in literature.

In addition to having been most likely considered to be a historical text by Wace and his contemporaries, as well as by historians after him, the *Roman de Brut* is also one of the fundamental works of medieval French literature, as it introduces to the French-speaking public of England and France the theme of King Arthur and his court. It also includes the first written account of the Round Table, which Wace developed with remarkable inventiveness. In the Middle Ages the distinction between romance and history was not as clear-cut as it is today; for example, there were close thematic, lexical, and structural ties between the *Brut* and the *romans antiques* which we consider fictional, the *Thèbes* (1150), the *Eneas* (1160), and the *Troie* (1165) (also referred to as the *romans d'antiquité*). The *Roman de Brut* also contains the earliest example of the term *roman* with the meaning 'French vernacular text' (v. 14866). This term was soon applied to the genre of romance itself.[1] A number of themes are common to both historical writing and literature—family, war, chivalry, kingship, power, wealth, the possession of land, the power of love, marriage—themes that would become fundamental to the development of European

[1] For further reading, see the section 'Editions and Translations of the *romans antiques*' in the Select Bibliography, xli.

literature over the centuries. One of the most prolific of twelfth-century vernacular authors, Wace is best known for his two verse chronicles (histories), the *Roman de Brut*[2] and the *Roman de Rou* (1160–*c.*1174), but he is also the author of three surviving hagiographical works, the *Conception Nostre Dame* (*c.*1130–*c.*1140), and the first French lives of St Margaret (also *c.*1130–*c.*1140) and St Nicholas (*c.*1150).[3]

Wace was born in Jersey, probably sometime between 1100 and 1110, perhaps closer to 1110 as it appears that he was still writing in the mid-1170s. As nothing definite is heard of him after *c.*1174, it is possible that he died between 1174 and the early 1180s. In the surviving manuscripts of his works his name occurs in a number of forms: Wace, Gace(s), Gasce, Grace, Guace(s), Vacce, Vace, Vuace.[4] He tells us that he was from Jersey though we don't know how long he lived there. While still quite young, he was taken to the ducal capital of Caen and sent to school there (in his words he was 'mis a letres', *Rou*, III, v. 5307). In Caen he could have attended the school of the abbey of Saint-Étienne, which took boys from the secular world and educated them alongside those who were destined for the cloister.[5] Wace would have studied Latin at this school, and it was perhaps at an early age that he learned to translate and adapt Latin narratives, skills he developed into such a fundamental aspect of his career as a writer.

The information that Wace was born in Jersey and studied in Caen comes from a passage in the *Rou* (III, vv. 5299–318); other passages provide further biographical information. He also tells us that he was

[2] *Le Roman de Brut de Wace*, ed. Ivor D. O. Arnold, 2 vols (Paris: SATF, 1938–40); *Wace's Roman de Brut: A History of the British; Text and Translation*, trans. Judith Weiss (Exeter: University of Exeter Press, 1999; 2nd edn 2002) (contains Arnold's text in facing page with emendations and notes; see xxv–xxvii on Weiss's methodology for the presentation of the text).

[3] For further reading, see the section 'Editions and Translation of Wace's Other Works' in the Select Bibliography, xl–xli.

[4] Although we cannot be certain whether the name Wace was a personal name or a family name, it has recently been demonstrated that the name 'Robert', used in connection with this author, was a misnomer (see Hans-Erich Keller, 'Le Mirage Robert Wace', *Zeitschrift für romanische Philologie*, 100 (1990), 465–6).

[5] See Judith Everard, 'Wace, the Historical Background: Jersey in the Twelfth Century', in Glyn S. Burgess and Judith Weiss (eds), *Maistre Wace: A Celebration: Proceedings of the International Colloquium Held in Jersey 10–12 September 2004* (St Helier: Société Jersiaise, 2006), 10.

educated in France, which at that time was the area now known as the Île-de-France. While it is possible that he went to Chartres, Paris provided the finest available education in theology and in the subjects of the trivium (grammar, logic, and rhetoric), so it was probably in this environment, which was developing as a new centre of royal government as well as of learning, that he qualified as a magister, thus acquiring the right to teach (*licentia docendi*). He subsequently returned to Caen where, he tells us, he began to compose works in the vernacular. As vernacular literature was already established throughout the Norman and Anglo-Norman realm, Caen may have been a place where translations and adaptations from Latin had more appeal than they did to the Latin-based intelligentsia in Paris. Unlike monks, who were obliged to write their chronicles and other works in Latin, Wace, as an independent secular author, would have had the opportunity to write in French.[6]

One of Wace's best-known statements about himself is that he held the office of *clerc lisant* during the time of three Henrys: Henry I, Henry II, and Henry the Young King (who was crowned in June 1170, but never lived to reign) (*Rou*, III, vv. 179–80). The post of *clerc lisant* seems to have been a secular one. Its duties are not clear, but they may well have involved studying, teaching, interpreting and reciting texts, plus various forms of administrative tasks, such as acting as a notary.

Wace presumably continued to live in Caen, but at some unknown date (probably in the mid- or late 1160s) King Henry II granted him a prebend (*provende*) in Bayeux (*Rou*, III, vv. 171–5, 5313–18). Just what this prebend consisted of is not clear. A prebend could be an endowment of lands, churches, or rights from the estates of abbeys or cathedrals. In Wace's case it seems to have been the status of

[6] Although the *Roman de Brut* is often considered to be an Anglo-Norman text (see e.g. Ruth J. Dean, *Anglo-Norman Literature: A Guide to Texts and Manuscripts*, with the collaboration of Maureen B. M. Boulton (London: ANTS, 1999), 2–4), since nine of the nineteen complete or nearly complete manuscripts are Anglo-Norman, and of the fifteen incomplete copies that survive either as extracts or as manuscript fragments ten are Anglo-Norman, the author's language was most likely Norman-based French (the number of fragments and extracts increases if different extracts within the same manuscript are counted separately). We are indebted to Ian Short for his clarification of the most recent count of *Brut* MSS, as well as for the assessment that Wace's language was a 'Norman-based Schriftsprache' (private communication).

non-dignitary canon at the cathedral of Bayeux.[7] He may have had no specific duties other than the requirement to be present to witness abbey transactions, but he might also have been obliged by the bishop to attend monthly chapter meetings in Bayeux. The distance from Caen to Bayeux is under 30 kilometres, so he could have continued to live in Caen.[8] We don't know why Henry gave Wace the prebend; it could have been a reward for the progress he had made on the *Rou* or a belated acknowledgement of his earlier *Brut*, which had been completed in 1155.

Those seeking further confirmation concerning Wace's presence as a cleric in Caen or Bayeux may consult several charter attestations that include the name Wascius (or variants). There are four charters of interest from the cartulary of the cathedral of Bayeux, printed as *Livre noir*, and those of the priory of Le Plessis-Grimoult and the abbey of Saint-Martin de Troarn, which remain in manuscript.[9] The earliest occurrence (although it is a copy in a much later document) is an agreement, dated February 1169, between Bishop Henry of Bayeux (1165–1204) and Abbot Gislebert of Saint-Martin de Troarn, which resolves a dispute over the benefices and churches that formed the liberty of the abbey. A Wacius (the form in the text is 'Wacio', as attestations are recorded in the ablative case) is among the witnesses named as canons. In another of Bishop Henry's charters, now dated *c.*1170–3, a 'magister Wacius' is a witness to the confirmation by the bishop of Bayeux and others of the privileges and possessions of the

[7] The cathedral of Bayeux had extensive holdings, so, if lands were involved, Wace's prebend could have been elsewhere in the Bessin, and possibly in Caen. In his first reference to the prebend Wace states that King Henry had it given to him ('cil me fist doner . . . une provende', *Roman de Rou*, III, vv. 173–4) and in the second reference that it was simply given to him by Henry ('m'en fu donee . . . une provende', *Rou*, III, vv. 5315–16). For further biographical information, see the general introduction to Jean Blacker, Glyn S. Burgess, and Amy V. Ogden, *Wace, The Hagiographical Works: The Conception Nostre Dame and the Lives of St Margaret and St Nicholas* (Leiden: Brill, 2013), 1–8.

[8] In its regular business the cathedral would have dealt with such things as property transactions with other religious houses or confirmations of donations by benefactors.

[9] These attestations have recently been examined by Judith Everard, who has redated them where necessary and printed summaries and witness lists (see the appendix 'Charter Attestations by Canon Wace', in Valentine Fallan with Judith Everard, 'Master Wace: A Cross-Channel Prosopographer for the Twelfth Century?', in David Roffe (ed.), *The English and Their Legacy, 900–1200: Essays in Honour of Ann Williams* (Woodbridge: Boydell, 2012), 61–77, at 75–7.

regular canons of the priory of Le Plessis-Grimoult. This wording conforms to Wace's designation of himself as 'Maistre / Mestre Wace'.[10]

In terms of Wace's links to known individuals or families, in the *Rou* he makes a reference to his father, whom as a boy he heard say that the number of ships that set off from Saint-Valéry, in preparation for the invasion of England, was seven hundred less four (III, vv. 6423–8). Was he then the son or grandson of a shipbuilder who worked on William's invasion fleet? Or did his father just hear this information from someone who was involved in the crossing? Also, does Wace say that his maternal grandfather or great-grandfather was Turstin [or Thurstan], chamberlain to William the Conqueror's father, Robert the Magnificent of Normandy (1018–35) (*Roman de Rou*, III, vv. 3223–5)? *Rou* MS B (Paris, Bibliothèque nationale de France, fr. 375) reads: 'De par sa mere fu mis auves' ('was my ancestor through his mother'). This led literary historian Gaston Paris to suggest emending the line to read 'de par ma mere fu mi aives' ('was my ancestor through my mother').[11] Whether Wace was related to Turstin, as grandson or great-grandson, must remain speculation.

Wace could have been connected to the Wac/Wach/Vac family that held lands not only in Jersey and Guernsey, but also in the Bessin, the Cotentin, and parts of England. One member of this family was a Roger Wac, who in 1154 held lands in St Jean des Chênes in Jersey from the abbey of Saint-Sauveur in the Cotentin and has previously been noted as possibly connected to Wace.[12] Also named in earlier

[10] See the *Conception Nostre Dame*, v. 2; the *Life of St Nicholas*, v. 1546; and the four examples in the *Brut*, vv. 7, 3823, 13282, 14866, and in the *Rou* (*Chronique Ascendante*, v. 3, II, v. 443; III, vv. 158, 11439).

[11] MS A (British Library, Royal 4.C.XI) of Wace's *Rou* states that 'Tosteins, ki *ert* ses chamberlencs, | De sa chambre maistre gardeins | —De par sa mere fu sis aives' ('Turstin, who was his chamberlain, chief guardian of his chamber, was his ancestor [grandfather/great-grandfather] through his mother'). The phrase 'through his mother' probably means on his mother's side. The emendation suggested by Gaston Paris carries a good deal of conviction, but it cannot be regarded as indisputable; see Gaston Paris, 'Sur un épisode d'Aimeri de Narbonne', *Romania*, 9/3 (1880), 515–46, at 526–7. The Old French term *aive* has the general sense of 'ancestor, forebear', but it can also mean 'grandfather'.

[12] See e.g. Glyn S. Burgess, introduction to his translation of Anthony J. Holden's text of *Wace, the Roman de Rou* (St Helier: Société Jersiaise, 2002), xix n. 21.

studies is a later canon of Bayeux, Richard Wace.[13] Canon Richard, whose name occurs in the form 'Ricardus Wacii' ('Richard son of Wacius'), could have been the poet's son (or nephew); for if Wace were in lower (secular) orders, he would have been able to marry and have children.[14]

It would seem that Wace began to compose vernacular works after his return from France to Caen. In the *Rou* he twice mentions writing *sirventes* (lyric poems not concerning love), but these have either not survived or have not yet been identified in any manuscript (II, v. 4148; III, v. 153).[15] Rather than lyric poems, Wace appears to have preferred what he calls *romans*, that is lengthier works in the vernacular language, translated and adapted from Latin sources (including his religious narratives). Moreover, in spite of their modern titles containing the word *roman*, the *Brut* and the *Rou* still rely heavily on Latin histories as sources, and they are fundamentally chronicles composed *en romanz*, rather than stories of love and chivalry as in the case of the romances of Chrétien de Troyes and other contemporaries.

As far as the end of Wace's career is concerned, we know that he began the *Rou* in 1160 (*Chronique Ascendante*, vv. 1–4).[16] At some

[13] While there is no direct evidence linking Richard Wace with Roger Wac, or linking our author to either of them, Valentine Fallan has suggested that 'if Wace was (or thought he was) a family member this would present a cohesive picture of the many co-incidences of names and holdings' found in the *Rou* (Fallan with Everard, 'Master Wace', 66).

[14] Fallan has identified several individuals of different generations with the surname Wac (sometimes Wach, Wasce, or Vac) in Jersey, Guernsey, the Bessin, the Cotentin, and parts of England. She has demonstrated that most are related to the Roger Wac who held the fief of St Jean des Chênes in Jersey. The fact that other combatants named in the *Rou*, and unknown in 1066, are now identified as contemporaries—even neighbours—of Wace, suggests that he was at the very least a member of the same feudal milieu, that of the vicomtes of the Bessin and earls of Chester. For further details, see Fallan with Everard, 'Master Wace'.

[15] The full texts read: 'Mais (o)re puis jeo lunges penser, | Livres escrire e translater, | Faire rumanz e serventeis' ('But now I can put in a great deal of effort, write and translate books, and compose [works in the vernacular] and *serventeis*', *Rou*, III, vv. 151–3); 'A Chaem lunges conversai, | De romanz faire m'entremis' ('I stayed in Caen for a long time and set about composing works in the vernacular', III, vv. 5310–11).

[16] The *Chronique Ascendante des ducs de Normandie* provides a summary of the *Roman de Rou* in reverse chronological order, beginning with the year 1066 very briefly, then mentioning the generosity of Henry II and Eleanor, Henry's prowess, a reference to the Siege of Rouen in 1174, going back to Rollo in the early tenth century. However, its status within Wace's oeuvre and its date of composition remain uncertain.

stage, perhaps around the early or middle 1160s, he stopped working on it, only resuming his task somewhat later, perhaps around 1170. The *Chronique* (v. 62) mentions the Siege of Rouen, a historical event that took place in 1174 and, although we have no precise confirmation of this, Wace could have abandoned the *Rou* at around this date. In the final lines of the *Rou*, he tells us that King Henry II withdrew his patronage and commissioned a new version by a Maistre Beneeit, probably the Benoît de Sainte-Maure, who a few years earlier had composed the *Roman de Troie* (*Rou*, III, vv. 11420–4). We do not know why Henry chose to act in this way.[17] At this stage Wace had probably been composing vernacular works for well over forty years, yet he clearly still thought he had more output left in him. By the time he finished writing, romance as a genre was in full swing, and he himself had had a significant influence on it,[18] saints' lives were enjoying great popularity and, following in the footsteps of Geffrei Gaimar, who had written his now-lost *Estoire des Bretuns* in the 1130s, the earliest extant Old French chronicle,[19] he had completed two lengthy historical works. Thus, Wace's range is extraordinary, having been a *clerc lisant*, a recognized author for nearly a half-century, and a pioneer in at least two major genres: hagiography—including *enfances*, *passio*, and miracle narratives—and chronicles. We also learn that Wace participated in important political events—in connection with recent Norman history, not

[17] Suggestions include the possibility of Wace's advancing age; that perhaps Wace preferred truth to the propaganda desired by Henry; perhaps he showed favouritism towards Henry's brother, Robert Curthose, who disputed Henry's right to the throne; or perhaps, simply, Wace's progress was just frustratingly slow and Henry's patience ran out (see *The History of the Norman People: Wace's Roman de Rou*, trans. Glyn S. Burgess (Woodbridge: Boydell, 2004), Introduction, xii-xiii, and Jean Blacker, '"La Geste est grande, longue e grieve a translater": History for Henry II', *Romance Quarterly*, 37 (1990), 387–96). Whatever the reason, we know that Wace was not happy to be cast aside in favour of a rival. He brings his work to an end on a somewhat disgruntled note and with an enigmatic final statement: 'Quin velt avant faire sin face' ('Anyone who wants to do more, let him do it', *Rou*, III, v. 11440).

[18] On Wace's influence on romance, see esp. Margaret M. Pelan, *L'Influence du Brut de Wace sur les romanciers français de son temps* (Paris: Droz, 1931; repr. Geneva: Slatkine, 1974). See also Geffrei Gaimar, *Estoire des Engleis/History of the English*, ed. and trans. Ian Short (Oxford: Oxford University Press, 2009).

[19] Geffrei Gaimar's recent editor, Ian Short, dates the *Estoire des Engleis* to between March 1136 and April 1137 (edn., xii).

just the history of the Britons—such as the moving of the remains of dukes Richard I and Richard II to a more elevated position behind the main altar at Sainte-Trinité in Fécamp, in 1162, in the presence of Henry II (*Rou*, III, vv. 2241–6).

The *Rou* is also important for our understanding of the *Roman de Brut*, given the amount of self-reflective material Wace includes.[20] For example, in the *Rou* Wace tells us that he travelled to the forest of Brocéliande in Brittany to see 'Arthurian sites' for himself, and felt like a fool for having done so since he didn't find any:

Issi soleit jadis ploveir	Thus in days past, it used to rain
En la forest e environ,	In the forest, and around,
mais jo ne sai par quel raison.	But I don't know why.
La seut l'en les fees veeir,	People used to see fairies there,
se li Breton nos dient veir,	If the Bretons are telling the truth,
e altres mer(e)veilles plusors;	And many other marvels;
aires i selt aveir *d'ostors*	There used to be hawks' nests there
e de grant cers mult grant plenté,	And large stags in abundance,
mais vilain ont *tot* deserté.	But peasants have ruined it all.
La alai jo merveilles querre,	I went there looking for marvels,
vi la forest e vi la terre,	I saw the forest and I saw the land,
merveill quis, mais nes trovai,	I sought marvels, but I didn't find any,
fol m'en revinc, fol i alai;	I came back a fool, and went a fool;
fol i alai, fol m'en revinc,	I went a fool, I came back a fool,
folie quis, por fol me tin*c*.	I sought folly, I considered myself a fool.

(*Rou*, III, vv. 6384–98)[21]

Wace comments discouragingly on the 'fables' told by the Breton tale-tellers—here 'Breton' probably means 'Breton' and not 'Briton', but, since the same form is used for both in Old French, it can often be ambiguous[22]—because he was concerned to relate Arthurian material as he heard it, while at the same time worrying about the

[20] On the self-reflective material that Wace includes in the *Rou*, see esp. J. Blacker, 'Narrative Decisions and Revisions in the *Roman de Rou*', in Burgess and Weiss (eds), *Maistre Wace*, 55–71.

[21] Blacker's translation. Other translations of the *Rou* are from Burgess's 2002 edn. Translations from the *Brut* in this Introduction are from the prose translation in this Oxford World's Classics edition.

[22] See n. 30.

'unprovability' of that material, as well as of Merlin's predictions.[23] In fact, Wace's concern for the 'unprovability' of the Arthurian material as well as all historical narrative can be seen as quite modern, since he was apparently aware that the past was 'unrecoverable', that language always stands between the 'facts of history' and historians, though historians should always try to reproduce what they can in order to move human knowledge forward.[24]

The Roman de Brut *in Context*

Wace himself tells us at the very end of his work (vv. 14865–6) that the *Brut* was completed in 1155, but a work of this length would have been started several years earlier, perhaps shortly after the completion of the *Nicholas*, around 1150.

Although we should not—and will not—dismiss the literary context of this very complex text, Wace's *Brut* should ultimately be viewed less as a precursor to the medieval French romance tradition[25]

[23] With respect to Merlin's refusal to pronounce on Arthur's 'death', Weiss aptly comments: 'One accords a certain respect to Wace's skeptical reporting of Arthur's end and the legends of his survival; the only certain thing here is uncertainty itself' (Weiss, xxii).

[24] Wace's provision of multiple perspectives (in the *Rou* primarily) reveals an apparent lack of confidence in any historian's ability to access the 'absolute truth', which exists beyond the 'facts' narrated in texts—because those narrations are perforce dependent on the imperfect tool of language—and is a very modern position, in fact a postmodern one; an outstanding characteristic of the postmodern condition, according to Jean-François Lyotard, is the disbelief in *métarécits*, great heroes, great dangers, great goals ('En simplifiant à l'extrême, on tient pour "postmoderne" l'incrédulité à l'égard des métarécits . . . La fonction narrative perd ses foncteurs, le grand héros, les grands périls, les grands périples et le grand but', *La Condition postmoderne: Rapport sur le savoir* (Paris: Éditions de Minuit, 1979), 7–8). Gabrielle Spiegel reminds us that 'if, as Lyotard argues, there are no longer any master narratives, still less are there any certainties about the nature and status of history itself, whether as an object of study or a subject of practice. Our confidence in the totality and ultimate unity of the greater historical enterprise is gone. Like so much else, history has been subject to the fracturing and fragmentation that has beset all aspects of postmodern thought. Not only are there no master narratives, there is no consensus of even the possibility of historical knowledge uncontaminated by the hermeneutic circle' (Spiegel, *The Past as Text: The Theory and Practice of Medieval Historiography* (Baltimore: Johns Hopkins University Press, 1997), xxi-xxii).

[25] For scholarship on Wace's *Brut*, see Blacker, *Wace: A Critical Bibliography*, with the collaboration of Glyn S. Burgess (St Helier: Société Jersiaise, 2008), 46–118.

and more as a historical text, a central conduit of the Latin tradition to the Anglo-Norman, Continental French, and English vernacular historical traditions.[26] The *Brut* introduced the Arthurian world, a world that was to capture the imagination of the vernacular public of Wace's time, all the way up to the modern period, where we see a burgeoning of scholarship on Geoffrey of Monmouth in particular, and Arthur, as well as in popular culture, novels, and films centring on versions of the Arthurian world—the 'Arthurian industry', as Arthurian scholar Richard Barber has aptly termed it.[27]

When seen in the larger context of the Galfridian tradition (that is, Geoffrey of Monmouth's and associated texts),[28] among the many distinguishing thematic features of the *Brut* are Wace's tendency to 'equalize' the enemies, that is to 'depoliticize' the presentation of factions in favour of a more universal, fatalistic view;[29] the creation of

[26] In terms of the English historical tradition—which we do not have space to discuss here—the earliest text is Laȝamon's English verse *Brut* (*c.*1200). See esp. Françoise H. M. Le Saux, *Layamon's Brut: The Poem and Its Sources* (Cambridge: D. S. Brewer, 1989); Le Saux (ed.), *The Text and Tradition of Layamon's Brut* (Cambridge: D. S. Brewer, 1994); Lawman, *Brut*, trans. Rosamund Allen (New York: St Martin's Press, 1992), introd., xiii-xxxvi; and Rosamund Allen, Jane Roberts, and Carole Weinberg (eds), *Reading Laȝamon's Brut: Approaches and Explorations* (Amsterdam: Rodopi, 2013).

[27] Richard Barber, *King Arthur: Hero and Legend* (New York: St Martin's Press, 1961; repr. 1986), 199.

[28] The Galfridian tradition refers to Geoffrey of Monmouth's vulgate *Historia* (most recently edited by Michael D. Reeve and translated by Neil Wright, in Geoffrey of Monmouth, *The History of the Kings of Britain: An Edition and Translation of the De gestis Britonum [Historia Regum Britanniae]* (Woodbridge: Boydell, 2007)) and the First Variant, which Wace also used. The majority of scholars concur that Geoffrey's text came first (*c.*1140), but some, including most recently David Burchmore, the first English translator of the text, argue that the First Variant was the original and Geoffrey's vulgate derivative (Geoffrey of Monmouth, *The History of the Kings of Britain: The First Variant Version* (Cambridge, MA: Harvard University Press, 2019)). See also the lengthy introduction by Neil Wright, including work on Wace, in his critical edition of *The Historia Regum Britannie of Geoffrey of Monmouth, II: The First Variant Version* (Cambridge: D. S. Brewer 1988), and R. William Leckie, Jr's chapter on Wace and Laȝamon's English verse *Brut* (*c.*1200) in *The Passage of Dominion: Geoffrey of Monmouth and the Periodization of Insular History in the Twelfth Century* (Toronto: University of Toronto Press, 1981), 102–19.

[29] Some scholars have misinterpreted my intentions in coining this phrase as applied to Wace's *Brut*. I did not mean that Wace eliminated all political content from his text, but that, for example, he tended to praise figures such as Julius Caesar, whom Geoffrey viewed as enemies of the Britons, as well as neutralizing Geoffrey's animosity towards the Saxons, and other groups or individuals, by focusing on etymology, genealogy, and geographical definitions, as if to set the history in a more universalizing context. The addition of nostalgia, a major theme of the Norman poet, intertwined with the theme of the

a continuum of power, ranging from Gormund's nearly total destruction of the Britons as he makes his 'Donation' to the Saxons, and the Saxon heirs' subsequent lack of desire to assimilate with the remaining Britons, to Arthur's more culturally tolerant, albeit nonetheless colonialist strategies; and the coexisting tension between Arthur's role as civilizer and equalizer, despite his irregular barbarian origins, and his hunger for power and world domination.

In addition, it is important to note the major textual differences—absences and additions—between the *Brut* and the Galfridian tradition (based on Geoffrey of Monmouth's *Historia Regum Britanniae*): Wace's refusal to include the book of Merlin's Prophecies; Wace's inclusion of the Round Table—the first time this feature is found in writing; and the 'Breton hope', which is found in other texts but not in as positive a way as in Wace, who in no way minimizes or ridicules the hope—on the part of the Britons or Bretons—that Arthur will one day return in good health to lead his people.[30] In this introductory section to the *Brut*, we will touch here on the distinguishing thematic features listed above, as well as the textual and structural differences, tracing them as they appear in the text.

passage of time and Fortune's wheel, also serves to dilute the political content (Jean Blacker, 'Transformations of a Theme: The Depoliticization of the Arthurian World in the *Roman de Brut*', in Mary Flowers Braswell and John Bugge (eds), *The Arthurian Tradition: Essays in Convergence* (Tuscaloosa: University of Alabama Press, 1988), 54–74).

[30] Although in the scholarship, the 'Breton hope' has traditionally been associated with the Bretons rather than with the Britons—or both—the ambiguity of Old French (and modern, for that matter) with respect to the adjective *breton* (Anglo-Norman *bretun*), which can mean either 'Briton' or 'Breton', coupled with the fact that Wace is leaving things very open-ended, particularly here (and he is often equivocal elsewhere), suggests the possibility that Wace could have meant either 'Bretons' or 'Britons' or perhaps both. On this point Rachel Bromwich writes: 'Notwithstanding the ambiguity in Wace's use of the word "Bretun", and the possibility that the reference to *li Bretun* and the Round Table may be an allusion to insular rather than to continental Britons, the reference to *li Bretun* in connection with the return of Arthur seems to be the latter' ('Brittany and the Arthurian Legend', in Rachel Bromwich, A. O. H. Jarman, and Brynley F. Roberts (eds), *The Arthur of the Welsh: The Arthurian Legend in Medieval Welsh Literature* (Cardiff: University of Wales Press, 1991), 249–72, at 263). On the ambiguity of the term 'Breton' in Wace, see also Margaret Houck, who concludes that context suggests that, except for the references to the tale-tellers' fables concerning the Round Table and the expectation of Arthur's return, Wace's use of the term 'Breton' in Old French refers to the insular Britons, not the continental Britons, adding equivocally 'or he may mean simply Britons as a whole, without thinking of any distinction between insular and continental' (*Sources of the Roman de Brut of Wace* (Berkeley and Los Angeles: University of California Press, 1941), 255–6).

Predecessors: Earliest Texts by Gildas, 'Nennius', and Bede

The texts by these three authors all precede the Galfridian tradition and have differing influences on it. Just how much Geoffrey (and the redactor of the First Variant version) relied on Gildas's *De Excidio et conquestu Britanniae*[31] is difficult to say, but it is important to note that, although the latter text is actually a sermon in which its author decries the acts of his contemporaries and blames them for the decay of Britain, it is possibly the only significant source for sub-Roman Britain of the fifth and sixth centuries, as it is the only source written by a contemporary of many of the events. Although Arthur does not yet appear, Ambrosius Aurelianus (an important Romano-British fifth-century war leader according to Gildas) is credited with the Britons' victory over the Saxons at the Battle of Badon Hill.

'Nennius', as the author of the *Historia Brittonum* is sometimes called, is thought to have written his narrative in the first half of the ninth century. It survives in many recensions of the eleventh century and later. The work has been seen as anonymous, and the attribution to Nennius is considered to be a forgery by some scholars.[32] It is the earliest source to present Arthur as a historical figure, and it is the source of numerous stories and legends that have been amplified by other sources, most notably Geoffrey of Monmouth. In the *Historia Brittonum*, chapter 56 recounts the twelve battles fought and won by Arthur—who is described as a *dux bellorum* ('battle leader') rather than as king—including that of Badon Hill, where Arthur was supposed to have felled 960 Saxons single-handedly. This text, as well as the *Annales Cambriae*, the Welsh Triads, and other sources have stimulated a tremendous amount of scholarship with respect to both the legends of Arthur and their possible historical contexts.[33]

Bede's *Historia Ecclesiastica Gentis Anglorum* (finished in 731), while not a direct source for Geoffrey's *Historia* since it contains so

[31] Gildas, *The Ruin of Britain and Other Works*, ed. and trans. Michael Winterbottom (London: Phillimore, 1978).

[32] 'Nennius', *British History and the Welsh Annals*, ed. and trans. Michael Winterbottom (London: Phillimore, 1980); 'Nennius', *The Historia Brittonum, 3: The 'Vatican' Recension*, ed. David N. Dumville (Cambridge: D. S. Brewer, 1985).

[33] For major scholarship on the *Historia Brittonum*, the *Annales Cambriae*, and the Welsh Triads, see the items by Rachel Bromwich, David Dumville, Peter J. Field, Thomas Green, and Nicholas Higham in the Select Bibliography.

little on the Britons or Arthur, had a tremendous influence on Geoffrey. It was, in fact, a counterpoint for the latter, given its influence on the entire English historiographical tradition.[34] Among Geoffrey's many motives for writing the *Historia* was the need he felt to write the marginalized Britons 'back' into English history, to argue against Bede's view that the Saxon takeover of the island was an 'achievement'. This was not only Bede's view, but that of Geoffrey's contemporaries from the first half of the twelfth century, especially William of Malmesbury—often sceptical, as seen for example in his negative comments on the old wives' tales of the 'Breton hope'—and Henry of Huntingdon[35]—less sceptical than William. In fact, Henry was fascinated by the text of the *Historia* which Robert of Torigini, Norman historian and abbot of Mont Saint-Michel, showed him there in 1139.[36] In practical terms, Henry could not completely rewrite his already very long and involved *Historia Anglorum* in order to take account of the new information he had discovered, but he did write the *Epistola ad Warinum* (purportedly composed for 'Warin the Breton'), which on many levels was a summary of the high points of the *Historia*.[37]

Geoffrey of Monmouth

Central to the development of Arthurian history and fiction are primarily Geoffrey of Monmouth's 'vulgate' *Historia* (1130s) and secondarily the First Variant (and other variants, 1140s–1150s). There has been so much scholarship generated around Geoffrey of Monmouth

[34] See esp. Neil Wright, 'Geoffrey of Monmouth and Bede', in Richard Barber (ed.), *Arthurian Literature VI* (Cambridge: D. S. Brewer, 1986), 27–59.

[35] See William of Malmesbury, *Gesta Regum Anglorum: The History of the English Kings*, ed. and trans. R. A. B. Mynors† (completed by R. M. Thompson and M. Winterbottom), vol. I, Oxford Medieval Texts (Oxford: Clarendon Press, 1998); Henry of Huntingdon, *The History of the English People 1000–1154*, ed. and trans. Diana Greenway, Oxford World's Classics (1996, 2002, 2009); see also Henry, Archdeacon of Huntingdon, *Historia Anglorum: The History of the English People*, ed. and trans. Diana Greenway, Oxford Medieval Texts (Oxford: Clarendon Press, 1996; Latin facing-page).

[36] Henry of Huntingdon, *History*, ed. and trans. Greenway, xxviii–xxix.

[37] Neil Wright, 'The Place of Henry of Huntingdon's *Epistola ad Warinum* in the Text-History of Geoffrey of Monmouth's *Historia regum Britannie*: A Preliminary Investigation', in G. Jondorf and D. N. Dumville (eds), *France and the British Isles in the Middle Ages and Renaissance: Essays by Members of Girton College, Cambridge, in Memory of Ruth Morgan* (Woodbridge: Boydell, 1991), 71–113.

that one can well appreciate historian Richard Barber's allusion to it as 'the Arthurian industry'. It is as if, through the invention and cultivation of Arthur, Geoffrey met not only a political need but also a psychic need, one which is still apparently felt today, given the vast amount of fiction and film generated surrounding Arthurian myth and culture.[38] As eminent French critic Emmanuèle Baumgartner and leading Anglo-Norman scholar Ian Short have put it: 'Si Arthur n'avait pas existé, il aurait sans doute fallu l'inventer' ('If Arthur hadn't already existed, one would no doubt have had to invent him').[39]

Found in over two hundred manuscripts, fifty from the twelfth century alone, it is no exaggeration to say that in the *Historia* Geoffrey of Monmouth created one of the most popular narratives in European history.[40] In addition to Geoffrey's need to write the Britons 'back' into the history of the island, addressing the marginalization of the Britons in much historical narrative about England was the sending of a message aimed at the Anglo-Norman ruling elite during the civil war following the death of Henry I, warning them of the damaging effects of political discord. By further developing the myth of Trojan ancestry, Geoffrey was providing the Anglo-Norman ruling house with a genealogy more glorious than that from which the Franks were descended; Geoffrey aimed to glorify the Britons' civilizing influence—primarily through Arthur—for the benefit of the Anglo-Norman ruling house principally in opposition to the kings of France rather than in opposition to the English. In addition, Geoffrey aimed to construct a *récit total* ('a complete narrative'), consciously setting out to integrate the three central *matières* ('subject matters') as found in history of the early to mid-twelfth century, those of Rome (*le roman antique*), of France (*la chanson de geste*), and the 'matter of Britain' (*la matière*

[38] See esp. John Gillingham, 'The Contexts and Purposes of Geoffrey of Monmouth's *History of the Kings of Britain*', *Anglo-Norman Studies*, 13 (1990), 99–118; repr. in Gillingham, *The English in the Twelfth Century: Imperialism, National Identity and Political Values* (Woodbridge: Boydell, 2000), 19–39.

[39] Emmanuèle Baumgartner and Ian Short (eds and trans), *La Geste du roi Arthur, selon le Roman de Brut de Wace et l'Historia regum Britanniae de Geoffroy de Monmouth* (Paris: Union générale d'éditions, 10/18, 1993), 7.

[40] Jaakko Tahkokallio, 'Early Manuscript Dissemination', in Georgia Henley and Joshua Byron Smith (eds), *A Companion to Geoffrey of Monmouth* (Leiden: Brill, 2020), and Julia C. Crick, *The Historia regum Britannie of Geoffrey of Monmouth, III. A Summary Catalogue of the Manuscripts* (Woodbridge: Boydell, 1989).

de Bretagne).[41] It is also thought that Geoffrey wrote his narrative of sovereignty, colonization, conquest, domination, and assimilation primarily from a Welsh perspective, as a 'powerful rejoinder' to English writers—and the Anglo-Norman elites—the majority of whom increasingly viewed the 'colonials' as barbarians (including Britons from Cornwall and in the north of the kingdom), as cultural inferiors to those in power who practised the high civilization of the French and, by association, the English.[42]

In addition to these theories as to why Geoffrey wrote this tremendously popular work, it must be noted here that much of the material in his *Historia* is of his own invention, both peoples and places.

Scholars have demonstrated that Wace also used the First Variant (FV) (though probably not the second or other variants), though some think that he used it almost exclusively.[43] The majority of scholars believe that the largely Anglocentric First Variant was a redaction of the vulgate, the redactors trying to bring it back into the Bedan orbit by removing Geoffrey's 300-year extension of Briton rule (or sometimes shared Briton–Saxon rule) before the rule of Athelstan in the tenth century.[44] Wace does have difficulty reconciling the two versions, particularly at the end of his *Brut*, where he needs to explain how England was named after the Saxons, trying to finesse the circumstances with an etymological reasoning that the Saxons were descended from the Angles (rather than there having been two separate groups), and thus the Angles became the 'English' ('les Anglais') and Britain became 'Angleterre'.[45]

[41] Jean-Yves Tilliette, 'Invention du récit: La "Brutiade" de Geoffroy de Monmouth (*Historia regum Britanniae*, §6–22)', *Cahiers de civilisation médiévale*, 39 (1996), 217–33.

[42] Gillingham, 'Contexts and Purposes', 39.

[43] I agree with Laurence Mathey, who argues that Wace uses both the vulgate and the FV, often in equal measures, alternating at will ('De la Vulgate à la Variant Version de l'*Historia regum Britannie*: *Le Roman de Brut* de Wace à l'épreuve du texte source', in Hélène Tétrel and Géraldine Veysseyre (eds), *L'Historia regum Britannie et les 'Bruts' en Europe, I* (Paris: Classiques Garnier, 2015), 129–39. Since it is unlikely that Wace had access to two different manuscripts, it is quite possible that he used a MS such as c, Cardiff, South Glamorgan Central Library 2.611, which is a conflate MS of the vulgate and the FV (ed. Wright, II, cv).

[44] But recently David Burchmore has renewed the argument, posed by Robert Caldwell in the 1930s, that Geoffrey revised the FV, which came first (trans., Burchmore, vii-xxix, including numerous references to Robert Caldwell's work). See also Wright's explanation of the various arguments concerning the relative dating of these two texts and the major differences between them (ed. Wright, II, xii–lxx).

[45] See notes to pp. 56 and 202 in the Explanatory Notes.

Audience and Literary Context

Wace's *Brut* does not have addressees, unlike Geoffrey, some of whose manuscripts of the so-called 'vulgate' *Historia Regum Britanniae* (*HRB*) were addressed to Robert of Gloucester, Henry I's eldest illegitimate son, to King Stephen (though many manuscripts are without attribution), and the Prophecies of Merlin to Alexander, archbishop of Lincoln. Laȝamon states, in his Middle English *Brut* (*c.*1200, a work based largely on Wace) that Wace presented the *Brut* to Eleanor of Aquitaine, but we do not *know* this for a fact,[46] although in the *Rou* Wace mentions that Henry gave him a prebend in Bayeux, which some have surmised may have been in payment for the *Brut*. We cannot answer definitively the questions of whether Wace shared many of Geoffrey's goals, or what Wace's goals were. But a close reading of the text suggests that Wace embraced the idea of more inclusion of the Britons in the history of the island, arguing against the prejudices of 'barbarian' levelled against the Britons, the importance of the new ethos of *cortoisie* under the civilizing influence of Arthur's court, and arguing for the avoidance of civil strife and warfare for the benefit of the Anglo-Norman audience, though ironically Wace certainly does portray battles with gusto. Whether or not these can be considered goals, we do regularly observe Wace's passions for seafaring, battles on land and sea, etymology, and toponymics.[47] There are times when politics seem less important than do these passions, unless in the context of Arthur, who is portrayed as the tolerant colonizer and also civilizer.

We cannot know how many other vernacular traditions—other than the nascent vernacular historiographical tradition—Wace may have been familiar with, but his *Brut* was produced in the context of the *romans antiques*, as well as the Arthurian tales of Chrétien de Troyes and others. From the early thirteenth century onwards, there is striking manuscript evidence that Continental audiences thought of the *Brut* as parallel with other *romans antiques*, such as the *Roman d'Eneas* and the *Roman de Troie*, works that also relate the Trojan foundation myth. The Continental manuscripts also bind, and thus

[46] See Karen Broadhurst's well-placed scepticism on Henry and Eleanor's patronage in 'Henry II of England and Eleanor of Aquitaine: Patrons of Literature in England?', *Viator*, 27 (1996), 53–84.

[47] See n. 56 below.

associate, the *Brut* with romances of Chrétien, whereas the Anglo-Norman manuscripts bind the *Brut* almost exclusively with Latin history, religious texts, and Gaimar's *Estoire des Engleis*.[48] We do know that Wace was familiar with oral tales of Arthur, as evident in his comments in the *Roman de Rou* that he had gone to the forest of Brocéliande in search of proof of tales of Arthur,[49] i.e. the fables the fablers told, as seen in the passage in the *Brut* on the *aventures* that Wace says took place during the twelve-year peace of Arthur's reign:

> En cele grant pais ke jo di,
> Ne sai si vus l'avez oï,
> Furent les merveilles pruvees
> E les aventures truvees
> Ki d'Artur sunt tant recuntees
> Ke a fable sunt aturnees.
> Ne tut mençunge, ne tut veir,
> Tut folie ne tut saveir.[50]
> Tant unt li cunteür cunté
> E li fableür tant flablé
> Pur lur cuntes enbeleter,
> Que tut unt fait fable sembler.
> (*Brut*, vv. 9787–98)

> During this great peace I am describing (I do not know whether you have heard of this), marvels manifested themselves and adventures were encountered, and tales were told so frequently about Arthur that they were turned into fables. They were neither all lies nor entirely the truth, neither all foolishness nor entirely based on fact. The storytellers told their tales and the raconteurs invented their yarns in order to embellish their accounts in such a way that they made everything appear to have been invented. (p. 145)

Interestingly, at this point, Continental MS H of the *Brut* (Paris, BnF, fr. 1450) inserts after v. 9798 six texts, five of which are romances by Chrétien, as if to offer examples or proof of the 'aventures' mentioned by Wace (*Erec et Enide, Perceval* (and its anonymous First Continuation), *Cligès*, *Yvain*, and *Lancelot* [frag.]). After this very

[48] See the updated chart of *Brut* MSS in their codicological contexts in J. Blacker, '"But That's Another Story": Wace, Laȝamon, and the Early Anonymous Old French verse *Bruts*', *Arthuriana*, 31/4 (2021), 47–102, at 83–92.

[49] See xvi above.

[50] For this line, Weiss restores a reading from MS P: 'Ne tut folie ne tut saveir'.

lengthy insertion of six romance texts at v. 9799 of Wace's *Brut*, Wace's *Brut* resumes and continues to the end, v. 14866.

Foundation Myth; the Saxons, Picts, and Scots; and Arthur's Many Roles

Given that Gaimar's *Estoire des Bretuns* is no longer extant, Wace's text is the first interpretation in the French vernacular of the Latin historiographical tradition, which was essentially inaugurated by Geoffrey of Monmouth, focusing on the Trojan foundation myth in Britain.[51] This foundation myth instructs the Anglo-Norman audience about the beginnings of civilization in Britain, their new 'extended' home, connecting them with the Trojans, and thus also with the Normans whose historians, such as Dudo of St Quentin, also tried to cement ancient history with modern history via Troy. The romance texts of the *Roman d'Eneas* and the *Roman de Troie* also sought to invoke the Trojans as a foundation myth for the French.

Regarding the foundation myth, Wace follows Geoffrey closely, but he parts ways, for example, in the story of the giants who were allegedly the island's inhabitants before the arrival of the Trojans. Whereas Geoffrey has Corineus kill the giants' leader Goemagog (Gogmagog) (*HRB*, §21.470, 475, 480) and chase the remaining giants into the hills in the west, Wace relates that all the giants were killed, as well as their progeny, a process he refers to as a 'cleansing'. Wace writes 'Quant la terre fud neïee | Des gaianz e de lur lignee' (vv. 1169–70; 'When the land was cleansed of the giants and their lineage', p. 20).[52] If 'e de lur lignee' were not added, we might be able

[51] See esp. Ian Short, 'What was Gaimar's *Estoire des Bretuns*?', *Cultura Neolatina*, 71 (2011), 147–9.

[52] Interestingly, one manuscript avoids the image of genocide altogether, as vv. 1169–70 are missing in H (Paris, BnF, fr. 1450, 13th century, an unusual MS containing four complete romances and one fragment by Chrétien de Troyes, the First Continuation of the *Perceval* interpolated between lines 9798 and 9799 of the *Brut*); in MS G vv. 1169–70 are missing altogether, while G adds more details in twenty-two lines between 1168 and 1169, narrating how the giants were chased into the mountains and were slaughtered there, such that not one was left standing ('Onc ne lor eschapa un pié', 'Not a single one survived'; the twenty-first line added by MS G, ed. Arnold, I, 66; see Weiss, 30, n. 6). Other MSS have similar renditions of what has been reported by Arnold and retained by Weiss (though the latter does not note the variants here). For v. 1169 Arnold and Weiss both have 'neïee', C has 'finee' [When the land was *finished* with the giants, and

to interpret the killing of the giants as referring to the twenty giants who had accompanied Gogmagog. But the thoroughness with which the line/lineage was wiped out is inescapable. There were no more giants hiding anywhere who could reproduce. Once this removal of the giants has taken place, the Trojans, who have now become Britons, have also become an ersatz native people of Britain, as if they were the original inhabitants; the slate has been—quite literally—wiped clean: an ironic image of cultural genocide inflicted upon the indigenous giants (who may not have been considered human at all) by the Britons who were later to take the place of the natives in the eyes of the Saxons.[53]

Wace does not display the same degree of animosity towards the Saxons as Geoffrey does, perhaps because he does from time to time use the First Variant, which was certainly more Anglocentric than the vulgate. The Picts and the Scots are also the targets of less anger than

their lineage]; S has 'delivree' [When the land was *delivered* from the giants and their lineage]; and J, A, and K and G have variations of 'neïee'—'nesiee', 'neie', and 'nestoiee' respectively (variants for v. 1169, ed. Arnold, I, 66). The Royal *Brut* (in MS B) reports that Brutus's people killed nineteen of the twenty giants they encountered, except for 'Geomagog' (v. 995, *Anglo-Norman Brut (Royal 13.A.xxi)*, ed. Alexander Bell (Oxford: Basil Blackwell for the Anglo-Norman Text Society, 1969)), who soon perishes at the hands of Corineus at 'Gogmagog's Leap', saying nothing about any others (vv. 994–1000).

[53] At the risk of oversimplification, it can be said that giants in this period were not ordinarily considered fully human beings, even though they were often depicted as having human or human-like features. Nonetheless, the complete wiping out of any group presented as an acceptable practice is disconcerting at the least, certainly for modern sensibilities. Sylvia Huot writes that 'the elimination of giants, in short, is essential to the process of establishing civilization and furthering God's plan, whether in the Holy Land or in Britain. Whereas Britain under the giants remained in a state of wilderness, Brutus and his men divide it up, according to a system of feudal government, build cities, and "improve" the land through agricultural management. Tellingly, neither Geoffrey of Monmouth nor Wace addressed the question of where the British giants came from, or how they might have lived before the arrival of the Trojan settlers' (*Outsiders: The Humanity and Inhumanity of Giants in Medieval French Romance* (Notre Dame, IN: University of Notre Dame Press, 2016), 37–8). On images of the monstrous and the role of monsters in Galfridian material, see Jeffrey Jerome Cohen, *Of Giants: Sex, Monsters, and the Middle Ages* (Minneapolis: University of Minnesota Press, 1999), esp. 39–61, and Huot, *Outsiders*, 37, 42–3, 65–6, 70–4, 141–2. Especially pertinent to remember is Cohen's observation with regard to Geoffrey, but it certainly holds for Wace here, that 'the irony, of course, is that the Celtic ("British") peoples, whose history Geoffrey is writing, stand exactly in this aboriginal position to the Anglo-Saxons, who "settled" the island'—that is, in the preconquest account of English history, the Celts occupy the place of the Galfridian giants, the invading Germanic tribes that of the glorified British' (*Of Giants*, 34–5).

in the vulgate, especially the latter, to whom Arthur shows a great tolerance, particularly when appealed to by the Scottish women. Wace's differing views on the Saxons and the Scots are seen in the tableau at Loch Lomond, which differs significantly from its two main written sources.[54] First, in this scene Wace has eliminated the Picts, thus deviating from both the vulgate and First Variant; in fact, the Picts figure in the *Brut* far less frequently than in the vulgate or the First Variant, where they are almost a matched set with the Scots, particularly in Geoffrey's text where the Scots are rarely mentioned without the Picts. Secondly, Wace expands the narrative on the blockade to starve out the Scots:

> Tant les assailli e guarda,
> Tant les destrainst e afama,
> A vinz, a cenz e a milliers,
> Chaeient morz par les graviers.
>
> (vv. 9451–4)

> He attacked them so much, watched them so much, and assailed and starved them so much that in their twenties, in their hundreds, and in their thousands they fell down dead on the shore. (p. 140)

Although Wace may have done this for purely poetic effect, it is nonetheless noteworthy, for it is followed by Arthur's making short work of the Irish king, Gillamarus, chasing him and his troops back to their ships, forcing them to depart, before turning back to the lake where he had left the Scots.

At this point, Wace adds no more about Arthur's resumption of the slaughter of the Scots (as found in the vulgate). In Wace, Arthur may be a barbarian king, but he is no butcher, as will be seen below in the contrast between Arthur and Gormund. Instead, Wace moves on directly to the two pleas for mercy without describing any more killing and death. In Wace's text the second plea is original and far more complex than that of his sources. In the vulgate and First Variant, the plea is reported in the third person, as it is delivered by bishops and other clergy, 'official' representatives of the people, and more learned and of higher social status than their flocks. Wace devotes four lines to this third-person plea from the clergy, but then he adds a forty-five-line

[54] It is impossible to know with any certainty whether Wace relied on oral sources for his Loch Lomond passage, or if he relied on his own invention.

speech that becomes the focal point of the passage. The speech is made by Scottish women—not those from the noble elites but simply women—who plead for the remaining men, women, and children to be spared.[55]

Not only does Wace achieve significant dramatic effect by adding this speech, but also the contents of the speech are remarkably complex, as if to display contemporary negotiating tactics in addition to the contents of the arguments themselves,[56] including criticism of Arthur and of the Saxons, and the importance of Christian solidarity. The women ask Arthur for mercy, but it would appear that they do not expect any further reply than the most central—that is, other than that he cease ravaging the Scots and recognize the validity of their arguments.[57]

The different arguments involved in this elaborate speech are: why have you destroyed the land?; why continue to destroy the land?; if you don't have mercy on the men, then have mercy on the women and children; we have already paid sufficient penalty when the Saxons came—we didn't invite the Saxons who ravaged our

[55] The forty-five-line speech that becomes the focal point of the passage is found in vv. 9477–520. On Wace's use of direct address in the *Brut*, see Françoise H. M. Le Saux, *A Companion to Wace* (Cambridge: D. S. Brewer, 2005), 106–7, 134–7, 140.

[56] Wace is known for his interest in warfare and sea battles, so it is not unreasonable to think that negotiating tactics and other forms of diplomacy also fascinated him. On Wace's penchant for military vocabulary and war narratives, as well as his expertise, see Matthew Bennett, 'The Uses and Abuses of Wace's *Roman de Rou*', in Burgess and Weiss (eds), *Maistre Wace*, 31–40, and Bennett, 'Wace and Warfare', in R. Allen Brown (ed.), *Anglo-Norman Studies XI: Proceedings of the Battle Conference 1988* (Woodbridge: Boydell, 1989), 37–57. On Wace's familiarity with seagoing vessels and navigating military manœuvres on water, as well as maritime vocabulary in general, see William Sayers, 'A Norse Etymology for Luff, "Weather Edge of a Sail"', *American Neptune*, 66/1 (2001), 25–38, and 'Arthur's Embarkation for Gaul in a Fresh Translation of Wace's *Roman de Brut*', *Romance Notes*, 46/2 (2006), 143–56. On Wace as a historian, see also Elisabeth van Houts, 'Wace as Historian', in K. S. B. Keats-Rohan (ed.), *Family Trees and the Roots of Politics: The Prosopography of Britain and France from the Tenth to the Twelfth Century* (Cambridge: Boydell, 1997), 103–32 and on the ocean voyages leading up to and involved in the Norman Conquest, see also Van Houts, 'The Ship List of William the Conqueror', in *Anglo-Norman Studies X: Proceedings of the Battle Conference 1987*, ed. R. A. Brown (Woodbridge: Boydell, 1988), 159–93, and Bennett, 'Poetry as History?', 21–39.

[57] In the vulgate Geoffrey constructs the passage so that the clergy tell Arthur that the people and the land have been ravaged enough, that there was no need to kill every last one, and that if need be, they would live in slavery if they had to, if granted a small portion of their country (*HRB*, §149.169–75).

land; 'If we accommodated them, they harmed us all the more' (p. 140; 'Si nus les avum hebergiez, | Tant nus unt li plus damagiez', vv. 9495–6); they seized our property and sent it home to their lands; we had no one to defend us; they had the power and we endured it; the Saxons were heathen and we [the Scots] were Christians; 'They treated us badly, but you are doing worse to us' (p. 140; 'Mal nus unt fait, tu nus faiz pis', v. 9509); no honour or fame will come to you by killing those who ask for mercy; you have conquered us, but let us live; we are Christians like you; 'Wherever it may be, hand over some land to us' (p. 140; 'Quel part que seit, terre nus livre!', v. 9514); we are willing to be slaves if we can continue to live, and as Christians, since 'We follow the faith that you follow' (p. 141; 'Nus tenum la lei que tu tiens', v. 9518); Christianity will be brought low if this land is destroyed; and lastly, the women say that the Scots are willing to be slaves if they can continue to live as Christians.

The arguments fall into four groups: first, demanding Arthur's justification for what he has done, if only as a rhetorical ploy. Secondly, the defencelessness of the Scots is accentuated, in the face of the Saxons and now before Arthur as well—the Scots are victims, and not of their own doing; this argument acts as a veiled reminder of Vortigern's invitation to the Saxons to settle in Britain, as seen in Bede, but it is not clear how many members of Wace's audience—unless they were 'professional' historians—might have been aware of Bede's presentation of the *adventus Saxonum*, unless that version had already passed into legend, reaching beyond those who were able to read Gildas and Bede in the original Latin. Furthermore, the Scots are victims of the Saxons, just as the Britons, and thus the Scots and the Britons may have more in common than they might otherwise have thought. In other words, the Scottish women seek to set up at least a 'psychic' alliance between the Scots and the Britons. Thirdly, that Christians should form a community, not fight one another, and that the result of Christians fighting Christians would be destruction of the whole land. Lastly, the Scots would be willing to hold any land at all—a more conciliatory position than in the vulgate *Historia* where the clergy ask on their behalf that they specifically be allowed to keep a portion of *their own* lands ('sineret illos portiunculam habere patriae, perpetuae seruitutis iugum ultro gestauros', *HRB*, §149.172–3, 'if he let them keep a small portion of their country, they would willingly bear the yoke of slavery forever')[58] and live, even as slaves.

This passage also serves to draw the Scots closer to Arthur and the Britons, if only as two parts of a larger community of Christians, if not as Britons, at least as non-Saxons. Here Wace appears to attempt to mitigate the previously adversarial position the Scots held vis-à-vis the Britons in the *Historia Regum Britanniae*—that is, as a traditional enemy of the Britons[59]—as if to say that it is better to band together as enemies of the Saxons than to fight each other. Through this speech Wace reminds his audience yet again of the Saxons' perfidy. According to the Scottish women, when the Scots took them in and protected them, the Saxons treated them even more poorly. This is another anti-Saxon element, and also one which draws the victimized cultures together.

In addition, due to Arthur's conquest, in broad terms a colonial situation is established, whereby the Scots are essentially the colonized and the Britons the colonizers (although the analogy does not work perfectly (and is anachronistic), since in the text Arthur's 'peoples' had no explicitly articulated plans to settle the region).[60] Arthur's

[58] Thorpe treats this passage somewhat differently: 'He should allow them to have some small tract of land of their own' (Geoffrey of Monmouth, *The History of the Kings of Britain*, ix.6, trans. Lewis Thorpe (Harmondsworth: Penguin, 1966; repr. 1982), 219–20). This implies that they could keep some land for themselves, for their own use, without accentuating who had held the land previously, that it had been 'their own'. As Michael A. Faletra states: 'The bishops also asked that Arthur allow the besieged to have some little plot of land of their own, seeing that they would be bearing the yoke of servitude anyway' (Geoffrey of Monmouth, *The History of the Kings of Britain*, §149, trans. M. A. Faletra (Toronto: Broadview Press, 2008), 169).

[59] As seen e.g. in §91.59–62, where 'foul crowds of Scots, Picts, Norsemen, Danes and other allies' ravage the land of the Britons following the departure of the Romans, as well as in Cadwallader's final lament: 'Woe to us sinners . . . His mighty retribution is upon us, to uproot from our native soil us whom neither the Romans once nor later the Scots, the Picts or the deceitful treachery of the Saxons could drive out' (*HRB*, §203.532, 534–6).

[60] Technically speaking, the situation involving Arthur and the Scots in this instance might more properly be called one of 'lordship' and not of 'colonization', but I am invoking a colonial situation to emphasize the absolute nature of domination by conquest, those in power vs. those not in power. In a particularly useful study on the distinctions between the terms 'lordship' and 'colony' in the Middle Ages, focusing on medieval Ireland but having much broader implications, R. R. Davies points out that the terms cannot be used interchangeably for a number of reasons, primarily that 'colony' connotes a more dependent relationship than 'lordship' does, 'it is the governmental dependence which is perhaps even more clearly the hallmark of colonial status' ('Lordship or Colony?', in

status is increased since it is now up to him as victor—albeit potentially a fellow Briton[61]—not only to grant the Scots mercy but also to give them permission to live on the land(s) they had formerly held.[62]

In the *Brut*, following the speech of the Scottish women, Arthur shows compassion (though without tears), sparing all the living Scots and their progeny; 'He granted them life and limb, took homage from them, and departed' (p. 141; 'Vie e membre lur parduna, | Lur humages prist sis laissa', vv. 9525–6); this is one of his many acts of magnanimity which balances out his fierceness in battle. In perhaps a nod to the alliance proposed by the Scottish women—material unique in the *Brut*—peace is restored, the Scots are no longer enemies of the Britons, and Arthur divides Scotland among three high-born British lords.[63]

James Lydon (ed.), *The English in Medieval Ireland: Proceedings of the First Joint Meeting of the Royal Irish Academy and the British Academy, Dublin, 1982* (Dublin: Royal Irish Academy, 1984), 142–60, at 152). In addition, 'colonisation included the cultivation of new land and in some degree the displacement of the native population' (151), which is not the case here with Arthur and the Scots. See also Ania Loomba's discussion of the distinction between administrative colonialism and settler colonialism, including references to the Roman Empire (*Colonialism/Postcolonialism* (3rd edn, Abingdon: Routledge, 2015), 22–5).

[61] On the modernist assumption of 'fellow Celt' feeling, see Patrick Sims-Williams who claims that 'self-conscious Celtic solidarity cannot be traced back beyond the modern period' . . . and that any proposed alliances of Scots, Irish, and Welsh leaders were based primarily on 'common grievance against the English rather than their ethnic kinship' ('Celtomania and Celtoscepticism', *Cambrian Medieval Celtic Studies*, 36 (1998), 1–36, at 11 and also Matthew H. Hammond, 'Ethnicity and the Writing of Medieval Scottish History', *Scottish Historical Review*, 85/1 (2006), 1–27, at 17).

[62] With respect to the relationships between the British territories/kingdoms and England in the Galfridian material and how Geoffrey's goals as he was writing during the reign of Stephen may have been received by the Anglo-Norman elites, Alan MacColl proposes that 'if the history of Geoffrey's Britannia is to be read primarily as a warning of the dangers facing England at the time the work was written, the interpretative emphasis is shifted away from imperial and expansionist concerns to the governance of England itself . . . In the early years of Stephen's reign (1135–54), one imagines that Geoffrey and his intended audience would have been less interested in dreams of a pan-Britannic empire than in the immediate problems of ensuring stable government and securing England against Welsh rebellion and incursions by the Scots' ('The Meaning of "Britain" in Medieval and Early Modern England', *Journal of British Studies*, 45 (2006), 248–69, at 252).

[63] It is possible that Wace meant this to be more than a 'psychic' alliance, as it seems to presage, for example, Arthur's trust in the Scottish king Agusel (albeit one of his barons) as he places the latter at the head of his first battalion in preparation for war with the emperor Lucius (vv. 12358–9). Although Wace follows the vulgate (*HRB*, §152.201–5) and FV (§152.2 'Uranium sceptro Murefensium insigniuit') in Arthur's dividing the land north of the Humber into three parts, thus restoring ancestral rights of rulership as they were before the Saxon incursions—Scotland to be ruled by Agusel, Lothian to be ruled

It is virtually impossible to summarize Arthur's importance, except through providing lists of aspects of his reign as seen in this early material.[64] Baumgartner highlights three major aspects of Arthur's reign: the triumph of the Christian faith; the establishment, by force if necessary, of the *pax arthuriana*; and the blossoming of new codes of social life, which define the term *cortoisie*.[65] As can be seen so clearly in the text itself, Arthurian *cortoisie* is often dominated by warfare and its ethos, which can be surprising to many who have come to associate *cortoisie* almost exclusively with love, good manners, politeness, consideration for others, and, of course, with the court and the nobility, not necessarily with the battlefield. Arthur is associated with the zenith of the civilization of the Britons, but also with the 'Breton hope', the belief that Arthur would one day return to rule his land in peace, bringing the Britons once again to their rightful place in English history.

In terms of Arthur's conception and birth, Wace follows the general outlines of the vulgate and First Variant, without significant departures. However, there are aspects of his birth and rise to power that can be emphasized. In terms of the symbolism of Arthur's conception, involving Merlin's transformation of Uther into the guise of Gorlois so that Uther could lie with his wife, Ygerne, French critic Denis Hüe proposes that the conception is based on a very archaic heroic saviour motif in the Indo-European tradition, in which Arthur

by Loth, and Moray by Urien (see note to p. 139) (v. 9632, Urien, 'Cil ki sire ert de Mureifens'). He de-emphasizes that the Scots had once been enemies of the Britons, and appears to construct a melding of sorts, albeit with Arthur as king over all (vv. 9614–40). However, this 'melding of sorts' is all the more complicated because if Arthur is giving ancestral lands to high-born British lords who had previously ruled territories north of the Humber, who were the peoples they supposedly ruled? Britons? Those who eventually became Scots? Probably not the Scots as Geoffrey perceived them, i.e. as invading enemies nearly as pernicious as the Saxons. This is not an answerable question since we have no way of telling who Wace thought those people were, nor can we address definitively the extent of anachronism in the *Brut*. We also do not know to what extent Wace may have taken into consideration the multilayered complexities between the era the Galfridian material is supposedly referring to and Wace's own lifetime.

[64] A group of Arthurian romances in French prose, *c.*1210–30. Probably written by Cistercian monks, the cycle is comprised of *L'Estoire del Saint Graal*, a *Merlin* based on Robert de Boron's, and the Prose *Lancelot*, made up of the *Lancelot* proper, the *Queste del Saint Graal*, and the *Mort Artu*.

[65] 'Passages d'Arthur en Normandie', in Letellier and Hüe (eds), *Le Roman de Brut, entre mythe et histoire*, 20.

is made to conform simultaneously to three requirements. The hero had to represent new blood, yet be of noble lineage; be the son of a king, yet a bastard; and be born of an adulterous, yet faithful, mother.[66] It is not necessary, however, as Hüe points out, for Wace to seek to reconcile the mythical and the legendary with the historical, forsaking some of the former elements, in order to reinforce belief in the latter, because these factors can—and do—all exist simultaneously. In fact, the power of the myths which intersect with Arthur, the 'political' figure, are inseparable from him as a leader and a historical artefact.[67]

The symbolic paradigm originating in the Galfridian material, beginning with Arthur's conception aided by Merlin, and including Wace's additions, particularly the Round Table and his enhancement of the 'Breton hope', has elements which point to Arthur's status as insider or outsider, and sometimes as both. Each status contributes to Arthur's protean nature as a literary/historical figure across the eras and genres of historiographical or romance narrative: Arthur is an illegitimate son, thus an outsider (his conception aided through Merlin's use of herbs and other forms of deception to disguise Uther); he is also son of a king and future queen, an insider; he inherits the throne thus, by extension, through magical means, and in that way, Arthur is again an outsider;[68] Arthur earns the right to be king through his own seemingly transcendental prowess and is characterized as the 'greatest king', and is thus an insider; Arthur belongs to a 'barbarian group' when seen from the perspective of the soon-to-be-dominant group, the Saxons (Angles, mentioned in some texts, in the eleventh hour), and therefore again an outsider; Arthur functions as a civilizer through his founding of the Round Table, which carries sociolinguistic as well as sociopolitical connotations, making him an

[66] Hüe, 'Les Variantes de la séduction: autour de la naissance d'Arthur', in Letellier and Hüe (eds), *Le Roman de Brut entre mythe et histoire*, 67–88, at 68–9.

[67] I am defining 'historical artefact' here as an element of a text or cultural remnant that is *believed* to be true, i.e. *believed* to have existed in 'actual history' without our necessarily having any scientific corroboration.

[68] Absent from the Galfridian material, the motif of the test of Arthur pulling the sword from the stone in order to prove his descendance from the regal line apparently enters the written tradition in Robert de Boron's late twelfth–early thirteenth century *Roman de Merlin*; see Rosemary Morris, *The Character of King Arthur in Medieval Literature* (Cambridge: D. S. Brewer, 1982; repr. 1985).

insider; he is a member of both a colonizing group (conquering foreign lands) and a colonized group (the Britons as colonized by the Saxons), thus a conqueror and a member of the conquered, both an insider and outsider; and lastly, Arthur dies, and yet does not die—he is both a human and messianic figure, notably through the 'Breton hope', both within the human realm and outside it, the consummate insider/outsider.

That Arthur is both a civilizer and also a world conqueror may seem contradictory, but Wace combines them in a vision of tolerance and protection. First, Arthur's foreign conquests including Ireland, Orkney, Gotland, and Wenelande capitulate to him, as does Iceland; he also conquers France. These conquests are distinguished by the fact that Arthur brings the countries into his orbit, yet he does not demand subservience from the populations, leaving them to live as they had been before they came into Arthur's world. Arthur is seen as a defender of his realm against the Romans, who figure extensively in the *Brut*, and certainly not as a butcher, unlike Gormund, who, following Arthur's 'death', slaughters innumerable Britons and gives the island to the Saxons. The Round Table brings together the leaders of the entire kingdom, seated in such a way that none could claim superiority over another (admittedly these are all members of the nobility, so the equality is not spread throughout the levels of society, even if it is implied that it trickles down to affect all subjects). All the members of the Round Table seem to understand one another, as if they need no translator to help them understand their different languages or dialects. During the plenary court and the twelve years of peace—the *pax arthuriana*—when Arthur is officially crowned, Wace includes over four hundred lines containing a narrative of music, games, and other festivities, in a passage which has no parallel in early vernacular historiography, or, for that matter, in romance texts either.

Perhaps the most important aspect of Wace's characterization of Arthur, beyond the king's demonstrated superiority to Rome, is the poet's nuanced treatment of the 'Breton hope'. Wace emphasizes that he cannot pronounce on Arthur's fate one way or the other, but must leave that to Merlin—an unusual move for Wace since he had almost exclusively avoided Merlin in his text (he certainly avoided the book of Prophecies). We will not learn what happens to Arthur, because only Merlin knows. The mystery surrounding Arthur's 'death' is what enables Wace to create a unique and highly symbolic presence for the monarch.

Laȝamon scholar Rosamund Allen reminds us that Geoffrey does not mention Arthur's return, 'but speaks of him as mortally wounded and taken to Avalon so that his wounds could be tended to, which Wace echoes but adds that the Britons await his return, and he [Wace], will say no more than Merlin did: that his death would be doubtful'.[69] However, it should be added that Wace, as usual, occupies the middle ground: like Geoffrey, he says that Arthur was taken to Avalon, but Wace adds that the king is still *in* Avalon, awaited by the Britons, 'as they say and understand', but not committing himself completely, using the third person: 'ne volt plus dire de sa fin' (v. 13283; 'Master Wace . . . does not wish to say any more about his end', p. 196), emphasizing that Merlin is right about the doubtful nature of Arthur's end:

> Encore i est, Bretun l'atendent,
> Si cum il dient e entendent;
> De la vendra, encore puet vivre.
> Maistre Wace, ki fist cest livre,
> Ne volt plus dire de sa fin
> Qu'en dist li prophetes Merlin;
> Merlin dist d'Arthur, si ot dreit,
> Que sa mort dutuse serreit.
> Li prophetes dist verité;
> Tut tens en ad l'um puis duté,
> E dutera, ço crei, tut dis,
> Se il est morz u il est vis.
> (vv. 13279–90)

> He is still there. The Britons are waiting for him, as they say and understand. From there he will come, and he will go on living. Master Wace, who composed this book, does not wish to say any more about his end than the prophet Merlin does. Merlin says about Arthur, and he is right, that his death would remain in doubt. The prophet told the truth. Since then, it has always been doubted, and will be doubted, I believe, for all time, whether he is dead or alive. (p. 196)

Geoffrey of Monmouth wrote a highly political history. It depends, however, on one's perspectives as to what form Geoffrey's politics

[69] In Judith Weiss and Rosamund Allen (trans.), *The Life of King Arthur: Wace and Lawman* (London: Dent, 1997), note to vv. 14281–2, 14290–7.

took, beyond bringing the Britons into history by legitimizing their role in historical narrative, by demonstrating their long-standing claims and the legitimacy of their rivalry as equals with the Saxons, though ultimately relegated to the geographical fringes of the island. For Wace, Arthur becomes more of a symbol of an outsider who, through strength, wisdom, and ambition, rises to help his people without transforming the other outsiders (for example, the Scots) into marginalized groups—though for the Saxons, his wish to do so is hard to deny. While Arthur may have wanted to triumph over the Saxons, he is not depicted as destroying or subjugating others, and through the Round Table Wace's Arthur is seen to establish a seat of government where all are equal, and none are first among equals. Arthur refuses to capitulate to the Romans, setting an example of tolerant behaviour, though not without feistiness and a determination to prevail over those who choose to dominate him or the Britons.

But it is Laȝamon who takes Wace's symbolism a step further, building in a way on Wace's work, out of time and space. By saying that the Britons await '*an* Arthur' rather than '*the* Arthur',[70] the king becomes a symbol for all those who are downtrodden, all those waiting to be saved from marginalization, to be brought back to their rightful place in history, to be brought to the table as equals among equals, natives among newcomers, regardless of how 'other' they may seem to some who judge them by their differences, and not by their common humanity. This universal symbolism of Arthur both contributes to his place in history and historical writing and takes him beyond history, and undoubtedly contributes to the monarch's lasting appeal both to scholars and within popular culture. He acts as an illustration of how necessary myth, i.e. uplifting myth, is to the global imagination. Although it may be true, as Nicholas Higham concludes, that 'we can now agree to discount King Arthur as a "real" figure of the past, leaving him and his deeds to the "smoke" and "highland mist" of make-believe and wishful thinking . . . [that] it is there that he properly belongs',[71] the 'highland

[70] Michael A. Faletra, 'Once and Future Britons: The Welsh in Lawman's *Brut*', *Medievalia and Humanistica*, 28 (2001), 1–23, at 15.

[71] Nicholas J. Higham, *King Arthur: The Making of the Legend* (New Haven: Yale University Press, 2018), 279.

mist of make-believe' is nonetheless crucial to the global imagination because it has the capacity to pull us all out of separatism, towards dreams of building a more equal, just, and hopeful world, dreams which Wace himself must surely have shared to at least some degree.

NOTE ON THE TRANSLATION

THE present translation of Wace's *Roman de Brut* is based on the edition by Ivor Arnold, published in two volumes by the Société des Anciens Textes Français (SATF) (1938–40). The work itself survives in nineteen complete or nearly complete manuscripts and in fifteen fragments or extracts.[1] Arnold's edition is based on a composite version of two manuscripts, P and D (see 'List of Manuscripts', p. 228). The translation aims to render the text's octosyllabic rhyming couplets in as straightforward a manner as possible. Occasionally, however, in order to improve the fluency of the translation, long sentences are broken into two or more shorter sentences. Also, in order to make the relationship between the sentences a little clearer, short sentences are sometimes expanded by the addition of an 'and', a 'but', or a 'for', etc. Past and present tenses oscillate in Old French, and where Wace has used a present tense when a past tense seems more appropriate in English the relevant changes have been made. When there are breaks in the text that are incorporated into Arnold's text, these breaks have been retained in the translation. Further breaks are added throughout the work in order to give the reader a breather in what is a long text. For a similar purpose, explanatory headers have been added from time to time to draw attention to the various divisions in the narration. References are to the line numbering in Arnold's edition. We make no attempt to reproduce the editor's original punctuation. An asterisk in the translation indicates the presence of a note in the Explanatory Notes. For clarification, modern place names are given in square brackets, e.g. [Southampton] or [York].

[1] For further details concerning manuscripts beyond the list accompanying the Introduction, see Arnold, I, vii–xiv, Blacker, '"But That's Another Story"', Appendix I, 83–92, Dean and Boulton, item 2, 2–3, Le Saux, *Companion*, 85–6, and Weiss, xxviii–xxix.

SELECT BIBLIOGRAPHY

Primary Sources

EDITIONS AND TRANSLATIONS OF THE *ROMAN DE BRUT*

Arnold, Ivor D. O. (ed.), *Le Roman de Brut de Wace*, SATF, 2 vols (Paris: SATF, 1938–40).

Arnold, Ivor D. O., and Pelan, Margaret M. (eds), *La Partie arthurienne du Roman de Brut (extrait du manuscript B.N. fr 794)*, Bibliothèque française et romane, série B: textes et documents, 1 (Paris: C. Klincksieck et Centre de philologie romane et de littérature romanes de la Faculté des Lettres de Strasbourg, 1962, repr. 2002).

Baumgartner, Emmanuèle, and Short, Ian (eds and trans), *La Geste du roi Arthur, selon le Roman de Brut de Wace et l'Historia Regum Britanniae de Geoffrey de Monmouth*, Bibliothèque médiévale, 2356 (Paris: Union générale d'éditions, 10/18, 1993).

Glowka, Arthur Wayne, *Wace, Le Roman de Brut: The French Book of Brutus*, Medieval and Renaissance Texts and Studies, 279 (Tempe: Arizona Center for Medieval and Renaissance Studies, 2005).

Weiss, Judith (trans.), *Wace's Roman de Brut, A History of the British: Text and Translation* (Exeter: University of Exeter Press, 1999; 2nd edn, 2002).

Weiss, Judith, and Allen, Rosamund (trans.), *The Life of King Arthur: Wace and Lawman*, Everyman's Library (London: Dent, 1997).

EDITIONS AND TRANSLATIONS OF WACE'S OTHER WORKS

Blacker, Jean, Burgess, Glyn S., and Ogden, Amy V., *Wace, The Hagiographical Works: The Conception Nostre Dame and the Lives of St Margaret and St Nicholas*, Studies in Medieval and Reformation Traditions, 169, Texts and Sources, 3 (Leiden: Brill, 2013).

Burgess, Glyn S. (trans.), *The History of the Norman People: Wace's Roman de Rou*, with notes by Glyn S. Burgess and Elisabeth van Houts (Woodbridge: Boydell, 2004).

Burgess, Glyn S. (trans.), *Wace, the Roman de Rou*, with the text of Anthony J. Holden and notes by Glyn S. Burgess and Elisabeth van Houts (St Helier: Société Jersiaise, 2002).

Holden, Anthony J. (ed.), *Le Roman de Rou de Wace*, SATF, 3 vols (Paris: Picard, 1970–3).

Laurent, Françoise, Le Saux, Françoise H. M., and Bragantini-Maillard, Nathalie (eds and trans), *Vie de sainte Marguerite, Conception Nostre Dame,*

Vie de Saint Nicolas by Wace, édition bilingue: Publication, tradition, présentation et notes, Champion Classiques, Moyen Âge, 50 (Paris: Champion, 2019).

EDITIONS AND TRANSLATIONS OF THE *ROMANS ANTIQUES*

Le Roman d'Énéas, édition bilingue: Édition et traduction du manuscrit A, présentation et notes, eds and trans Wilfrid Besnardeau and Francine Mora-Lebrun, Champion Classiques, Moyen Âge, 47 (Paris: Champion, 2018).

Le Roman de Thèbes, édition bilingue, publication, traduction, présentation et notes, ed. and trans. Aimé Petit, Champion Classiques, Moyen Âge, 25 (Paris: Champion, 2008).

Le Roman de Thèbes and the Roman d'Eneas, trans. Glyn S. Burgess and Douglas Kelly (Liverpool: University of Liverpool Press, 2021).

Le Roman de Troie par Benoît de Sainte-Maure, publié d'après tous les manuscrits connus, ed. Léopold Constans, 6 vols (Paris: Firmin Didot, 1904–12).

Roman de Troie par Benoît de Sainte-Maure, trans. Glyn S. Burgess and Douglas Kelly, Gallica, 41 (Cambridge: D. S. Brewer, 2017).

OTHER VERNACULAR TEXTS AND TRANSLATIONS

An Anglo-Norman Brut (Royal 13.A.xxi), ed. Alexander Bell, Anglo-Norman Texts, XXI–XXII (Oxford: Basil Blackwell for the Anglo-Norman Text Society, 1969).

Geffrei Gaimar, *Estoire des Engleis / History of the English*, ed. and trans. Ian Short (Oxford: Oxford University Press, 2009).

Lawman, *Brut*, trans. Rosamund Allen (New York: St Martin's Press, 1992).

LATIN TEXTS AND TRANSLATIONS

Bede, *Ecclesiastical History of the English People*, ed. Bertram Colgrave and R. A. B. Mynors, Oxford Medieval Texts (Oxford: Clarendon Press, 1969; repr. 2007).

Geoffrey of Monmouth, *The Historia Regum Britannie of Geoffrey of Monmouth, II: The First Variant Version: A Critical Edition*, ed. Neil Wright (Cambridge: D. S. Brewer, 1988).

Geoffrey of Monmouth, *The History of the Kings of Britain: An Edition and Translation of the De gestis Britonum [Historia Regum Britanniae]*, ed. Michael D. Reeve, trans. Neil Wright, Arthurian Studies, 69 (Woodbridge: Boydell, 2007).

Geoffrey of Monmouth, *The History of the Kings of Britain*, trans. Michael A. Faletra (Toronto: Broadview Press, 2008).

Geoffrey of Monmouth, *The History of the Kings of Britain*, trans. Lewis Thorpe (Harmondsworth: Penguin, 1966; repr. 1982).

Geoffrey of Monmouth, *The History of the Kings of Britain: The First Variant Version*, trans. David W. Burchmore, Dumbarton Oaks Medieval Library, 57 (Cambridge, MA: Harvard University Press, 2019).

Gildas, *The Ruin of Britain and Other Works*, ed. and trans. Michael Winterbottom, Arthurian Period Sources, 7 (London: Phillimore, 1978).

Henry, Archdeacon of Huntingdon, *Historia Anglorum: The History of the English People*, ed. and trans. Diana Greenway, Oxford Medieval Texts (Oxford: Clarendon Press, 1996) [with Latin facing-page].

Henry of Huntingdon, *The History of the English People 1000–1154*, ed. and trans. Diana Greenway, Oxford World's Classics (Oxford: Oxford University Press, 1996, 2002, 2009).

'Nennius', *The Historia Brittonum, III. The 'Vatican' Recension*, ed. David N. Dumville (Cambridge: D. S. Brewer, 1985).

'Nennius', *British History and the Welsh Annals*, ed. and trans. Michael Winterbottom, History from the Sources, 8 (London and Chichester: Phillimore, 1980).

William of Malmesbury, *Gesta Regum Anglorum: The History of the English Kings*, ed. and trans. R. A. B. Mynors† (completed by R. M. Thompson and M. Winterbottom), vol. I, Oxford Medieval Texts (Oxford: Clarendon Press, 1998); vol. II, General Introduction and Commentary, R. M. Thompson in collaboration with M. Winterbottom (Oxford: Clarendon Press, 1999).

Secondary Sources

Allen, Rosamund, Roberts, Jane, and Weinberg, Carole (eds), *Reading Laȝamon's Brut: Approaches and Explorations*, DQR Studies in Literature, 52 (Amsterdam: Rodopi, 2013).

Barber, Richard, *King Arthur: Hero and Legend* (New York: St Martins, 1961; repr. 1986).

Baumgartner, Emmanuèle, 'Passages d'Arthur en Normandie', in Letellier and Hüe (eds), *Le Roman de Brut entre mythe et histoire*, 19–33.

Bennett, Matthew, 'Poetry as History? The *Roman de Rou* of Wace as a Source for the Norman Conquest', in R. Allen Brown (ed.), *Anglo-Norman Studies V: Proceedings of the Battle Conference 1982* (Woodbridge: Boydell, 1983), 21–39.

Bennett, Matthew, 'The Uses and Abuses of Wace's *Roman de Rou*', in Burgess and Weiss (eds), *Maistre Wace*, 31–40.

Bennett, Matthew, 'Wace and Warfare', in R. Allen Brown (ed.), *Anglo-Norman Studies XI: Proceedings of the Battle Conference 1988* (Woodbridge: Boydell, 1989), 37–57.

Blacker, Jean, 'Anglo-Norman Verse Prophecies of Merlin', critical edn and trans., *Arthuriana*, 15/1 (2005), 1–125 (guest-edited volume); repr. with revisions as a book (Dallas, TX: Scriptorium Press, 2005).

Blacker, Jean, '"But That's Another Story": Wace, Laȝamon, and the Early Anonymous Old French Verse *Bruts*', *Arthuriana*, 31/4 (2021), 47–102.

Blacker, Jean, *Faces of Time: The Portrayal of the Past in Old French and Latin Historical Narrative of the Anglo-Norman Regnum* (Austin: University of Texas Press, 1994); rev. electronic version available through Amazon Kindle, 2019.

Blacker, Jean, '"La Geste est grande, longue e grieve a translater": History for Henry II', *Romance Quarterly*, 37 (1990), 387–96.

Blacker, Jean, 'Transformations of a Theme: The Depoliticization of the Arthurian World in the *Roman de Brut*', in Mary Flowers Braswell and John Bugge (eds), *The Arthurian Tradition: Essays in Convergence* (Tuscaloosa: University of Alabama Press, 1988), 54–74.

Blacker, Jean, *Wace: A Critical Bibliography*, with the collaboration of Glyn S. Burgess (St Helier: Société Jersiaise, 2008).

Blenner-Hassett, Roland, *A Study of the Place-Names in Lawman's Brut*, Stanford University Publications, University Series, Language and Literature, 9/1 (Stanford, CA: Stanford University Press, 1950).

Blenner-Hassett, Roland, 'Geoffrey of Monmouth's *Mons Agned* and *Castellum Puellarum*', *Speculum*, 17/2 (1942), 250–4.

Bratu, Christian, '*Translatio*, autorité et affirmation de soi chez Gaimar, Wace et Benoît de Sainte-Maure', *Medieval Chronicle*, 8 (2013), 135–64.

Breeze, Andrew, 'The Historical Arthur and Sixth-Century Scotland', *Northern History*, 52/2 (2015), 158–81.

Broadhurst, Karen, 'Henry II of England and Eleanor of Aquitaine: Patrons of Literature in England?', *Viator*, 27 (1996), 53–84.

Bromwich, Rachel, 'Brittany and the Arthurian Legend', in Rachel Bromwich, A. O. H. Jarman, and Brynley F. Roberts (eds), *The Arthur of the Welsh: The Arthurian Legend in Medieval Welsh Literature* (Cardiff: University of Wales Press, 1991), 249–72.

Burgess, Glyn S., 'Women in the Works of Wace', in Burgess and Weiss (eds), *Maistre Wace*, 91–106.

Burgess, Glyn S., and Weiss, Judith (eds), *Maistre Wace: A Celebration: Proceedings of the International Colloquium Held in Jersey 10–12 September 2004* (St Helier: Société Jersiaise, 2006).

Caldwell, Robert, 'Wace's *Roman de Brut* and the Variant Version of Geoffrey of Monmouth's *Historia Regum Britanniae*', *Speculum*, 31 (1956), 675–82.

Cohen, Jeffrey Jerome, *Of Giants: Sex, Monsters, and the Middle Ages*, Medieval Cultures, 17 (Minneapolis: University of Minnesota Press, 1999).

Crick, Julia C., *The Historia Regum Britannie of Geoffrey of Monmouth, III. A Summary Catalogue of the Manuscripts* (Woodbridge: Boydell, 1989).

D'Alessandro, Domenico, '*Historia Regum Britanniae* et *Roman de Brut*: Une comparaison formelle', *Medioevo Romanzo*, 21 (1994), 37–52.

Davies, R. R., 'Lordship or Colony?', in James Lydon (ed.), *The English in Medieval Ireland: Proceedings of the First Joint Meeting of the Royal Irish Academy and the British Academy, Dublin, 1982* (Dublin: Royal Irish Academy, 1984), 142–60.

Dean, Ruth J., *Anglo-Norman Literature: A Guide to Texts and Manuscripts*, with the collaboration of Maureen B. M. Boulton, Anglo-Norman Text Society, Occasional Publications Series, 3 (London: ANTS, 1999).

Dumville, David N., 'The Historical Value of the *Historia Brittonum*', in Richard Barber (ed.), *Arthurian Literature VI* (Cambridge: D. S. Brewer, 1986), 1–26.

Dumville, David N., '"Nennius" and the *Historia Brittonum*', *Studia Celtica*, 10/11 (1975–6), 78–95; repr. in Dumville, *Histories and Pseudo-histories of the Insular Middle Ages* (Aldershot: Variorum, 1990), X, 78–95.

Durling, Nancy Vine, 'Translation and Innovation in the *Roman de Brut*', in Jeanette Beer (ed.), *Medieval Translators and Their Craft*, Studies in Medieval Culture, 25 (Kalamazoo, MI: Medieval Institute Publications, 1989), 9–49.

Everard, Judith, 'Wace the Historical Background: Jersey in the Twelfth Century', in Burgess and Weiss (eds), *Maistre Wace*, 1–15.

Faletra, Michael A., 'Once and Future Britons: The Welsh in Lawman's *Brut*', *Medievalia et Humanistica*, 28 (2001), 1–23.

Fallan, Valentine, with Everard, Judith, 'Master Wace: A Cross-Channel Prosopographer for the Twelfth Century?', in David Roffe (ed.), *The English and Their Legacy, 900–1200: Essays in Honour of Ann Williams* (Woodbridge: Boydell, 2012), 61–77.

Faral, Edmond, *La Légende arthurienne études et documents: Première partie, les plus anciens textes*, 2 vols (Paris: Champion, 1929; repr. New York: AMS Press, 1973).

Field, Peter J., 'Arthur's Battles', *Arthuriana*, 18/4 (2008), 3–32.

Field, Peter J., 'Nennius and His History', *Studia Celtica*, 30 (1996), 159–65.

Finke, Laurie, and Shichtman, Martin B., 'The Mont St. Michel Giant: Sexual Violence and Imperialism in the Chronicles of Wace and Laȝamon', in Anna Roberts (ed.), *Violence against Women in Medieval Texts* (Gainesville: University Press of Florida, 1998), 56–74.

Flutre, Louis-Fernand, *Tables des noms propres avec toutes leurs variantes figurant dans les écrits en français ou en provençal et actuellement publiés* (Poitiers: Centre d'études supérieures de civilisation médiévale, 1962).

Foulon, Charles, 'Wace', in Roger Sherman Loomis (ed.), *Arthurian Literature in the Middle Ages: A Collaborative History* (Oxford: Clarendon Press, 1959), 94–103.

Gallais, Pierre, 'La *Variant Version* de l'*Historia Regum Britanniae* et le *Brut* de Wace', *Romania*, 87 (1966), 1–32.

Gillingham, John, 'The Contexts and Purposes of Geoffrey of Monmouth's *History of the Kings of Britain*', *Anglo-Norman Studies*, 13 (1990), 99–118; repr. in Gillingham, *The English in the Twelfth Century: Imperialism, National Identity and Political Value* (Woodbridge: Boydell, 2000), 19–39.

Glowka, Arthur Wayne, 'Masculinity, Male Sexuality, and Kinship in Wace's *Roman de Brut*', in Rosamond Allen, Lucy Perry, and Jane Roberts (eds), *Lazamon: Contexts, Language and Interpretation* (London: King's College London, Centre for Late Antique and Medieval Studies, 2002), 413–31.

Green, Thomas, *Concepts of Arthur* (Stroud: Tempus, 2007).

Grisward, Joël, 'A propos du thème descriptif de la tempête chez Wace et chez Thomas d'Angleterre', in *Mélanges de langue et de littérature du Moyen Âge et de la Renaissance offerts à Jean Frappier*, 2 vols., Publications romanes et françaises, 112 (Geneva: Droz, 1970), I, 375–89.

Hammond, Matthew H., 'Ethnicity and the Writing of Medieval Scottish History', *Scottish Historical Review*, 85/1 (2006), 1–27.

Henley, Georgia, and Smith, Joshua Byron (eds), *A Companion to Geoffrey of Monmouth*, Brill's Companions to European History, 22 (Leiden: Brill, 2020).

Higham, Nicholas J., *King Arthur: The Making of the Legend* (New Haven: Yale University Press, 2018).

Houck, Margaret, *Sources of the Roman de Brut of Wace*, University of California Publications in English, 5/2 (Berkeley and Los Angeles: University of California Press, 1941), 161–356.

Howell, Raymond, 'The Demolition of the Roman Tetrapylon in Caerleon: An Erasure of Memory?', *Oxford Journal of Archaeology*, 19/4 (2000), 387–95.

Hüe, Denis, 'Les Variantes de la séduction: Autour de la naissance d'Arthur', in Letellier and Hüe (eds), *Le Roman de Brut entre mythe et histoire*, 67–88.

Hüe, Denis, and Le Bossé, Michel Vital (eds), *Wace et l'Église, les princes et la foi* (Orléans: Paradigme, 2019).

Huot, Sylvia, *Outsiders: The Humanity and Inhumanity of Giants in Medieval French Romance* (Notre Dame, IN: University of Notre Dame Press, 2016).

Keller, Hans-Erich, 'De l'amour dans le *Roman de Brut*', in Norris J. Lacy and Gloria Torrini-Roblin (eds), *Continuations: Essays on Medieval French Literature and Language in Honor of John L. Grigsby* (Birmingham, AL: Summa Publications, 1989), 63–81.

Keller, Hans-Erich, *Étude descriptive sur le vocabulaire de Wace* (Berlin: Akademie-Verlag, 1953).

Keller, Hans-Erich, 'Le Mirage Robert Wace', *Zeitschrift für romanische Philologie*, 100 (1990), 465–6.

Keller, Hans-Erich, 'Two Toponymical Problems in Geoffrey of Monmouth and Wace: Eustreia and Siesia', *Speculum*, 49 (1974), 687–98.

Keller, Hans-Erich, 'Wace et Geoffroy de Monmouth: Problèmes de la chronologie des sources', *Romania*, 98 (1977), 1–14.

Keller, Hans-Erich, 'Wace et les Bretons', in *Actes du 14e Congrès international arthurien*, 2 vols (Rennes: Presses universitaires de Rennes, 1984), I, 354–70.

Kooper, Erik, 'Guests of the Court: An Unnoticed List of Arthurian Names (British Library, Add. 6113)', in Catherine M. Jones and Logan Whalen (eds), *Li premerains vers: Essays in Honor of Keith Busby* (Amsterdam: Rodopi, 2011), 223–34.

Lacy, Norris J., 'The Form of the *Brut*'s Arthurian Sequence', in Hans R. Runte, Henri Niedzielski, and William L. Hendrickson (eds), *Jean Misrahi Memorial Volume: Studies in Medieval Literature* (Columbia, SC: French Literature Publications Company, 1977), 150–8.

Langille, Édouard, '"Mençunge ou folie?": Commentaire sur la mise en "romanz" de Wace', *Dalhousie French Studies*, 39–40 (1997), 19–32.

Leckie, R. William, Jr., *The Passage of Dominion: Geoffrey of Monmouth and the Periodization of Insular History in the Twelfth Century* (Toronto: University of Toronto Press, 1981).

Le Saux, Françoise H. M., *A Companion to Wace* (Cambridge: D. S. Brewer, 2005).

Le Saux, Françoise H. M., *Layamon's Brut: The Poem and Its Sources*, Arthurian Studies, 19 (Cambridge: D. S. Brewer, 1989).

Le Saux, Françoise H. M. (ed.), *The Text and Tradition of Layamon's Brut*, Arthurian Studies, 33 (Cambridge: D. S. Brewer, 1994).

Le Saux, Françoise H. M., 'Wace's *Roman de Brut*', in W. J. R. Barron (ed.), *The Arthur of the English: The Arthurian Legend in Medieval English Life and Literature* (Cardiff: University of Wales Press, 1999; new paperback edn, 2001), 18–22.

Le Saux, Françoise H. M., and Damian-Grint, Peter, 'The Arthur of the Chronicles', in Glyn S. Burgess and Karen Pratt (eds), *The Arthur of the French: The Arthurian Legend in Medieval French and Occitan Literature* (Cardiff: University of Wales Press, 2006; paperback version, 2009), 93–111.

Letellier, Claude, and Hüe, Denis (eds), *Le Roman de Brut entre mythe et histoire: Actes du colloque, Bagnoles de l'Orne, septembre 2001*, Medievalia, 47 (Orléans: Paradigme, 2003).

Loomba, Ania, *Colonialism/Postcolonialism* (3rd edn, Abingdon: Routledge, 2015).

Lyotard, Jean-François, *La Condition postmoderne: Rapport sur le savoir* (Paris: Éditions de Minuit, 1979).

MacColl, Alan, 'The Meaning of "Britain" in Medieval and Early Modern England', *Journal of British Studies*, 45 (2006), 248–69.

McKee, Arielle C., and Pirzadeh, Saba, 'Arthurian Eco-Conquest in Geoffrey of Monmouth, Wace, and Lazamon', *Parergon*, 34 (2017), 1–24.

Marx, Jean, 'Wace et la matière de Bretagne', in *Mélanges de langue et de littérature du Moyen Âge et de la Renaissance offerts à Jean Frappier, Professeur à la Sorbonne, par ses collègues, ses élèves et ses amis*, 2 vols, Publications romanes et françaises, 112 (Geneva: Droz, 1970), II, 771–4.

Mathey, Laurence, 'De l'*Historia Regum Britanniae* de Geoffroy de Monmouth au *Roman de Brut* de Wace: Étude d'un écart à valeur idéologique', in Jean-Claude Aubailly et al. (eds), *'Et c'est la fin pour quoy sommes ensemble': Hommage à Jean Doufournet*, 2 vols (Paris: Champion, 1993), II, 941–8.

Mathey, Laurence, 'De la Vulgate à la Variant Version de l'*Historia regum Britannie*: *Le Roman de Brut* de Wace à l'épreuve du texte source', in Hélène Tétrel and Géraldine Veysseyre (eds), *L'Historia regum Britannie et les 'Bruts' en Europe, I* (Paris: Classiques Garnier, 2015), 129–39.

Mathey, Laurence, '*Le Roman de Brut* de Wace: Une œuvre inclassable?', in Marianne Bouchardon and Michèle Guéret Laferté (eds), *L'Œuvre inclassable: Actes du colloque organisé à l'Université de Rouen en novembre 2015* (Rouen: Publications numériques du CÉRÉDI, 2016), 1–6.

Matthews, William, 'Where was Siesia-Sessoyne?', *Speculum*, 49 (1974), 680–6.

Morris, Rosemary, *The Character of King Arthur in Medieval Literature* (Cambridge: D. S. Brewer, 1982).

Morris, Rosemary, 'Uther and Igerne: A Study in Uncourtly Love', in Richard Barber (ed.), *Arthurian Literature IV* (Woodbridge: D. S. Brewer, 1985), 70–92.

Noble, James, 'Patronage, Politics, and the Figure of Arthur in Geoffrey of Monmouth, Wace and Layamon', in Keith Busby (ed.), *Arthurian Yearbook II* (New York: Garland, 1992), 159–78.

Paradisi, Gioia, 'Remarques sur l'exégèse onomastique et étymologique chez Wace (*expositio, ratio nominis*)', in Burgess and Weiss (eds), *Maistre Wace*, 149–65.

Paris, Gaston, 'Sur un épisode d'Aimeri de Narbonne', *Romania*, 9/3 (1880), 515–46.

Pelan, Margaret, *L'Influence du Brut de Wace sur les romanciers français de son temps* (Paris: Droz, 1931; repr. Geneva: Slatkine, 1974).

Pickens, Rupert T., 'Arthur's Channel Crossing: Courtesy and the Demonic in Geoffrey of Monmouth and Wace's *Brut*', *Arthuriana*, 7 (1997), 3–19.

Pickens, Rupert T., 'Arthurian Time and Space: Chrétien's *Conte du Graal* and Wace's *Brut*', *Medium Aevum*, 75 (2006), 219–46.

Pickens, Rupert T., 'Vasselage épique et courtoisie romanesque dans le *Roman de Brut*', in Jacques Chocheyras (ed.), *De l'œventure épique à l'œventure romanesque: Mélanges offerts à André de Mondach par ses amis, collègues et élèves* (Bern: Peter Lang, 1997), 165–200.

Pomel, Fabienne, 'Le Déni de la fable chez Wace: La Parole de l'historiographe, du conteur et du prophète dans le *Roman de Brut*', in Letellier and Hüe (eds.), *Le Roman de Brut entre mythe et histoire*, 143–62.

Queillé, Anaïg, 'La Violence des origines dans le *Roman de Brut* de Wace', in R. J. Carluer (ed.), *Violence et société en Bretagne et dans les pays celtiques, colloque international, Brest, 18–20 mars 1999*, Études sur la Bretagne et les pays celtiques (Brest: Université de Bretagne Occidentale, 2000), 69–104.

Rider, Jeff, 'The Fictional Margin: The Merlin of the *Brut*', *Modern Philology*, 87 (1989), 1–12.

Rollo, David, *Historical Fabrication, Ethnic Fable and French Romance in Twelfth-Century England*, Edward C. Monographs on Medieval Literature, 9 (Lexington, KY: French Forum, 1998).

Sargent-Baur, Barbara N., '*Dux bellorum/rex militum/roi fainéant*: The Transformation of Arthur in the Twelfth Century', in Edward Donald Kennedy (ed.), *King Arthur: A Casebook* (New York: Garland, 1996), 29–43.

Sargent-Baur, Barbara N., 'Veraces historiae aut fallaces fabulae', in Norris J. Lacy (ed.), *Text and Intertext in Medieval Arthurian Literature* (New York: Garland, 1996), 25–39.

Sayers, William, 'A Norse Etymology for Luff, "Weather Edge of a Sail" ', *American Neptune*, 66/1 (2001), 25–38.

Sayers, William, 'Arthur's Embarkation for Gaul in a Fresh Translation of Wace's *Roman de Brut*', *Romance Notes*, 46/2 (2006), 143–56.

Schmolke-Hasselmann, Beate, 'The Round Table: Ideal, Fiction, Reality', in Richard Barber (ed.), *Arthurian Literature, II* (1982), 41–75.

Short, Ian, 'What was Gaimar's *Estoire des Bretuns*?', *Cultura Neolatina*, 71 (2011), 147–9.

Sims-Williams, Patrick, 'Celtomania and Celtoscepticism', *Cambrian Medieval Celtic Studies*, 36 (1998), 1–36.

Spiegel, Gabrielle M., *The Past as Text: The Theory and Practice of Medieval Historiography* (Baltimore: Johns Hopkins University Press, 1997).

Sturm-Maddox, Sara, ' "Tenir sa terre en pais": Social Order in the *Brut* and in the *Conte del Graal*', *Studies in Philology*, 81 (1984), 28–41.

Tahkokallio, Jaakko, 'Early Manuscript Dissemination', in Georgia Henley and Joshua Byron Smith (eds), *A Companion to Geoffrey of Monmouth*, Brill's Companions to European History, 22 (Leiden: Brill, 2020), 155–80.

Tilliette, Jean-Yves, 'Invention du récit: La "Brutiade" de Geoffroy de Monmouth (*Historia regum Britanniae*, §6–22)', *Cahiers de civilisation médiévale*, 39 (1996), 217–33.

Trachsler, Richard, *Clôtures du cycle arthurien: Études et textes*, Publications romanes et françaises, 215 (Geneva: Droz, 1996).

Van Houts, Elisabeth, 'The Ship List of William the Conqueror', in R. A. Brown (ed.), *Anglo-Norman Studies X: Proceedings of the Battle Conference 1987* (Woodbridge: Boydell, 1988), 159–93.

Van Houts, Elisabeth, 'Wace as Historian', in K. S. B. Keats-Rohan (ed.), *Family Trees and the Roots of Politics: The Prosopography of Britain and France from the Tenth to the Twelfth Century* (Cambridge: Boydell, 1997), 103–32; repr. in Burgess (trans.), *The History of the Norman People*, xxxv–lxii.

Walters, Lori J., 'Reconfiguring Wace's Round Table: Walwein and the Rise of National Vernaculars', *Arthuriana*, 15/2 (2005), 39–58.

Walters, Lori J., 'Re-Examining Wace's Round Table', in Keith Busby and Christopher Kleinherz (eds), *Courtly Arts and the Art of Courtliness: Selected Papers from the Eleventh Triennial Congress of the International Courtly Literature Society* (Cambridge: D. S. Brewer, 2006), 721–44.

Warren, Michelle, 'Memory Out of Line: Hebrew Etymology in the *Roman de Brut* and *Merlin*', *Modern Language Notes*, 118/4 (2003), 989–1014.

Wright, Neil, 'Geoffrey of Monmouth and Bede', in Richard Barber (ed.), *Arthurian Literature VI* (Cambridge: D. S. Brewer, 1986), 27–59.

Wright, Neil, 'The Place of Henry of Huntingdon's *Epistola ad Warinum* in the Text-History of Geoffrey of Monmouth's *Historia regum Britannie*: A Preliminary Investigation', in G. Jondorf and D. N. Dumville (eds), *France and the British Isles in the Middle Ages and Renaissance: Essays by Members of Girton College, Cambridge, in Memory of Ruth Morgan* (Woodbridge: Boydell, 1991), 71–113.

Wulf, Charlotte A. T., 'A Comparative Study of Wace's Guenevere in the Twelfth Century', in Friedrich Wolfzettel (ed.), *Arthurian Romance and Gender / Masculin / féminin dans le roman arthurien médiéval / Geschlecterrolen in mittellalterlichen Artusroman* (Amsterdam: Rodopi, 1995), 66–78.

York, Ernest C., 'Wace's *Wenelande*: Identification and Speculation', *Romance Notes*, 22 (1981), 101–4.

Zatta, Jane, 'Translating the *Historia*: The Ideological Transformation of the *Historia Regum Britanniae* in Twelfth-Century Vernacular Chronicles', *Arthuriana*, 8 (1998), 148–61.

Further Reading in Oxford World's Classics

Chaucer, G., *The Canterbury Tales*, ed. David Wright and Christopher Cannon.

Malory, T., *Le Morte Darthur*, ed. Helen Cooper.

Mandeville, J., *The Book of Marvels and Travels*, ed. Anthony Bale.

Sir Gawain and the Green Knight, trans. Keith Harrison, ed. Helen Cooper.

The Song of Roland and Other Poems of Charlemagne, ed. Simon Gaunt and Karen Pratt.

SUMMARY OF THE TEXT

1–1050 Aeneas escapes the Greeks who conquered Troy; the birth of Brutus; Brutus and the Trojans leave Greece and head for Spain and France; the Trojans defeat the French (with the help of Corineus, a Trojan lord already in France) and leave for Britain.

1051–2050 When they arrive, Corineus defeats the giant Gogmagog (Cornwall is named after Corineus); Brutus names Britain after himself and founds New Troy; he gives Britain to his three sons, Locrinus (Logres), Kamber (Kambrie, i.e. Wales), and Albanactus (Albany, i.e. Scotland); Ebrauc (Ebraucus) and his fifty sons and daughters; King Leir and his three daughters; Leir dies and is buried in Leicester.

2151–3240 Reigns of a number of kings; the brothers Belin (Belinus) and Brenne (Brennius) fight each other and then defeat the Romans; Brenne remains in Rome and Belin returns to Britain founding Carleon, the City of Legions ('Kaerusc', 'town on the River Usk'), and 'Belinsgate' in London ('Billingsgate' on the Thames).

3241–976 More kings; Caesar arrives in Britain and demands tribute from Cassibellan.

3977–4834 Britons attack the Romans but are forced to capitulate and pay the tribute; the Romans retreat; Wace declares that he did not know if 'England ever paid tribute until Caesar had conquered her' (4816–20) (he uses the word 'England' here, rather than 'Bretaine' ('Britain', 'Britannia') as in the *HRB*).[1]

4835–5198 Cassibellan lives for seven years after Caesar leaves and his nephew, Tenuancius, reigns after him; then the son of Tenuancius, Kimbelin becomes king and pays the tribute as well; after the latter's death, the emperor Claudius wants to restore the tribute which

[1] It is worth noting that Wace uses the word 'Engleterre' already in v. 4, although his primary focus for the work is a history of the Britons, and he often uses 'Bretaine' as well, at times apparently interchangeably. However, 'Bretaine' is still used far more frequently, and it tends to not be a political usage, but rather a geographione. Cf. Alan MacColl who states: 'Wace omitted Geoffrey's opening description of Britain, supplying instead his own introduction, which instructs us to read what follows as the history of England. He will explain, he says, "who they were, and whence they came, who once upon a time were the rulers of England (Engleterre)". The result is a reorientation of the whole narrative' ('The Meaning of "Britain" in Medieval and Early Modern England', 255–6).

Wider, elder son of Kimbelin, had left by the wayside; Arviragus, younger son of Kimbelin, reconciles with Claudius, marries his daughter, and rules Britain; Marius kills Rodric, the king of the Picts, and gives Caithness to the Picts, but the Britons refuse to give them wives, so they cross to Ireland to get wives for themselves.

5199–272 King Luces (son of Coil, grandson of Marius) asked Pope Eleutere (Eleutherius) to send preachers to convert the Britons to Christianity; bishops Dunian and Fagan come, teach Luces the laws, convert him, and the rest of the Britons follow suit; through the king dioceses are established and divided into parishes.

5273–651 The Roman senator Sever (Septimius Severus) is sent to Britain; narrative events include his building of a dyke ('un fossé', v. 5309) across the land—which could refer to Sever's building of a defensive wall, which has been linked to either the reinforcing of the Antonine Wall (*c.* AD 208) or, most frequently, to the rebuilding of Hadrian's Wall (*c.*208–11); the Romans beg that when Sever is killed he be buried with honour, which he is, in York.

5652–942 When King Choel dies, Constant marries his daughter Eleine, who becomes the mother of the emperor Constantine (of the house of Constantine); Eleine and Constantine travel to Jerusalem, where she finds the 'True Cross'; although Cunan should have inherited Britain, Maximien steals it from him, later giving him Brittany to rule; Maximien promises to get rid of all its inhabitants, making Brittany solely for the Britons.

5943–6140 Maximien brings over 100,000 peasants from Britain to till the land; he also wants the Britons in Brittany to shun native women, and thus asks Dionot, king of Britain, to send his beautiful daughter Ursula, along with 11,000 marriageable girls; but they are lost at sea, and those who survive are raped and killed by Wanis, king of Hungary, and Melga, lord of Scythia; Wace thus identifies this story with the legend of the martyrdom of St Ursula and the 11,000 virgins.

6141–258 The Britons fight Wanis and Melga; the Romans help the Britons, the former build the Antonine Wall and then finally give up, telling the Britons that they can no longer constantly make the voyage to Britain to protect the Britons from the Huns and other ravaging hordes; the Romans leave Britain.

6259–674 Seeking help from Brittany, the Britons elect Constantine king; but Vortigern makes Constant (the monk), Constantine's eldest son, king; Vortigern sends for Pictish mercenaries, who kill Constant and make Vortigern king.

6675–7075 The guardians of Constant's two younger brothers, Uther and Aurelius, fear for the boys' lives at the hands of Vortigern and so they take the boys to Brittany; the arrival of the Saxon brothers Hengist and Horsa, or, as it is known in historical narratives, the beginning of the *adventus Saxonum*; the Saxons help Vortigern against the Picts; upon Hengist's request, Vortigern gives him land to build a castle that becomes 'Thongcastre'; after completion of the castle, eighteen ships arrive filled with Hengist's kin, knights, and followers, and Ronwen, Hengist's daughter with whom Vortigern falls madly in love; although she is a pagan, Vortigern marries her; Hengist asks for more land, this time in Scotland, for his son Octa and the latter's cousin Ebissa (Eosa).

7076–308 The Britons rebel, overthrowing Vortigern and making his son Vortimer king; Vortimer restores to the Britons what they had lost through the Saxons and rebuilds churches; in Bede and *HRB*, St Germanus and St Lupus come to fight the Pelagian heresy, but in Wace Hengist is instead blamed for the fall from the true religion; Ronwen poisons her stepson and Vortigern is restored to the throne; Hengist brings 300,000 armed men from Germany because he fears the Britons, and plans the treachery of the 'night of the long knives' wherein the Saxons, having hidden knives in their boots, proceed to slaughter 460 Britons at a peace parley on the calends of May (1 May); the Saxons want to kill Vortigern, but Hengist lets him escape with his life, the king having given them London, Winchester, Lincoln, York, and Chichester; Wace provides a false etymology to the effect that Sussex, Essex, and Middlesex were named after the Saxon word for knives, and the English then proceeded to change the word for knives, given their shame at what their ancestors had done.

7309–542 Vortigern abandons everything to the Saxons and flees across the Severn, deep into Wales; he tries to build a castle but it keeps crumbling, so he asks his soothsayers, who recommend that he find the blood of a fatherless boy, kill him, and sprinkle it upon the mortar so that his castle would remain standing; they find the fatherless Merlin and ask the governor for him; Merlin declares Vortigern's soothsayers to be liars and proceeds to explain why the towers will not stand: the pool beneath needs to be drained to reveal two sleeping dragons in two hollow stones, one all white, the other 'red as blood'; Vortigern begs Merlin to tell him what the dragons mean, and Merlin makes his prophecies, which Wace declines to translate, saying he does not know how to interpret them, 'as I would not like to say anything, in case what I say does not happen' (both MS D and MS L have the Prophecies inserted into Wace's text, the former in decasyllables, the latter in alexandrines).

7543–82 Merlin foretells of Vortigern's death; Aurelius and Uther want to avenge their brother Constant; Aurelius will be king first, then he is poisoned; Utherpendragon will then reign, but he too will be poisoned and die; his son, the 'boar of Cornwall', will 'devour the traitors and destroy all your kin . . . valiant and brave, conquering all his enemies'.

7583–8178 The brothers arrive from Brittany, and the Britons, whom Hengist had chased into the woods, make Aurelius their king; Vortigern flees to Wales, building a castle in Hergrin (see *HRB*, §119.33, Hergign), near the river Wye, on top of Mount Cloart (*HRB*, §119.34, Doartius). Hengist flees to Scotland; Aurelius' army fights Hengist and defeats him; Eldulf beheads Hengist; Octa, the latter's son, begs Aurelius for mercy, which the latter grants, also giving him land in Scotland; Aurelius wants to erect a monument to commemorate those who died during the 'night of the long knives'; Uther is chosen to go to Ireland to fetch the stones, the Giants' Dance, from Mount Killomar in Ireland, but only Merlin can help the Britons accomplish this task; the stones are brought to Amesbury to form Stonehenge.

8179–406 Ambrosius is poisoned by one of Vortigern's sons, Paschent; Merlin reads the omen of this event in the extraordinarily bright comet; part of the omen reveals that there will be a son who will 'conquer all the land beyond France'; the daughter will be married in Scotland and 'many good heirs will be born from her'; Uther heeds Merlin's words, prepares himself for battle, and kills Paschent; Uther has two golden dragons made, one of which he carries into battle and the other he gives to Winchester; Uther is now called Pendragon or 'Dragon's Head'.

8407–822 After killing Paschent, Uther becomes king; Octa attacks the Britons; Uther defeats Octa and invites all his lords and their wives to London for a feast; Gorlois, count of Cornwall, realizes that Uther is falling in love with his wife, Ygerne, and so leaves the banquet precipitously, taking her to Tintagel; suffering from unrequited love, Uther begs for Merlin's help, counselled by Ulfin, and Merlin agrees to disguise Uther as Gorlois so that he can lie with Ygerne, unbeknownst to her that he was not her husband; that night Arthur is conceived; Uther later marries Ygerne, Gorlois having died in battle, and they have many happy years together, also conceiving Arthur's sister, Anna, who is eventually given to Loth of Lothian.

8823–9008 Uther reigns in peace for many years until he kills Octa and Eosa in battle, eventually being poisoned by the Saxons; after his death, he is buried at Stonehenge beside his brother Aurelius.

9009–272 Arthur is crowned at the age of 15 by the Britons; he vows to never let the Saxons have peace as long as they are in the land; the Battle of Lincoln takes place; the Saxons are spared; they leave, but then return and lay waste to Devonshire, Somerset, and a large section of Dorset; Arthur leaves Scotland, where he was defeating the Scots, and heads to Bath.

9273–586 The Battle of Bath; Arthur dons his finest armour, his sword Caliburn, his shield Pridwen on the inside of which an image of the Virgin Mary is depicted, so that he would always see her when he was in battle; he alone kills four hundred Saxons, more than his whole army; the defeat and death of Colgrin and Baldulf; Arthur heads for Loch Lomond; the Scots beg for mercy through their bishops and their womenfolk; tales of the marvellous lakes.

9587–730 Arthur's men praise him; he stays in York until Christmas Day, feasting at Christmas; Arthur restores York, giving the peasants work, restoring inheritances to the dispossessed nobles, and granting them revenues, including three royal brothers Loth, Agusel, and Urien to whom he restores lands north of the Humber: he returns Moray to Urien, Scotland to Agusel, and Lothian to Loth, whose son Walwein (Gawain, Gauvain) was still a small boy; Arthur marries Guinevere; after conquering Ireland, he conquers Iceland; Orkney, Gotland, and Wenelande capitulate to him in Ireland; he is welcomed back to England with great joy.

9731–10170 The twelve years' peace; Arthur establishes the Round Table; goes to Norway to make his brother-in-law, Loth, king there; he should have inherited the throne from King Sichelin, as he was his nephew and sole heir; Arthur then invades France, fighting Frollo the Roman legate in single combat as a result of the latter's suggestion, so as not to damage Paris more than necessary; Arthur defeats Frollo and conquers all of France, giving Anjou and Angers to Kay his seneschal, Normandy to Bedivere his cupbearer, Flanders to Holdin, Le Mans to his cousin Borel, Boulogne to Ligier, and Ponthieu to Richier.

10171–11058 After making all his friends rich, Arthur returns to England; he summons all his barons to Caerleon for Pentecost; list of all the barons who attend the court, including many Welshmen and their sons; Arthur is crowned with great pomp, as is his queen Guinevere; there are many games and entertainments; on the fourth day gives many gifts, and while doing so, twelve white-haired men appear with a message from Lucius, the ruler of Rome, who demands tribute in keeping with the traditions of times past; furious, Arthur prepares for war after sending a message to the Romans, saying that he would never pay tribute and that instead he would demand tribute of Rome.

11059–608 The messengers return to Rome, and convey Arthur's message, while reporting that the king is admirable; Lucius prepares for war; Arthur summons his barons and prepares his army; the king entrusts the kingdom to Mordred and sails for France; Arthur's dream; they disembark at Barfleur and Arthur goes to Mont Saint-Michel to engage with the giant there; Eleine's nurse tells Bedivere the story of Eleine's rape and murder; Arthur fights the giant; Hoel grieves for his niece, and they build a chapel to St Mary in her memory, which is now called Eleine's Tomb (Tombeleine).

11609–13076 When the Irish and the others arrive, Arthur proceeds through Normandy to Burgundy; the battle begins to determine whether Arthur or the Romans—each of whom had conquered it—should have France; Gawain carries a message to Lucius; the Romans pursue the messengers and the war is on; Petreius is captured and the Romans ambush the Britons; ambush is foiled by Guitart; Lucius heads to Langres; Arthur arranges his troops, addresses them, and Lucius does the same for his own troops; the armies meet; Boccus kills Bedivere and Hyrelgas avenges him; the Britons reach the Roman standard; Gawain engages Lucius; Morvid's troops help the Britons win; Arthur sends Lucius' body back to Rome on a bier, with the message that whosoever would demand tribute would be sent back in the same way; Kay who had built the castle of Chinon is mortally wounded; Mordred usurps Britain and takes Arthur's wife as well.

13077–298 Arthur heads back, mourning Gawain and Agusel of Scotland; Arthur's ships land at Sandwich; Mordred flees to Cornwall; Guinevere goes to Caerleon and enters an abbey; the last battle is engaged at Camlaan (by the river 'Camble') in Cornwall; both Arthur and Mordred are mortally wounded; Arthur has himself borne away to Avalon to have his wounds tended, 542 years after the Incarnation; to Cador, Constantine's son, he gives his kingdom until he could return; the 'Breton hope'.

13299–384 Constantine has both of Mordred's sons beheaded; Constantine reigns for three years; next his nephew Cunan reigns, then Malgo, then Cariz.

13385–624 Gormund inherits his father's kingdom in Africa, but he does not want it since he did not conquer it himself; he sails to Ireland, conquers it, and comes to Britain; the Saxons strike a bargain with him, that he should conquer Britain and give it to them as a fief; the pagans wreak havoc on the island; the Britons are besieged; Gormund gives his 'Donation' to the Saxons, destroys much of Britain—including Chichester which is conquered through the stratagem of the sparrows—and leaves for France with king Louis's nephew, Ysembard (Isembard).

13625–82 Reprise of how Gormund lays ruin to Britain; how the 'Donation' leads the Saxons to rename themselves 'English'; the Saxons rename everything in their own language, not wishing to give up their own customs or language; the English cannot settle on a king and thus there is chaos and no support for Christianity for over a hundred years.

13683–946 St Gregory, the pope, sends St Augustine to convert the English; in Dorchester, the inhabitants mock Augustine by hanging rays' tails on his vestments, and God punishes them by humiliating them with tails (the legend of the 'tailed Englishmen'); God comforts Augustine and helps him establish Cerne abbey (Cernel); when the English and the Saxons have all been baptized, Augustine goes to Bangor Abbey where the abbot Dionot and over 300 monks refuse to be subject to him since they already had a prelate in Caerleon, ratified by Rome; Augustine's anger at this refusal leads him to orchestrate a gathering of knights and foot soldiers at Leicester who proceed to slaughter 2,200 Bangor monks like sheep.

13947–99 The Britons make Chatwan (Cadwan) king, and he holds off the Saxons until they beg for mercy; a war is averted and Elfrid, king of Northumbria, has the land north of the Humber and Chatwan the land south.

14000–638 Peace is kept between them; Elfrid's son Edwin and Chatwan's son Chadwalein are brought up together, but Edwin wants to be consecrated and Chadwalein, sympathetic, is overruled by his barons, and battle preparations begin; Edwin seizes Chadwalein's kingdom; Brien feeds the latter flesh from his own thigh to save his life; Brien kills the soothsayer Pellit; Chadwalein becomes an ally of Peanda, king of Mercia; Edwin is killed at the Battle of Hatfield; Peanda loses many men at the Battle of Hevenfeld; Chadwalein—following the advice of Margadud, lord of South Wales—sets Peanda against Oswi, who was also an English ruler; both are killed.

14639–774 Chadwalein rules the land justly for forty-eight years; at his passing he is mourned greatly and buried in London; his son, Cadwallader, is the last king of the Britons to rule England; there is a great famine; not knowing what to do, Cadwallader goes to Brittany, to King Alain, a good friend and nephew of Salomun, who had shown great affection for Cadwallader's father; the Saxons send for more of their people who come in swarms and rename everything in their language, but they distribute the lands and lordships just as the Britons had first set them out; at that time Athelstan was king, the first Englishman to rule all England, except for Wales and Cornwall.

14775–842 Cadwallader wants to return to rule Britain, but a divine voice tells him that he must give up travelling to England and go to Rome; the English were to have Britain; the Britons were never to recover it until the time when Merlin's prophecy was fulfilled; nor could this happen until his remains were brought back from Rome and presented to Britain; Cadwallader summons his son Yvor and his nephew Yni and bids them to be 'lords of the Britons so that they do not descend into dishonour due to lack of a ruler'; eleven days before May, seventeenth day of April, seven hundred and one years after Christ's incarnation in holy Mary, Cadwallader dies.

14843–58 Yvor and Yni cross the sea with a large fleet, making the remainder of the Britons 'whom we now call Welsh, and who live over towards the north' their subjects; they never again had the power to regain Logres; they have degenerated 'when compared with the nobility, honour, customs, and way of life of their ancestors'.

14859–866 'Here ends the history of the Britons and of the line of barons who came from the lineage of Brutus and ruled England for a long time. Master Wace composed this narrative in French one thousand five hundred and fifty-five years after God became flesh for our redemption.'

THE ROMAN DE BRUT
OF
WACE

PROLOGUE

(1–8) WHOEVER wishes to hear about, and to know about, kings and heirs, as one passed to another, who they were and where they came from, about who first ruled England and which kings it had, in order, who came earlier and who came later, Master Wace, who is telling the truth about this, has translated this.*

AENEAS ESCAPES THE GREEKS WHO HAVE CONQUERED TROY

(9–66) As the book* sets forth, when the Greeks had conquered Troy and destroyed the whole country, in order to take vengeance on Paris, who had abducted Helen from Greece,* Duke Aeneas escaped the great slaughter with some considerable difficulty. He had a son, whom he took with him and whose name was Ascanius; he had no other son or daughter. He had twenty ships filled with his kinsmen, his household knights, and his riches. For a long time he wandered over the sea, and he was forced to endure a long period of hardship. He was forced to undergo many great perils, many great torments, and much suffering, but after a lengthy period of time he arrived in Italy. The land where Rome had been founded was then called Italy. There was no sign of Rome there at that time, nor would there be for some considerable time. Aeneas had toiled for a long time, sailed for a long time, and been at sea for a long time, crossing a very great expanse of water. He had reached the shores of Italy, a country of great abundance, where the Tiber flows into the sea, and which is very close to where Rome was situated. Latinus, a king who lived there, ruled this entire kingdom in peace. He was a very powerful and wealthy man, but he was old and well on in years. He honoured Aeneas greatly and gave him a large part of his kingdom on the coast. Against the wishes of the queen he promised to give him his daughter and make him heir to his kingdom; he had no other child or heir. After his death he would have all his wealth. The daughter was a very beautiful maiden, whose name was Lavinia. But Turnus, who was lord and duke of Tuscany, was to take her as his wife. This Turnus, who was his neighbour, was a very powerful man, and he knew that Latinus had given his daughter to Aeneas. He was grief-stricken and envious, for he had loved her for a long time, and she had been granted to him. Because of this, he waged a great war against Aeneas and fought with him in single combat. He was a bold and strong knight, but he was defeated and killed. Then Aeneas took the maiden; he became king and she queen. Afterwards, he never again encountered anyone who harmed him, nor anyone who withstood him in any way.

(67–106) After Aeneas had married Lavinia and conquered the whole of the land, he lived and reigned for four years. He fortified a castle and gave it Lavinia's name, calling it Lavinium. The wife and domain were his for four years, and in that fourth year, when his end came, Lavinia conceived, but she had not yet given birth to the child. Time passed quickly, however, and she had a son. His own name was Silvius, and his surname was Postumus. Ascanius, who came from Troy with his father, brought him up and held him in the highest affection. Ascanius' mother was Creusa. She was the daughter of King Priam, but in the tumult and the disruption there was when Aeneas was escaping from Troy he lost her in the great throng. After his father's death this Ascanius ruled the domain for a long time. He built a city that was called Alba Longa and he left this land to his stepmother, granting her free possession of the castle that Aeneas had built so that she would have it as long as she lived. But he took away the gods of Troy that Aeneas had placed there. He wanted to have them in Alba, but they could not remain there. He was never able to take them away in such a fashion that he could find them the next morning. They went back to the temple, but I do not know how this happened. He ruled the land for thirty-four years, during which time there was scarcely any conflict.

(107–48) When Ascanius died, his brother Silvius, who was born of Lavinia, inherited the land, and after Aeneas' death Ascanius had a son also named Silvius. He bore his uncle's name, but did not live long, lasting only for a short time. He had secretly been in love with a maiden who was a niece of Lavinia. He had relations with her, and she conceived. When Ascanius realized this, he had his soothsayers and his wise diviners come to him. Through them, he said, he wanted to know the nature of the child the lady was to bear. They drew lots and prophesied, and in their prediction they found that a son the lady would have would kill his father and his mother, and he would be thrown into exile. But later he would enjoy great honour. This came true as they stated, and it happened the way they promised, for on the due date, when he was born, the mother died and the child lived. She died in the act of giving birth, but the son was born safely and given the name Brutus. When he was no more than fifteen years old, he went hunting in the wood with his father, who brought misfortune upon him. Together they set off at an evil hour and encountered a herd of deer. The father drove them towards his son, who took a firm grip on a wooden bow shaft and fired an arrow at a deer he had spotted. But the arrow missed, striking his father and killing him. He did not do this intentionally. But, at this, all his kinsmen were furious. They drove Brutus out of the kingdom.

(149–60) Brutus crossed the sea and went to Greece, where he found amongst the Trojans the entire lineage of Helenus, one of the sons of King Priam, and also many other lineages which had been taken prisoner. There were many members of his own lineage there, but they were held as slaves. Brutus found there his kinsmen, of which there was a very large number in Greece. Since they were exiled, they had become more and more numerous.

(161–208) Brutus had not been there long when he gained a great reputation for audacity and prowess, as well as for learning and generosity. His kinsmen honoured him greatly, as did all the other prisoners. They gave him gifts, made promises to him, and very frequently said to him that, if he could, and if he dared, he should release them from captivity. There was a great company of men, and if they had a leader who would support them, instruct them, and lead them into battle, it would be distinctly possible for them to be freed from slavery. Amongst them there were more than a good seven thousand fine and brave knights, in addition to foot soldiers, servants, women, and children. If he were willing to lead them, they would have him raised to the rank of duke, for they would tolerate great hardship in order to live in peace and without slavery. There was no one who was displeased by this. In Greece there was a noble youth by the name of Assaracus. He was the son of a wealthy baron, one of the finest men in the whole region. But his mother was born in Troy. He was Greek through his father and Trojan through his mother. His mother was a concubine, but nevertheless his father had given him three fine castles as his heritage. Assaracus, who was a bastard, had by his father a brother who was born from his wife and in accordance with their law.* Refusing to accept that Assaracus should have any of the castles, he would deprive him of them if he could. Assaracus defended himself, and he held on to the land by force. He favoured the Trojans because he was of their race. They had no support in Greece from anyone other than him.

(209–52) It was through Assaracus' counsel and his acquiescence that they made Brutus their protector, and with his advice and his help they agreed to have Brutus as lord over them. He saw that he had a very large number of men with them and that the castles were strong. He had the three castles fortified, and he provisioned them in readiness for war. Then he assembled all the prisoners in the country, men, women, and children, and their beasts and their servants, of which they had a large number. He positioned them in the woods and the mountains. Then he had food and equipment brought, and straightaway he had a letter written, greeting the king of Greece and sending him this message:

'Through the ignominy and the disgrace of the noble people, and of the lineage of Dardanus, their fine ancestor, who was shamefully imprisoned for a long time, all the prisoners have joined together and formed a community, just like people who ought to be unified. They have made me their leader and withdrawn into these woods. They would prefer to live off roots, like beasts and wild animals, so that they could be free, rather than to live in plenty, but in captivity. They would rather live freely in poverty than have great plenty yet remain imprisoned. If they want to have their freedom, you ought not to be reluctant to let them have it, and you should not be surprised if it were their wish to acquire it for themselves. Each person desires and has the will to be free, and they have the right to be so. They beg you, and I inform you, that they should henceforth have their freedom where they are, and they should be able to go wherever they wish to go.'

(253–88) The king listened to what the letter had to say. It seemed to him to be an outrage that the Trojans were rebelling and demanding their freedom from him. They have undertaken an act of foolhardiness, he said, and embarked on a foolish endeavour. He summoned his dukes, princes, barons, and all his vassals, men on horseback and those on foot, and he rode towards those from Troy. The king told Brutus that he intended to secure the castles that Assaracus rightfully held and that Brutus was fortifying. If he were able to capture Brutus inside, he would do nothing other than hang him swiftly. Brutus heard very soon that the king was coming with his host. At a crossing, with which he was familiar, and through which the king was to pass, he lay in wait with three thousand armed men. Thinking that he could get through this pass, the king arrived and Brutus emerged from his hiding place, making a great slaughter of the king's troops. The Greeks, who were not armed, very quickly turned in flight. As they fled, a great number of them plunged into the very broad river Achalon. Brutus, who was chasing them, surrounded many of them in the water, making them fall headlong on to the banks of the river and drown in the deep water. Many of them were drowned and killed, but many were captured alive. The king himself fled, and the entire host departed.

(289–356) Antigonus, the king's brother, saw that Brutus was causing such havoc. He saw those who were dead and those who had drowned. He rallied his companions, and out of anger and wrath he went back to the fray. Then you would have seen a bitter battle, with many a blow from a lance and many from a sword, with many men still on their feet there and many felled, and with many fleeing and many fighting. They received many blows and delivered many. The Trojans cut right through them, killing many and knocking down many, binding some by oath, and capturing many. Antigonus was taken prisoner, as were the majority of his men. Brutus took them with him, seized, bound, and put on oath. Pandrasus was very upset by what had happened to his brother and to the other men. He assembled his men in the morning and laid siege to Sparatin. He thought that Brutus was there and had put his prisoners there, but he had entered the wood and taken his prisoners there. He had positioned knights in the castle, a full six hundred in addition to the archers. The king besieged the castle and arranged his barons round it, telling each one where he should be, and at what point he should assail them. He had belfries made and catapults constructed, frequently causing lances to be hurled and bows to be drawn. He had the belfry set up against the wall, and those who were on the battlements inside shot their arrows and their crossbow bolts. They threw large stones and large pieces of wood, and they hurled darts and sharp stakes. They had engineers, who worked swiftly and who had soon constructed mangonels to withstand the catapults; no one dared to remain there. The others prepared fire and cast it on to the belfry, reducing it all to cinders and ashes. Their opponents made every effort to defend themselves.

When the king saw that this was all to no avail, and that he could not capture them by assault, nor through any siege engine that he could create, he withdrew to higher ground and threatened them. He had the host closed in all round with a fine ditch and sharpened stakes. He allowed only three entry points, and these were well guarded. Then he swore that he would not leave there until he had captured the castle. Those who were besieged inside swore that they would never be captured unless they were first starved; they feared famine, for they had very little grain. There was a large number of them, but they had very little food. Because they were afraid that the food would run out, they sent word to their duke, telling him that he should help them, for, if help were a long time in coming, they would have to surrender through hunger, as they could not defend themselves against it.

(357–98) Brutus was very troubled as to how to rescue his men. He made up his mind about what he would do, and through which device he would help them. He would have to look for a stratagem, for he did not have the strength to cope with such a host. In order to destroy his opponent, he needed to construct a form of ruse or device, and in order to free his allies he had to take a great risk. He made up his mind in a very short time, then he ran forward very fiercely and grabbed a prisoner by the forelock. His name was Anacletus, and he had been captured along with the king's brother. Brutus drew him to him forcibly. In his hand he held his naked sword, and he made as if to kill him.

'Evil wretch,' he replied, 'you will soon die, and if you do not save yourself and him you will not outlive this day, neither yourself nor the king's brother. But you can save yourself and him, and get out of my prison.'

'You will do what you want,' he said, 'but if I can save the two of us tell me how I can do so.'

Brutus said: 'I shall let you know. Tonight, after the time one calls bedtime, you will go to those who are watching over the host. You will say to the guards that, thanks to a ruse and a trickster, you have escaped from my prison. You have rescued the king's brother from me, but you have left him behind in these woods. You did not dare to take him any further since I am having the woods watched. Let them come with you, and then take him away. When they arrive, I shall dart out of my hiding place and capture them all at the same time.'

(399–428) Anacletus agreed to Brutus's plan, and Brutus swore and promised to release him, life and limb. That night, when it was quite dark and people ought to be asleep, Brutus gathered his men together and entered a valley near the exit in these woods, which he had earlier reconnoitred. In the undergrowth, round the valley, he placed his companions in three locations. When Anacletus had made all his preparations, he took leave of him. He spurred swiftly towards the guards, as if he were taking flight. The guards caught sight of him, and some of them knew him well. They asked him how things were progressing. and what had happened to the king's brother.

'I have rescued him from prison and hidden him in this wood, for on his own he would not have dared to leave. Instead, you must come for him, for he is in chains and cannot walk, and I cannot carry him on my own. Come with me, I shall take you. I left him quite close to here. In giving him back to the king, you will have performed a great service for him.'

(429–56) They thought he was telling the truth. Who would have thought that he was lying? They had no suspicion of treason, so they made their way straight towards the woods. Anacletus set off. He himself was in front and the others behind. He led them straight to the spot where he knew Brutus was. Brutus, who was well protected, had them seized from all sides. Not a single one escaped, and no one survived to give the news to the host.

Then Brutus organized his army into three parts.

'Barons,' he said, 'you will go to the host and assault them from three sides. I shall go to the king's tent, taking some of you with me. But be very careful that none of you delivers a blow there, neither those in the front nor those in the rear, and take care that no word is uttered until I have blown the horn. When I have reached the king's tent, I shall sound my horn loudly, and as soon as you hear it woe betide you if you spare the Greeks. Attack them while they sleep, and kill them straightaway.'

(457–92) The knights did just as Brutus had outlined to them. They entered the host from three sides, and they came to a stop amongst the tents. Brutus was not slow to act. He went swiftly to the king's tent, and when he was about to enter it he sounded his horn forcefully. As soon as his men heard him, they spread out through all the tents. The Greeks were asleep, and before their sudden awakening their opponents had delivered many blows throughout the tents, cutting off many wrists, many arms, and many feet, and spilling out many brains and piercing many bowels. The Greeks had no opportunity to take up arms or to flee, for the Trojans, who were in front of them and behind them, captured them and did not shy away from killing them, wherever they managed to reach them. Wherever those who escaped their clutches thought they would have the best chance of escape, they plunged down the great cliffs, where they drowned in the deep rivers. They encountered difficulties on all sides. Brutus, who reached the king's tent, captured him alive and perfectly well. When the sun rose in the morning, he took him with him to the castle and ordered him to be watched over. Then he gathered the booty together and distributed it to the knights, issuing a command to those who were still alive that they should bury their dead.

(493–558) Next day he took the wisest of his men to one side. He asked their advice about what he should do with the king of Greece, whom he had captured: whether he should kill him, ransom him, or set him free. He wanted to act according to their advice, so that they could not blame him later in this respect. They had differing thoughts on this matter and gave differing advice. Some advised him to seek a part of his land, where their men could live in freedom and exempt from dues. Others advised, and it appealed to them greatly, that the king should let them go. They wanted to make their way to other realms with their children and their wives. While they were wondering which piece of advice they should adopt, Menbritius, a wise man, rose to his feet and, cried out:

'Why are you in doubt? Between all of you, you see absolutely nothing. So is not the right decision to seek permission to depart freely? As we sail in the ships, let the king give us gold and silver, and also ships and grain, and let him give us everything we need by way of provisions. Let him give the duke, our lord, his daughter Innogen as his wife. Then we shall go and seek dwellings in foreign parts, for should we remain with him any hardship we have known will just get worse. We shall never have peace with the Greeks, for they will never forget their kinsmen, their uncles, their brothers, or their other close friends, whom we have killed with our own hands. Know that they will avenge them as soon as they have the time and the opportunity to do so. He who expects anything else is a fool. As the saying goes, he who commits evil should not be trusted. I shall never believe that they will be merciful. From an old crime a new wound appears. We have done a great deal of harm to them, and I do not think that there is any one of them who has not suffered because of us, or who has not lost a friend or relative. Sons and cousins remain, whom we have orphaned and who will still seek vengeance. They will never forget this. We shall become fewer in number, and they will become more numerous. We shall go into decline, and they will prosper. If on one occasion they can get the upper hand, you will see whether it will be you or they who will survive. For all the Trojans will die, and we shall have deserved it. Because of such misfortune as I am describing to you I advise you to set out on your way, providing Brutus, our leader, agrees to this.'

(559–90) These words led to great commotion. 'Well said! Well said!', was the cry. Then they brought the king and made him stand before them. They all cried out that he would soon die, and that his brother would not survive if they were not given permission to leave, with a specified amount of money. Then they told him the precise amount, and about the ships, the grain, and the other provisions. They also asked him to marry his daughter to their leader. The king saw that they were in control, and he was very much afraid of dying. To one and all he granted freedom and permission to depart.

'You keep me in prison,' he said, 'and ask for my daughter. You will have my daughter. I can do nothing else. But it will be to my mortal enemy, a cruel and wicked man, that I shall be giving her, whether I like it or not. But to a certain extent I shall be comforted that a noble and brave man will be having her. The ships, the grain, the provisions, and the money I am being asked for I shall give you in abundance, and if you decided to remain in this country you would all be free and at liberty to do so, and by rightful judgement I would agree to give you a third of all my land.'

(591–610) They did not wish to remain, or to retract their demands. Then the king sent his messengers throughout Greece, to the ports and the shores. He assembled all the ships that were fit to sail over the sea, and the finest of them were chosen, the strongest and the largest. They were prepared and loaded with provisions. The country's finest and most costly possessions were placed in the ships. The king brought Innogen, his daughter, and gave her to the leader. He gave Brutus a great deal more than he had asked for. There was no vassal or baron to whom the king did not give a fine gift. Each man received the finest and most precious gift, according to his individual worth.

BRUTUS AND THE TROJANS LEAVE GREECE, HEADING FOR SPAIN AND FRANCE

(611–50) As soon as they had a favourable wind, they did not tarry long. They made their way to the ports and went aboard the ships, raising their masts and their sails. There were sixteen times twenty ships when they set off from Greece. They sailed for two days and one night without encountering any port or shore. In the evening of the second day they came to Leogice. They came to the island and climbed up it without finding a living soul. They found that the whole land was completely laid bare, so that there was nothing to be obtained from it. Pirates had totally laid it waste, driven the people away, and carried off their possessions. The whole land was a wasteland, but there was a large number of wild animals. The Trojans captured many of them and put a lot of them in their ships. The game, which was available in great abundance, lasted for a long time afterwards. They found a city that was laid waste and an ancient temple. The statue was of Diana, a prophetess, and she was a devil, who deceived people with spells. She took on the form of a woman in order to trick people. She had herself called Diana and took on the name 'Goddess of the Forest'. When the land was populated, the statue was worshipped and held in great honour. The ancients came there to enquire and hear about what the future would be. Diana gave them responses through signs and visions.

(651–90) Brutus took twelve of the elders, the most righteous and the wisest, and Gerion, a priest of their faith. Taking them with him, he came to the statue in the cave, leaving all his men outside. In his right hand he held a vessel, filled with wine and fresh milk, which, as Diana required, came from a white animal. Numerous times he prostrated himself, and he begged the goddess to give him a sign by way of a reply, or show him through a sign where he could find a region that was good and peaceful to inhabit. He said this prayer nine times in a low voice and with a demure countenance. On nine occasions he kissed the altar and walked round it nine times, carrying a goblet in his hand. Then he poured it into the burning fire, which he had lit in front of the statue, near the altar. Then he took the skin of the animal he had sacrificed. He spread it on the ground, lay down on it, and went to sleep. To him it seemed from where he was sleeping that the goddess was saying to him:

'Beyond France, far off in the sea towards the west, you can find a good and habitable land with very delightful dwellings. The soil is ripe for cultivation, and giants used to live there. Its name is Albion, and you will have that land, making it a new Troy. From you there will come a royal lineage that will be glorified throughout the world.'

(691–749) When the vision was completed and Brutus had a firm record of it in his mind, he gave thanks to the goddess and made a vow and a promise to her that if he were able to have this land, which she was promising him in his dream, he would build a temple and a statue for her. He would honour her for all time. Then he had the vision recounted to all his men, who were waiting for him in the temple, just as it was revealed to him. Then they all made their way to the ships. They sailed and rowed, benefiting from a good breeze and wind, until after around thirty days, they came to the Straits of Gibraltar.* But they continued on their journey and passed the Saline Lake and the altars of the Philistines. They went via Rucikadam and the mountains of Azaré, where they encountered pirates who impeded them considerably by doing battle with them. But the Trojans overcame them and seized a large amount of goods that were a source of wealth and riches for them. They passed by the river Malvan and docked in Mauritania. They disembarked and went in search of food and drink. They laid waste the entire land, stealing things from shore to shore, and seizing equipment and goods. Then they went on their way, sailing onwards and passing very close to the boundaries created by Hercules, two columns that he had established as a sign that he had conquered as far as the spot where he had placed his pillars. There they found the Sirens, who impeded their ships greatly. The Sirens are sea monsters, who, from the way their heads look, seem like women, but from the navel downwards they are fish. They have caused much harm to sailors, and they inhabit the oceans over towards the west. They have sweet voices and sing sweetly. They attract the foolish by their sweet song and attempt to deceive them. Foolish men, who hear their song and rejoice in their singing, forget and ignore where they are heading and fail to realize it in time. The Sirens make them drift up and down, frequently causing them to be shipwrecked, or at the very least to stray off course.

(750–72) Many a time the Sirens held on to the Trojan ships. They grabbed hold of them firmly, causing the Trojans to linger so much that they ran into rocks or were in danger of shipwreck. The Sirens did many things that made them afraid, for they were filled with treachery. It was not possible for anyone who was not on his guard to escape them. They represent the Devil, whose work is so delightful, and so sweet to uphold, that parting from them is very difficult. He who sticks to his task strays from his straight path and loses his course, just as he who spends too much time listening to the Sirens comes to grief. The Trojans spotted them. Hearing them sing, they recognized them. They had heard talk of them, and they had no wish to listen to them. The Sirens clung to their ships all round and almost caused the Trojans to drown. They escaped with great difficulty and then sailed close to Spain.

(773–92) On a shore there they found their Trojan race, four extensive generations, which Antenor, one of the barons, brought when they fled from Troy after the Greeks had conquered them. Corineus, who was their lord and ruler, protected them. He was very tall, and he was bold and as strong as a giant. He had heard and understood that these were men from Troy, who were in search of land they could possess in perpetuity. He was very pleased they had come, and accompanied by a very large part of his men he came and met up with them. Brutus loved him greatly, cherished him, and found in him a very fine friend.

(793–828) When they left the ports of Spain, they set their course towards Brittany. It was not yet called Brittany, rather it was called Armorica. On their right they passed Poitou, and they sailed and rowed until they reached the shore and came straight to the place where the Loire meets the sea. At the spot where this happens the entire fleet came together. They remained there for seven days, and they could see the country and the way things were. Geoffrey, who was king of Poitiers, sent his messengers to meet them in order to find out what sort of men they were, and whether they sought peace or combat. Humbert, who was a skilled orator, had the task of conveying the message. Corineus had disembarked, and from the ships he had entered into the woods with two hundred men in order to go hunting and to scour the countryside. The messengers met him and immediately asked him on whose advice, and on whose authority, he had gone hunting in the forest.

'The king', they said, 'has forbidden hunting, pursuing animals or tracking deer in the forest, except when he is participating himself. How dare you capture game, since the king has forbidden it!'

Corineus replied: 'If your king has forbidden it, I know nothing about this prohibition and I shall not adhere to it.'

(829–58) Humbert took a bow and stretched it. He intended to shoot at him, but the other man dodged out of the way. Angry, he jumped forward, seizing the bow that Humbert was holding. He plunged it into his head so deeply that, as a result, his brains spilled out. His companions fled, leaving Humbert lying there. They described to King Geoffrey how Humbert had been killed. The king wanted to go and avenge him, and to drive the men out of the land. What had happened to his servant upset him greatly. He was a powerful man and he summoned a large force of men. Brutus knew him through his spies. He prepared all his ships well, loading them with booty and provisions. He made all the army followers go on board. He told them that they should not leave there, whatever they might hear, until he came back to them, or sent them news of his whereabouts. He arranged his other divisions and went to oppose the king. The king approached and they engaged in battle, dealing great blows on all sides. The Poitevins attacked them well and the Trojans responded well. They fought for a long time without either side being victorious.

(859–900) Corineus, who was of great assistance in a crisis, was greatly ashamed that the Poitevins were so strong that they would never be conquered or killed. He arranged his men towards the right and had them launch an attack. He pierced the thick of the battle, killing many men both on the right and on the left. In this attack he lost his sword, but he procured an axe, which he got hold of by chance. Then the combat was very fierce. Anyone who was caught by the axe was split right through his body. The Trojans looked at him and everyone else was amazed. Displaying such audacious behaviour and delivering such great blows, he routed the entire host. No one dared to await his arrival. Corineus drove them away, and crying out behind their backs:

'Cowardly race! Why are you fleeing an enemy you are supposed to be attacking? Why are you turning your backs on us? Do you think you will defeat me by fleeing? Show us what you have been looking for here and defend your country. You are fleeing in a very wretched fashion when I am the only one from whom you flee. There are more than a thousand of you who are fleeing because of a single knight. You know of nowhere to which you can flee where I cannot kill you. But it is perhaps a precious comfort to you that you will die from this right hand of mine, with which I have dealt many fine blows and killed many thousands of men, cut many giants in half, and sent many to hell. Come here, four by four or three by three, and strike immediately!'

(901–30) Suharz, one of the king of Poitiers's men, heard Corineus' arrogant words and his fierce cries. With three hundred armed knights he turned towards him. They attacked their opponents on all sides and thought that they had already defeated him. But Corineus advanced and approached Suharz, giving him such a blow that he sliced his body right through from head to toe. Of the others he made such slaughter that it was like a lion killing sheep. No one had any more protection than sheep would have against a lion. With all his Trojans Brutus came to his assistance through the ranks. Then the uproar increased, as did the killing. Many a soul was sent flying out of its body. I shall tell you briefly how it ended: the Poitevins were defeated. Goffar, who was deeply troubled by this, went to France in search of aid, going to the twelve peers who were there and whose land was divided into twelve parts. Each one of the twelve was in charge and each called himself king. All twelve of them promised to avenge him in respect of his enemies, and he thanked them all. Then all the men were assembled.

(931–82) Brutus was delighted by the victory, and by the booty and the glory. He laid waste all the lands, burning and pillaging the cities. They ransacked them and laid them waste extensively. They came to a stop at a hillock and built a small castle on its peak. They had never before had a stronghold, a town, a city, or a dwelling. But, as we have read, through the efforts of these men he had begun to build the city of Tours, which still stands, and which received the name Tours because of an unusual occurrence. This will very soon be revealed to you, as I find it in writing. When the castle was completed, the Trojans withdrew to it. They had been there for two days after it had been fortified when, lo,* Goffar suddenly turned up with the French counts and kings. They saw that the hillock had a castle on it and this was extremely troubling to them.

'I am going mad with grief,' he said. 'Grief ought to drive me out of my mind. I see the wretches who have driven me away, who have pillaged my kingdom, and who in addition, against my wishes, have erected a castle in my domain. French barons, let us arm ourselves and attack them decisively!' Then they armed themselves and set off. They established twelve divisions of the French and came straight to the castle. Those inside emerged and the French struck them vigorously. Their opponents responded bravely to their blows. Lo, there was then a fully engaged battle. Each man made an effort to strike well. From the first blows, and in a short amount of time, the Trojans had the upper hand. They cast down dead more than two thousand of the French and wounded many. They pushed a huge number of them back, but the French were reinvigorated. Their forces were increasing all the time, for troops were constantly arriving. They stationed them in numbers at the castle, which was very pleasing for the French. They attacked the castle, until night came and caused them to disperse.

(983–1020) In the castle there was great commotion. They decided that at midnight Corineus would go out, taking his men with him, and they would hide in a wood that was very close by. When Brutus started the fight in the morning, Corineus would emerge swiftly from the wood. They would attack the French from the rear and surround them. Thus, they could destroy Goffar and his forces. They regarded this advice as good. Corineus and all his men emerged at cockcrow, and they were in the woods by the break of day. Brutus had the castle watched and he made most of his men remain awake. He set out very early in the morning, coming up to the French and attacking them. Then once again the battle was fierce. But straightaway, at the beginning, before Corineus had arrived, Brutus' nephew Turnus was killed. Turnus was a very bold man, and remarkably strong. He had no equal amongst the nobility in terms of strength or valour, and no one could strike as fiercely as he could, except Corineus. He had killed six hundred Frenchmen with his own hand and his sword, which was bathed in blood. He had moved away too far away from his men and pursued the French too intently. They surrounded him and wounded him. Together they knocked him down dead.

THE TROJANS DEFEAT THE FRENCH AND LEAVE FOR BRITAIN

(1021–62) BRUTUS dragged him away. He carried him back and buried him in the castle. After Turnus, who was killed there and buried in the castle grounds, the city was called Tours, and the surrounding region was called the Touraine. Brutus, intent on avenging his nephew, fought very hard. Corineus helped him and dealt many very powerful blows. He attacked the French from the other direction, where they were not paying attention. Then you would have seen some harsh combat, with many bodies pierced and many heads cut off. I could not describe to you the killing and the slaughter, the loss and the grief that the French suffered that day. They could not withstand them for long and very soon had to take flight. The Trojans pursued them and put them to the sword. Brutus had his bugles blown and made his men return. They decided they would leave and abandon this land. Then they captured booty and spoils and made straight for the ships. They loaded them up with their booty and departed from this land. Partly by the sun and the stars, and partly by their oars and their sails, the fleet reached Totnes in the port of Dartmouth.* This is the island the goddess promised them in a dream. Disembarking on to this land from the ships, they were very happy and filled with joy. Because of the land they had found, which they had sought and desired so fervently, they forgot all their travails and thanked the gods for it.

(1063–99) In this island there were giants; no one else lived there. The giants were immensely strong. They had grown bigger than any other races. I cannot recount all their names to you. I do not know any name except one. I can tell you the name of one of them; this one was Gogmagog, who was their lord. Through his strength and his size the others had made him their lord. Because of the Trojans, whom they hated and at whom they shot arrows, this giant and the others fled into the mountains and abandoned the flat lands. One day the Trojans held a feast in the manner of their ancestors. They held dances and games because of the joy they felt at the new places to which they had been directed and which were destined for both themselves and their lineage, to have as their heritage for all time. Lo, twenty giants appeared there, emerging from the caves in the mountains. Gogmagog, their lord and their leader, led them. They attacked the Trojans, killing a great many of them in a short time. With stones, clubs, and pikes they killed I do not know how many of them. As they tried to leave and go back to the mountains, the Trojans harassed them so much, and gave them such heavy blows with darts, lances, swords, and sharpened arrows, that they made them breathe their last.

(1100–32) Brutus spared the largest giant Gogmagog in order to see which of them was the stronger wrestler, Corineus or the giant, for they were both remarkably big and strong. Corineus darted forward as soon as he was aware that he had to fight. On an open plain near the sea, where there was a cliff and solid ground, Brutus arranged the combat and they all watched it willingly. Corineus rolled up his sleeves, braced himself, and adapted the shape of his body. He girded himself with the skirts of his coat and stiffened his flanks somewhat. Gogmagog readied himself and prepared himself for the fight. They grasped each other by the arms and wrapped their arms round. Lo, they were locked in combat, breast to breast, side to side. They embraced each other from the rear and wrapped their arms round one another very violently. Then you would have seen trick after trick, strength pitted against strength, feet forward, then feet withdrawn, ruse against ruse. Turning one way and then the other, each of them was strong and each man's anger grew. They pushed each other with their chests, so that their legs splayed out. Sometimes they were locked together such that they were immediately on top of each other.

(1133–68) Then you would have seen them breathing heavily, their noses puckering, and their brows running with sweat, their faces turning black, their eyes rolling, their eyebrows rising and falling, their teeth clenched, their colour changing, their heads rubbing against each other, then striking each other, thrusting, pulling, shoving, bending, holding in, up and down, testing their strength against each other, tripping each other up, and twisting. They tried many tricks and many moves. They used many tricks with their thighs, pulling them up and then dragging them back down. Each one wanted to surprise the other, and each one wanted to defend himself. Gogmagog strove mightily, stretching out his arms, wrapping his arms round him, and pulling Corineus towards him so fiercely that he broke three of his ribs. The giant wounded him severely and almost managed to knock him down beneath him. Corineus, who was wounded, got back his strength as best he could, and he pulled the giant with such power that he crushed his ribs. He raised himself back up a little and pulled him up against his breast. He carried him to the cliff, unconscious in his arms, and then he opened his hands and loosened his arms. The giant was heavy, and he came crashing down the cliff on to the rock in such a way that no bone remained unbroken. The sea became red all round him from the blood shed by his body. Later the place took the name of the giant who fell headlong there.

(1169–208) When the land was cleansed of the giants and their lineage, the Trojans felt more secure. They built houses, worked the land, erected cities and towns, and sowed and cultivated grain. The name of the land was Albion, but Brutus changed its name. He gave it a name taken from his own name, Brutus, and called it Britain. His companions, the Trojans, he called Britons, after Brutus. Corineus took possession of part of the land for his own use. This part he named Corinee, after Corineus. Then, later, I do not know through what error, it was called Cornwall. It still retains the beginning of its original name. The language they spoke at first, which they called Trojan, between themselves they called British. But the English later changed it to English. Both the language and the name lasted until Gormund arrived there. He drove the Britons away and handed the land over to the Saxons, who from Angle were called Angles, and they called it England. In this way all the Britons were driven out, so that they never regained power. Corineus had Cornwall and Brutus had the whole of Britain. Each drew his allies and his vassals to him from his own country. Soon the number of people had increased so much, and they had spread out so much throughout the land, that it seemed that Britain had been populated for a long time.

BRUTUS NAMES BRITAIN AFTER HIMSELF, FOUNDING NEW TROY AND DIVIDING THE LAND AMONG HIS THREE SONS

(1208–50) BRUTUS looked at the mountains and he saw the valleys and the plains, the marches and the thickets, the rivers and the shores, the fields and the meadows. He saw the ports and the fisheries, saw the people multiplying and the lands being cultivated. He thought he would build a city and restore Troy. When he had sought a suitable spot, one that was pleasing and delightful, he built his city on the river Thames. It was very well constructed and well positioned. In memory of his ancestors, he named it New Troy. Afterwards, the name became corrupted and was called Trinovant. But anyone who looks at the name finds that Trinovant is New Troy; this is evident in the way the make-up of the name has been corrupted. The terms for city are *urbs* in Latin, *citez* in French, *chester* in English, and *kaer* in British. Then, from Lud, a king who had a great affection for the city and lived there for a long time, it was named Kaerlu, after which Lud was corrupted and, because of Lud, they called it Lodoin. In the end, because of Lodoin, people said Londene in English and we now call it Lundres. Through many acts of great destruction perpetrated by foreigners, who often seized it, the land was often captured and often lost, and the cities and the regions all have different names from those first given to them by their founders who created them. At the time I am telling you about, there was a priest called El, from Judaea, and the ark and the law were carried off by the Philistines into their country.

(1251–302) When Brutus had built his city and attracted a huge number of people to it, he placed citizens and townspeople there, giving them precepts and laws so that they could maintain it in peace and concord. Under no circumstances would they do harm to one another. He ruled for twenty-four years and had three children with Innogen. His three sons were Locrinus, Kamber, and Albanactus. These three sons, who survived him, buried him in Trinovant, the city he had founded. Then they divided up the land, in love and companionship, so that each of them had his share. Locrinus, who was the firstborn and the strongest and the wisest, had as his share the region that was named Logres after Locrinus' own name. Kamber took over the land that was separated by the Severn, towards the north, and when he had taken possession of it he called it Kambrie after his own name. He built great palaces and great halls. But now Kambrie has the name Wales. It was once called Kambrie, and now it is Wales because of Guales the queen, or else Wales has the name Wales in memory of Duke Guales. He was a man of immense power, and the people talked about him a great deal. Albanactus, the third son, was the smallest, and it fell to his lot to take over a region covered in brush, which he called Albany after his own name. Albany took its name from Albanactus, and we call it Scotland. When the three brothers had separated, as good brothers and good friends, without wickedness or iniquity, they maintained fraternal relations between them. Humber, who was the king of the Huns, a man very much feared on the high seas, who went about laying waste islands and pillaging all the shores, arrived at a Scottish port and joined battle with Albanactus because of the land he was ravaging. He was a ruthless man, and he had a large number of troops with him. He defeated and conquered Albanactus, killing him and most of his men.

(1303–34) The others who escaped made their way to Locrinus in Britain. Locrinus and Kamber joined forces and went to avenge their brother. Humber, on this side of the Firth of Forth,* set off from a distance to attack them, but he was defeated and fled. He plunged into a river that after him is called the Humber; from Humber it is called the Humber. The river received the name Humber because of Humber, who died in it. He had been in Germany and had captured and laid waste a large amount of land there. He had kidnapped three maidens and left them behind in his ship. One maiden was the daughter of a king. Her name was Hestrild and she was very beautiful. No one could find a more beautiful girl on earth, nor one that was her like. When Humber had drowned to death, Locrinus and his brother Kamber went swiftly to the fleet of ships, to get his hands on the great amount of wealth. He found the three maidens whom Humber had taken there. Locrinus fell in love with Hestrild and ordered her to be looked after, saying that he would take her as his wife. He would never have another wife, for her beauty was very pleasing to him. She was handed over to be watched over.

(1335–71) Corineus was still alive, and he had a daughter whom Locrinus was intending to marry. But he abandoned her because of Hestrild and broke the agreement. Corineus was furious and he went in search of Locrinus until he found him. He came before him angrily and spoke to him arrogantly. With a large axe hanging round his neck, he said:

'Locrinus, foul traitor, foul rogue, no one can save you from inevitable death. Have you rejected my daughter, whom you had pledged to marry? What does it mean that you are not marrying her? Is this the thanks I get from you on behalf of your father, whom I served, and for the hardships I suffered from the wounds and from the combats I had undergone in my struggles with people from other countries? In order to advance your father's honour, I underwent much toil and tribulation, and you are rewarding me by abandoning my daughter Guendolien for I know not which foreign woman. I suffered many perils for your father, and now, even whilst you see me still alive, for some Hestrild you abandon my daughter, whom you were set to marry. As long as I have power in my limbs, which I raised when I killed the giants, this cannot go without revenge. You are dead, for you will soon be cut to pieces!'

(1372–96) Then Corineus moved towards Locrinus as if he intended to kill him, and perhaps he would have done so, had it not been for their allies, who darted between them and separated them. They appeased Corineus and advised Locrinus to keep to the agreement fully. He should marry her before worse happened as a result. So, in this way Locrinus took Guendolien as his wife, but he did not forget Hestrild, whom he made his concubine. Through one of his closest friends he had a cellar built in London, deep underground. Hestrild was kept there in secret. Locrinus retained her secretly in this way for seven years underground. When he wanted to tarry with her and spend a certain amount of time with her, he had his wife believe that he was making a sacrifice to God that he could not make otherwise than in this secret way.

(1397–452) Locrinus kept Hestrild there and remained with her until she gave birth to a daughter. Her name was Abren. She was very clear-skinned, and more beautiful than Hestrild, her mother, who was very beautiful and elegant. Guendolien also had a child, a boy, that very same year, and they called him Madan. As soon as Madan could walk, and could understand, and converse, he was sent to his grandfather to be raised and educated. The time came, as it must, when Corineus died, and Locrinus, who had no further fear of him, sent Guendolien away and honoured Hestrild so much that he raised her to the rank of queen. Guendolien was angry at the king, who had sent her away. To make her complaint, she went to Cornwall, where her father used to live. She gathered together so many of her kinsmen, and sought so many foreign troops, that she led a great host from Cornwall. She went to do battle with Locrinus, as a woman who was fierce and confident. On the river named Esture they met in combat in Dorset, but Locrinus was fatally injured. He fell to the ground and all his men fled. Guendolien, who was victorious, captured and seized possession of all the land. She had Hestrild and Abren sent tumbling into the river and drowned. But she commanded and established in honour of her husband, who had sired Abren, that the river should be named after him. Then the river into which she was thrown took its name Avren, from Abren; it flows into the sea at Christchurch. Guendolien was ferocious and a remarkable dispenser of justice. She had been with Locrinus for ten years, and after him she reigned for fifteen years. Then her son was able to rule the land and take possession of Britain. When she had passed everything on to him, she went back to Cornwall, retaining as much land as her father had ruled. At this time, Samuel was a prophet and Homer an esteemed poet.

(1453–92) Madan took a wife and had two sons: one was Malin and the other Menbriz. He was king for forty years, then he died, leaving his kingdom to his two sons. But the brothers fell out and fought over their kingdom. Each wanted to rule the entire domain and they could not come to an agreement. But Menbriz, who was a traitor, deceived his brother. He agreed and accepted a truce summoning him to a meeting in which no declaration of war would be made. The older brother killed the younger one, and thus Menbriz conquered the kingdom. At that time Saul was king of the Jews and Eristeus was king of the Greeks. Menbriz hated his entire lineage and everyone in his family. There would not have been a single nobleman with the right to good quality whom he would not have poisoned to death, or killed violently or treacherously. He abandoned his own wife and took up the evil profession from which the Sodomites perished when they were swallowed up in their city and fell, while still alive, into the abyss. He was king for twenty years, but in the twentieth year to his misfortune Menbriz went hunting in the forest. He became separated from his huntsmen behind him and entered a valley, following I know not what deer or beast. There he came across a group of enraged wolves; they devoured and consumed him. Thus, Menbriz was dismembered, torn limb from limb, and devoured.

(1493–548) Next, Ebrauc, his son by his wife, ruled his father's kingdom. He was very powerful, very tall, and very strong. He honoured his wealthy kinsmen and enhanced the lives of the poorest of them. There was no one with whom he would make war, or who would have dared to fight with him. He was the first one who set sail from England in search of booty. He assembled a huge fleet of ships, took part of his men and went to rob the French, the Flemings, and the Teutons. He pillaged all the coastal regions and took away a great amount of booty. England was honoured and blessed for a long time. In the era in which Ebrauc reigned, David instituted the psalter and built his city, Bethlehem, and the tower of Jerusalem. Silvius Latinus reigned and then Nathan issued his prophecies. Ebrauc, who was wealthy, built two cities over towards Scotland: one was called Kaer Ebrac and the other was called Alclud. The one that was called Ebrac was later called Eborac. The French later corrupted this name, and from Eborac they created Evrewic [York]. He situated the other city more towards the north, and on Mount Agned he built a castle that had the name the Castle of Maidens.* But I do not know why it was called the Castle of Maidens rather than of Damsels or Maidservants. I was not told why, and I cannot say why, and I have not heard everything or seen everything, or understood everything. For, if you had to provide a reason for everything, you would have to understand properly. Ebrauc lived for a very long time and he ruled the land very wisely. He lived for sixty years in all and had twenty sons with twenty wives, and thirty daughters in all. Hear what the names of the sons were: Brutus Green Shield [Vert-Escu], Margadud, Sisillius, Regin, Bladud, Moruid, Lago and Bodloan, Kimcar, Spaden, Gaül, Dardan, Eldad, Cangu, Kerim, Luor, Rud, Assarac, Buël, and Hector.

(1549–90) You have heard the names of the sons and now you must hear those of the daughters. The first was Gloigin, then came Otidas, Ourar, Innogin, Guardid, Radan, Guenlian, Angarad, Guenlode, Medlan, Mailure, Ecub, Tangustel, Stadud, Kamreda, Methael, Gad, Echeim, Nest and Gorgaon, Gladus, Ebren, Blangan, Egron, Edra, Aballac and Angues, Anor, Stadiald, and Galaes. Galaes was beautiful and noble, more so than any of the thirty. Methael was the ugliest and Guenlode was the most agreeable. Ourar was the hardest worker, Innogin the most eloquent, and Anor the most courtly* and the one who best displayed her finery. Gloigin was the eldest, the tallest, and the wisest. They were all well adorned and taken to Lombardy to King Silvius, their kinsman, who married them splendidly to the lineage of the Trojans. For it had been a long time since the ladies of Lombardy, as a result of some crime or other, had refused marriage to the Trojans or to members of their lineage. For this reason these maidens were summoned and given to the Trojans there. The brothers who had remained behind acquired arms and ships and made their way to Germany with the youths from Britain. Assarac, one of the most knowledgeable of them, took control over his brothers. They captured castles, towns, and cities, and they conquered the whole of the land.

(1591–626) Ebrauc retained Brutus, the eldest, with him; his name was Green Shield [Vert-Escu]. He ruled the kingdom after his father and was in charge of it for twelve years. Leil, his son, after his death, was then king for twenty-five years. He built a city towards the north, as the history tells us, so that he would be remembered; it was called Kaerleil [Carlisle]. He was a very brave man, but shortly before his death he began to deteriorate, so that he was not able to rule over the land. His vassals were quarrelling amongst themselves, and they would not desist for his sake or because of the distress he was feeling. Rightly or wrongly, they would do nothing for him. They had reduced him to a very low point, but one of his sons, Ruhundibras, was later a king who governed according to law, and he had brought the whole land to a state of peace. He brought peace to the barons, and he promised peace and maintained peace. He built Winchester and Canterbury, and also the castle of Chesterbury that was situated on Mount Paladur. Whilst walls were being built round this castle, it is said that an eagle spoke. But I do not know what it said or proclaimed. Forty years less one did he reign after the death of his father Leil. As we find in writing, Solomon reigned at that time. He founded the temple of Our Lord, just as God had ordained it. Preaching in Israel were Amos, Aggeus, and Iohel.

(1627–54) When Ruhundibras was dead, his son Bladud ruled Britain. He was a very powerful man and very skilled in sorcery. He founded Bath and constructed the baths; never before had there been any such as these. Bath was named from Bladud, by taking away the letter 'l'. Or it received its name from the baths because they were formed in a remarkable way. The baths were hot and efficacious, and most advantageous for the people. Near the baths he built the temple of Minerva. In order to show that she was being served, he established an eternal flame in a branch that would never be extinguished under any circumstances. Bladud worked many a miracle, and he delighted in such things. It was Bladud who wanted to fly in order to improve his reputation. It was he who boasted that he would fly, and would do so over London. He had wings constructed and made ready; he wanted to fly and intended to do so. But he came to a sorry end, for above the temple of Apollo he had an accident that broke every bone in his body. Thus, he came to a foolish end.

(1655–84) Bladud had ruled for twenty years after the death of Ruhundibras. He had to protect the domain after the death of his son Leir. Leir used his wealth to build a city in his name; its name was Kaerleir on the Soar; we now call it Leicester. Each name signifies 'city of Leir'. Once it was a very fine city, but a quarrel was later to lead to great destruction there. For sixty years continuously Leir ruled the domain in a very effective way. He had three daughters, but no other heir, and he could not have further children. The first child was Gonorille, then there was Ragau, then Cordelia. The youngest was the most beautiful and she was the one the father loved best. When Leir started to get somewhat weaker, as a man does who is getting old, he began to think about marrying off his three daughters.

He said he would marry them and share out his kingdom between them. But first he wanted to find out which one of them loved him the most. He wanted to bestow the majority of his wealth on the one who would cherish him the most.

(1685–728) He summoned each of them singly, starting with the eldest:

'My daughter,' he said, 'I want to know how much you love me, tell me the truth.' Gonorille swore to him by all the deities in heaven—she was filled with trickery—that she loved him more than her life:

'My daughter,' he said, 'you have loved me a great deal. You will be well rewarded, for you have valued my old age more than your own life or your youth. You will have such recompense for this that, if I can manage it, you can have as your husband the most esteemed baron you can select from my kingdom, and I shall share my land with you, giving you one third of it.' Then he asked for Ragau:

'My daughter, tell me, how much do you love me?'

Ragau had heard how her sister had responded, and how her father had been so grateful to her for loving him so profoundly. She wanted to have the same reward in her turn, so she said to him on oath:

'I love you above any other creature. I cannot express my love in any other way.'

'There is great love here,' said Leir, 'I cannot ask for more. I shall grant you a husband, along with a third of my domain.' Then he also spoke to Cordelia, who was the youngest daughter. Because he held her more dearly than Ragau, or the firstborn, he thought that she would know that he regarded her as his dearest daughter. Cordelia had listened carefully and noted clearly in her heart how her two sisters had spoken, and how they had flattered their father. She wanted to joke with him, and by joking she wished to show him that his daughters were cajoling him and feeding him a diet of flattery.

(1729–72) When Leir addressed her like the others, she said to him:

'Where is there any daughter who tells her father presumptuously that she loves him more than she ought to do? I do not know if there is any greater love than that between children and their father, or between children and their mother. You are my father, and I love you as much as I should love my father, and, to make you more certain of this, you have so much, you are worth so much, and I love you so much.' Then she fell silent, not wanting to say anything more. Her father was furious; he became livid with rage and misinterpreted her words. He thought that she was insulting him, and either not deigning to, not wanting to, or, out of malice, neglecting to declare that she loved him just as much as her sisters did, who had declared such love.

'You have treated me scornfully in not wanting to, or not deigning to, reply in the way that your sisters have done. To the two of them I shall give husbands and the whole of my kingdom in marriage. They will inherit everything, each of them having half of it. But you will not have a single foot of it. Nor will you ever have a husband through me, or a hand's breadth of what is mine. I cherished you and loved you more than any other woman, and I thought that you loved me more than the others. If you had deigned to do this, it would have been only right and proper. But you have spurned me to my face, indicating that you love me less than they do. All the time I held you more and more dearly, all the more you have been treating me with contempt. Never will you know joy from what is mine, and I shall never take any pleasure from what is yours.'

(1773–96) The maiden did not know what to reply. She thought she would collapse from anger and shame. She did not want to quarrel with her father, but he did not wish to listen to her. He did not delay any longer than he had to do before marrying off the two older girls. Each one was well married, one of them to the duke of Cornwall and the younger one to the king of Scotland. Arrangements were made that after him they would have the kingdom, and they would share it between them. Cordelia, who was the youngest girl, could do nothing other than wait, and I do not know what she could have done. The king offered her nothing, nor in his wickedness did he allow her to have a husband in his land. The maiden was filled with shame, and she felt deep anguish in her heart, more because he hated her wrongly than for the advantages she was losing as a result. She was grief-stricken because of her father's anger. But she was very beautiful and noble, and people talked about her a great deal.

(1797–828) Aganippus, one of the kings of France, heard Cordelia being praised and that she was still unmarried. He sent letters and messages to King Leir informing him that he would like to take his daughter as his wife, and if he sent her to him he would marry her. Leir had not forgotten, rather had he very frequently recalled, how his daughter had loved him. He sent word to the king of France, saying that he had divided up his whole realm and given it to his two daughters, half to the firstborn and half to the middle one. But if his daughter pleased him he could have the girl, but he would have nothing more. The king who had sought her hand thought that it was because of the king's affection for her that he was being denied her. So he desired her all the more and sent word to King Leir again that he was not asking for anything from him other than the grant of his daughter Cordelia. He should send her to him. Her father granted her to the king and sent her across the sea, but just the daughter and her apparel; she had no further garments with her. Then she was lady over the whole of France, and she was a very powerful queen.

(1829–82) The men who had married Cordelia's sisters, to whom the lands had been promised, could not wait to take over and possess the lands that their father-in-law had bestowed upon them and of which he had gladly divested himself. The duke of Cornwall, and Manglanus, the king of Scotland, waged war against him and oppressed him until they took his kingdom from him by force. Their father-in-law had left everything to them, but they made an arrangement with him that one of them would keep him with him and provide supplies for him, his squires, and his forty knights, so that he could travel with honour anywhere he desired. So they took over the kingdom and shared it out between them. Leir accepted their proposition and he relinquished the entire kingdom.

Manglanus had Leir with him, and at first he had him served him very well. But things soon got worse at court and provisions were cut back. The first thing was that the privileges diminished, then the provisions completely failed to materialize. Gonorille was very miserly. She took it as a great insult that her father ruled over a large household and yet did nothing. The costs of it all were upsetting her, and she often said to her husband:

'What use are all these people who are gathered here? By my faith, my lord, we are fools to have brought so many people here. My father does not know what he is doing. He is nothing but a troublemaker. He is an old man, and he is already acting like a disruptive child. Shame on anyone who now trusts his word or who will feed such people on his behalf. His servants quarrel with ours, and then one side shuns the other. Who could tolerate such a throng of people? The lord is mad and his men are degenerate. The more that is devoted to something the more that is wasted. No one who serves him will get anything back from it. He is a true fool who provides for such people. They have had too much, let them be on their way. My father has forty men here.

Henceforth, let there be just thirty with us, or let him depart with all his people. What does it matter to us?'

(1883–912) There are very few women without fault and in whom avarice does not take root. The lady exhorted her husband so much, and harried him so much, that he reduced the forty to thirty; he cut back the father's outgoings by ten. The father grew very annoyed at this. To him it seemed disgraceful that the number had been reduced. He went to his other son-in-law Hennim, who was married to Ragau and lived in Cornwall. But he had not been there for a year when they heaped shame upon him. If things were shameful before then, now they were much worse. Thirty men were reduced to ten. Then the number was reduced from ten to five.

'Woe is me,' he said, 'I was wrong to come here! If things were shameful there, they are worse for me here!' He went back to the first daughter, thinking that she would improve things and honour him as she had done at first. But she swore by heaven that no more than one knight would remain with him. The father had no choice but to agree. Then he began to feel very sad and to recall in his heart the many good things he had enjoyed but which he had now completely lost.

(1913–72) 'Woe is me,' he said, 'I have lived too long now that I have witnessed this wretched time. I have had so much and now I have so little. Where has everything I had gone to? Fortune, you change so much. You cannot remain fixed for a single hour. No one can trust in you. You make your wheel turn so swiftly and you have soon changed your colour. You are soon down, but you are soon back up again. The person on whom you wish to look kindly you have soon raised to great power, but as soon as you turn against them you soon reduce them to nothing. You have soon raised a villein on high and soon thrust him right back down. When you wish to do so, you ruin counts and kings, leaving them with nothing. As long as I had a certain degree of wealth, I had many relatives and servants. But, alas, as soon as I was impoverished, I lost friends, relatives, and servants. I have only one relative who would offer me any sign of affection. My youngest daughter, Cordelia, whom I blamed, told me the truth in telling me that in accordance with how much I had I would be esteemed that much and loved that much. I did not understand what she said, rather I blamed her and regarded her as a fool. As long as I had my own possessions, I was worth so much, praised so much, and loved so much. I found so many people who flattered me, but now if they see me, they turn away from me. Cordelia told me the truth, but I was not able to understand it, rather I blamed her and hated her for it. I drove her out of my land, giving her nothing. Now I have been failed by my daughters, who in the past were my friends and who loved me above everything else, as long as I had a certain amount of wealth. Now I must go in search of the one whom I drove to another land. But how shall I go about finding her, now that I have driven her from my kingdom? Nevertheless, I shall go and see if I can find anything to my advantage. She will never do less for me, or worse to me, than the elder ones have done. She said she would love me as one should love one's father. What more could I ask of her than that? Should she, who promised me a different form of love, love me better? She did this in order to deceive me.

(1973–2014) Leir lamented for a long time and thought for a long time. Then he came to the ships and went to France, arriving at a port in Chauz. He asked about the queen until very soon she was pointed out to him. He stopped outside the city to avoid being recognized by man or woman. He sent a squire to announce to the queen that her father had come to her and that he was seeking her out of necessity. He explained to her in orderly fashion how his daughters had thrown him out. Cordelia acted like a true daughter. She took a large amount of her wealth and handed it over to the squire, exhorting him to take it to her father on her behalf so that he could take comfort from it. With this money let him go secretly to a good town or city and get ready appropriately, feeding and dressing himself, washing and bathing. Let him also dress himself in royal garments and spend time there in great honour. He should also retain forty knights from the retinue that accompanied him. Later he should let the king know that he was coming to see his daughter. When he had received the money and heard the command, he took to his lord the news that was pleasing and welcome to him. They went to another city, took lodgings there, and dressed themselves well. When Leir was well rested there and was bathed, dressed, and equipped, and when his household had properly gathered there, well dressed and well attired, he sent word to the king that he was coming to him in order to see his daughter.

(2015–66) The king himself, out of nobility, and the queen, with great joy, advanced a long way out to meet him and they gladly honoured him. The king, who had never seen his father-in-law before, received him very warmly. Throughout the whole of his kingdom he had the word spread, and commanded his vassals that they should all serve him and do his bidding. He should tell them what he wanted, and whatever he said should be done, until his kingdom was restored and he was re-established in his domain. Thus, Aganippus acted in a courtly manner. He had all his Frenchmen gathered together, and through their advice and through their aid he prepared a large fleet of ships. He sent the ships to Britain with his father-in-law and handed Cordelia over to him so that she would be with the man who would have the kingdom after him, if they could retrieve it and take it out of the hands of his sons-in-law. They had soon crossed the sea and freed the whole of the land. They removed it from the wicked sons-in-law and took possession of all of it for Leir. After this, Leir lived for more three years. He ruled the entire kingdom peacefully and restored to his allies what they had lost. After three years he died. In Leicester, where his body lay, Cordelia buried him in the crypt of the temple of Janus. Then she ruled the domain for five years, but she was now a widow without a husband. After five years, two sons of her older sisters, whom Leir had married off, waged war on her and made a strong challenge for the land. Margan and Cunedagius hated their aunt because of the land she possessed. They fought on a number of occasions, often having the upper hand but also often being defeated. Finally, they captured Cordelia and imprisoned her. They refused to accept a ransom for her, keeping her for so long in prison that out of sorrow she killed herself in the jail, which was an act of folly.

(2067–120) When they had conquered the land, each of them had his own part of it: Cunedagius had the Humber in the west and Margan the area towards the north. Things remained like this for two years, but covetousness does not stay still. With him Margan had companions who were very envious and very wicked, and who had a distinct dislike of peace.

'You are a very wretched person when you divide all this into halves when you could claim the whole of it. Either you should have the whole of Britain or not even be left with a full foot of land. When you are the eldest, it is shameful that the next-born has most of it. Take possession of everything beyond the Humber. Take all of the lands outright.' Margan accepted their advice, but they deceived him badly. He crossed the Humber by force, burning and destroying, capturing and looting. Cunedagius, who had a large number of men with him, came and attacked him as best he could. But Margan did not dare wait for him or engage him in battle. He fled from place to place, with Cunedagius following him. Margan fled into Wales and his opponent followed him there. In Wales he was captured and killed, and there he was buried. The region in which he was killed, and in which he was buried, takes its name Margan from that of Margan; I know of no other explanation for it. Then Cunedagius had entirely to himself everything that had been shared between them. The king lived for thirty years and he ruled the country very peacefully. At that time Romulus and Remus built the city of Rome. They were brothers, but out of envy one of them robbed the other of his life. Hezekiah, whose life God extended by fifteen years because of the bitter tears he shed, was alive at that time and was king of Judaea. This happened at the time of Isaiah, who stated in a prophecy that a virgin would conceive, and from the virgin a son would be born whose name would be Emmanuel, and he would save Israel.

(2121–62) After Cunedagius' death, one of his sons, who was very wise, reigned. His name was Rival and he was very brave and greatly loved by all. In his time, rain, consisting of blood, came down for three days—I do not know what the meaning of this was—and there was a storm of flies from which many people became fatally ill. The scarlet-coloured rain that fell, and the truly remarkable flies, frightened everyone, and each one of them was afraid for his own safety. Then King Rival was dead, after him the kingdom was ruled by his son, who was called Gurgustius. After him the king was Sisillius, then Lago, the nephew of Gurgustius, then Kimare, son of Sisillius. Gorbodiagnes, who had two wicked and cruel sons, came next. The elder of the two was named Ferreus, and the younger one was called Porreus. They could never remain at peace with each other. Their father was still alive when, because of covetousness and envy, strife broke out with regard to the kingdom and the lordship. The older of the two said that he would have everything, and the other said he would take it all away from him. Porreus had a very wicked disposition. Through treachery or some ruse he wanted to kill his brother. Ferreus became aware of this, as he heard him talk of it, and he fled overseas to France, where he served King Suart until he returned with a large fleet of ships and knights. He fought with his brother, but things turned out badly for him, for he was the first to be killed, as were his knights.

(2163–80) Judon, their mother, who was still alive, regarded herself as dead and wretched because of the evil and the cruelty involved in the killing of one son by the other. She had loved the dead son more, so she conceived a great hatred for the other one. One night when he was lying down and sleeping securely, lo, this mother with her maid-servants and with sharp knives beneath their arms slit his throat. Was a mother ever more enraged? O God, who ever saw such a sin! They cut him to pieces. There was much talk for a long time of Judon and her vengeance. On account of one son she murdered the other, and on account of one son she lost two.

(2181–240) When Ferreus and Porreus were dead, no son or daughter was left, and there was no close heir from their lineage who could take over their heritage. Those with power fought each other, and the strong drove out the weak. Each man to the best of his ability defeated his weaker neighbours. Not a single one of them maintained what was right or upheld law or reason. They betrayed each other, and even kinsmen killed each other for their money and lands. Everywhere there were mortal combats. There were five* very powerful barons of splendid appearance, and they made the others submit to them and took over all the lands round them. Each one had taken over the surrounding domains and each one had himself called king. Each one made war on his peer and each one wanted to harry the other. In Scotland Stater reigned and Pinner was king of Logres. Rudac was king of Wales and Clotem ruled Cornwall. This Clotem ought to have had everything, for no more rightful heir was known. But those who were stronger than he was had no interest in coming to an agreement with him. Then Clotem had a very noble son, who possessed great audacity. He was brave and very tall, and his name was Dumwallo Molmuz. He was bold, handsome, and courtly, and he surpassed all the kings in Britain in audacity and beauty. As soon as he could bear arms, he never wanted to rest. He conquered the land of Logres, killing Pinner, who was its king. Then he went to capture Scotland and Wales, but the kings there intended to defend themselves. They formed an alliance against him through oath and through faith. They entered his land forcibly, destroying a great deal and laying waste a great deal. Rudac was there with the Welsh, and Stater with the Scots. They went about capturing castles and destroying estates and towns. Dumwallo, who had thirty thousand warriors, joined battle with them. As they first engaged, there was a great deal of uproar and blowing of horns, with many blows taken and given, many men killed and many wounded. Many shields were shattered, and many were pierced. Helmets were broken and hauberks torn.

(2241–70) The battle lasted for a long time, and they feared each other for a long time: which one would be the stronger and which one would win? Dumwallo was very subtle and very keen to win the battle. He took six hundred of his most trusted men with him, the boldest and the most proven. He had them arm themselves with the enemies' arms, which were lying round the battlefield, and he did the same. Then he said to them:

'Come with me and do what I do.' Then he watched closely and waited, and through spies he searched for where Rudac and Stater were and in which location they were fighting. Then he moved swiftly up beside them, as though he had been with him. He moved his men up alongside the two kings, crying out to them: 'Strike! Strike!' It was easy for them to strike their opponents, and they slaughtered them both. Then in close array they pulled back towards their own men, and when amongst them they put down their arms and took up their original ones, in order to prevent their own men from attacking and killing them, thinking they were someone else.

(2271–312) Once they had rearmed themselves and joined forces with their own men, they started to strike blows again, but their opponents could not withstand them. Because of the deaths of their leaders the divisions separated, and Dumwallo charged at them. They were discomfited in a very short time. When they had conquered the land, they created such peace throughout the kingdom that there was never any such peace before, and, I believe, there never will be again. He had a gold crown made for himself. I have never before heard tell of a king of Britain who had worn a crown of gold on his head. He established and confirmed an ordinance stating that all the temples and cities should have such great authority that no one, whatever wrong he had committed, if he could get access to one, would ever be seized by anyone before he had been pardoned for his deeds. He could go back in freedom to his lodging and possess freely everything he owned. Then he established that those who worked the plough should enjoy peace and not be troubled by anyone, nor should those who entered the cities on their way into the temples or markets. The life of anyone who harmed them would be in jeopardy as a criminal. He established the languages and the laws that still hold good today. He was king for forty years, then he died. His men buried him beside the temple of St Concord, a temple that he founded, as the history relates, in order to maintain peace and concord.

THE BROTHERS BELIN AND BRENNE FIGHT EACH OTHER, BUT THEN DEFEAT THE ROMANS

(2313–40) He had two noble sons with his wife; they were of noble lineage. The firstborn was called Belin and the second Brenne. Between them they ruled the kingdom. To Brenne, who was the younger, fell the task of ruling Northumbria, Caithness, and everything to the north of the Humber on that side. Belin was not willing to share any more of the land, and he made Brenne become his vassal so that he would serve and recognize him as his lord. Belin retained everything in his possession: Logres, Wales, and Cornwall. This lasted five years without either of them harming the other. But Brenne was surrounded by scoundrels, liars, and tricksters, who said so much and urged them so much that the brothers quarrelled. One of them was very treacherous and very deceptive in what he said. He was skilled at violating agreements and at stimulating antagonism, and he was good at concocting an accusation and altering a judgement. If there was any advantage in it for him, he had no concern for anyone who lost out.

(2341–74) 'We are amazed', he said, 'that, even though we do not want to tell you so, in this way you have taken control of such a tiny proportion of a great and extensive domain, which your father ruled in his lifetime. For the land that you do have—I do not know what service you will provide for it—you must serve your brother Belin and you must hold the land from him. Are you the son of a concubine, or a bastard? Were you baseborn and more cowardly, so that you must pay him homage? Are you not of the same lineage? The woman who bore you also bore him, and you were both from the same father. Since you are both brothers, born of one father and one mother, why does Belin have power over you and your heritage? Break the alliance and break the faith that exists between Belin and yourself, as it is a matter of dishonour for you. It will be a disaster if you regard him as your lord. Trust your barons, trust their advice. By my faith, I am amazed at a man as courageous as you are being shamed in this way. Belin divided up the land and made his choice. On what grounds did he divide it up? Some division needs to be made, but he who is more capable should have more of it. I have no knowledge of any more rightful method than that the best of the land should go to the best of the men.

(2375–404) 'You are the stronger and the bolder man. People realized this when you defeated Ceoflo, from whom you took Scotland when he was king of Moriane* and wanted to lay waste Scotland. It is possible that you have tolerated this, and kept your feelings to yourself, because we did not discuss the matter. We are discussing this now, and we are advising you to take everything and have everything. What are you afraid of? What is troubling you? We shall not fail you for the sake of our lives, and, if you do not trust us because the advantage in knights does not lie with you, go and seek help in Norway. King Elfinges will help you, and he has a daughter he will give to you. Marry his daughter, take her away, and strive to acquire some Norwegians. With so many Norwegians, so many Scots, so many foreigners, so many of our own men, you can bring together such a host, if you wish, that you can lay waste many a kingdom. Your brother will never oppose you, nor will he remain in the kingdom. Go quickly and come back even more quickly. Behave secretly so that Belin does not realize what you are doing and deceive you by his cunning.'

(2405–30) When he had delivered this advice and it had been praised by the others, Brenne willingly trusted them. He thought he could execute this well, but he failed to do so. He crossed the sea to Norway and asked Elfinges for his daughter. He granted her to him along with a large quantity of wealth. He said he would help him so much that he would have the whole of Britain. Many people told Belin about this, where he was going and what he was seeking. Belin thought and suspected that, since this affair had gone ahead without his leave, an act of treachery would soon be committed. So he met cunning with cunning. If Brenne intended to deceive him, he knew how to be on his guard against this. Belin went to capture Northumbria, seizing the castles and strengthening them. He did not fail to capture any castle where Brenne could take him by surprise. He placed guards throughout all the castles, thinking he could hold on to them permanently, so that his brother would never take possession of them. He had arms and grain brought.

(2431–74) Belin himself and his forces were positioned on the shores and at the ports, so that his brother would not push forward without opposition and without dispute. Brenne had heard the news that Belin had captured his land. He took his wife, did what he had to do, and returned with a large number of men. The lady was very beautiful and noble, but she was not pleased with this marriage. For a long time she had loved the king of Denmark, Gudlac, who had loved her in turn, and she was to be given to him. But Brenne had put paid to this. She had sent word to Gudlac and revealed to him the whole of the plan: Brenne had her and Gudlac would lose her. If he did not do something about this, he would never lie in her arms. Gudlac, the king of Denmark, was aware that Brenne was taking away his beloved. With as many ships as he could muster, he watched out for Brenne's return home. He intended to rescue her from Brenne if he could find the right opportunity. He would, he said, have had her if he had not lost her because of Brenne. The two fleets met each other, ships clashing with ships, blows being exchanged for blows, strength pitted against strength, knock against knock, plank against plank. Many a plank was shattered and smashed. Many men were killed and many drowned. On both sides, the men were strong. But Brenne's fleet yielded ground and withdrew in defeat. Gudlac himself happened by chance to approach one of their ships containing the lady, and he retained it. He was not interested in any of the other ships. He held this one and stayed behind. Brenne took flight, mourning deeply for his wife.

(2475–502) When Gudlac had captured his booty, he wanted to be back on dry land, and he was soon on his way home. But listen to the problem that ensued! A great storm blew up. The weather changed and the wind direction changed. It thundered and rained, and there were flashes of lightning. The sky turned black and the air darkened. The sea became choppy, and the waves reared, rising and falling. The ships were now at risk, and their planks and pegs started to break. The stitching broke and the planks split. The sails shattered and the masts broke. No one could lift up his head, so great was the storm. The ships were soon all separated, and they were dispersed to many lands. Things stayed this way on the tempestuous sea for five days, with a very high wind. Gudlac, with only three ships, sped down wind, and on the fifth day he docked in England. He was very happy when he reached land with the woman he loved. But he did not know, and was not aware of, what land he was in, as he had lost his way so completely.

(2503–50) Those who watched over the shores and guarded the ports captured Gudlac and his companions, his beloved, and his prisoners.

They brought them before Belin, who had them watched over, as he was waiting on the shore for his brother Brenne to arrive. Those who were captured along with the lady revealed the truth to the king of how Brenne had acted and had been to the king in Norway, and how Gudlac had encountered him and he had routed him. Brenne scarcely delayed. He once again established a great fleet of ships and arrived in Scotland with a large fleet and large forces. He sent word to his brother Belin and begged him through messengers not to hold on to his wife. He should free her and hand her over, liberate his castles, and go back to his land. If he did not hand her over at once, he would lay waste all his land. Belin did not fear his threats, or anything that Brenne could do. He refused him outright. When Brenne understood and saw that peace would achieve nothing, and that an entreaty would be of no value to him, he gathered his companions together and arranged his squadrons. Close to the forest of Calatere, the two brothers engaged in battle. One hated the other intensely, and they attacked each other. They rode towards each other and threatened each other. When the two hosts met, they fought each other with great ferocity. A large number of darts were thrown, and many stones, and there was also a great thrusting of lances and a great clash of swords. They threw, hurled, struck, shoved, fell, thrashed about, and breathed their last.

(2551–98) The Britons were the better fighters, whereas the Norwegians were merely mercenaries, who could not withstand their opponents for long. They were forced to flee to the ships. But Belin, who kept on striking them down, pursued them. In the fields and on the paths they died in their twenties, their hundreds, and their thousands. Brenne, who had started this wretched situation, escaped with great difficulty. He found a ship in the harbour and went on board with around a dozen men. He crossed over the sea towards France, having lost all his companions, who had been killed, wounded, or captured. When the dead had been buried, they were numbered at fifteen thousand, and not one of them escaped without being fatally wounded. When this affair was over, and his brother had fled, Belin held his council in York, inside the town. He asked for advice about what to do with King Gudlac, whom he was holding prisoner. From the prison where he was Gudlac had sent word to him that he would hold his domain from him as his liege lord, and from Denmark he would render him a tribute each year by proclamation. If he let him go free and take his beloved away, he would provide surety through hostages and pledges. On the advice of his barons he freed Gudlac and his beloved. But he took Gudlac's homage, and an oath and reliable hostage to guarantee that the agreement would be adhered to. Then he let him go, and thus Gudlac departed and went back to his land. He took with him his beloved, whom he had obtained as a result of great hardship.

(2599–628) Belin ruled the domain firmly, and he behaved very wisely. He was a peace-loving man who delighted in keeping the peace. He established peace and maintained peace. He journeyed through the regions and visited the lands. He saw the moors and the woodland, saw the rivers and the defiles, which could not be passed through easily, and he saw that cities were scarcely accessible from one to the other. Over valleys, moors, and hills he had roads and bridges constructed. He built good bridges and high roads made out of stone, sand, and lime. First, he made a roadway that is still visible; it is very long and runs the length of the land. The peasants call it Fosse, for it begins in Totnes and ends in Caithness. It starts in the area round Cornwall and ends in Scotland. From the port of Southampton on sea he had a paved road going right to St David's in Wales and finishing at the sea further on; it went from city to city as far as the land stretched. He had two further roads widened that crossed the breadth of the country.

(2629–70) When the king had finished building the roads, he ordered that there be peace. There should be complete peace and freedom, and if there was anybody in his domain who committed acts of violence their own domain would be forfeit. Brenne, who had gone to France, was ashamed and distressed because of what had happened to his land, and even more because of his wife, whom he had lost in such a dishonourable fashion. With eleven companions he served the king and his barons. He was a courtly and brave knight, and he was liked by everyone. He did not fail to hand over the provisions, the payments, or the gifts. He was highly praised for his bravery, and greatly loved for this generosity, for he acted very liberally, giving away a great deal and spending a great deal. When he had become well known and highly esteemed throughout the land, he asked for help and succour from the kings and the other lords in order to get back what Belin had stolen from him. He had travelled finally as far as Burgundy, to Duke Seguin, who treated him with great honour and gave him a large amount of his wealth. Brenne, who was a man of considerable breeding, spoke to him in courtly fashion. He knew about hunting and hawking by the river, and about all sorts of pleasures. He had a noble body and a handsome face, and he seemed to be like a man of very good lineage. The duke possessed great power, but he had no child or heir except for a daughter. Already a young woman, grown up and properly brought up, she was ripe for marriage.

(2671–708) Brenne was skilful at serving the duke and he pleased him through the elegance of his speech. His behaviour attracted the duke greatly, and he very much liked the fact that he remained with him. He gave his daughter to him as his wife and made him heir to his land, providing he himself did not have a son with his wife before he died. The inhabitants of the domain loved him very much and held him very dear. He knew how to inspire love through the elegance of his speech and through the gifts he gave. A year had not yet passed since Brenne was married when the duke, his father-in-law, died. Brenne became duke and received the domain. If it were possible, the barons who had loved him loved him more, for he gave them generous gifts and spoke to them pleasingly. The Burgundians, the knights and the barons, loved him greatly. He ruled a very large area of land, and had a considerable income and a beautiful and noble wife. But he had not forgotten that Belin had disinherited him and robbed him of the whole of his fief. As soon as he saw the time and the opportunity, he brought men together and sought for knights, begged neighbours, and hired mercenaries. He came to Normandy with a great host and prepared a fleet there. When he had completed this task and the wind was favourable, he crossed the sea in safety. Belin, who knew that he was coming, came to do battle against him with as many men as he could get hold of. Both of them had a large number of ferocious troops.

(2709–49) They were soon donning their arms, and striking and defending when between them came Tonuuenne, the mother of Belin and the mother of Brenne. Trembling, she came between the two armies; she was old and she moved swiftly,* asking for and seeking Brenne until the barons pointed him out to her. Throwing her arms round his neck, she kissed and embraced him repeatedly. She had not spoken to him for a long time, but she had long wished to do so. She tore all her clothing right down to below her waist, showing him her naked breasts, withered and hairy due to old age. In tears, she spoke to her son, and her words were interrupted by frequent sobs and profound sighs.

'Fair son,' she said, 'listen to me. Remember, remember these breasts, which you can see, and which suckled you many times. Remember that when you were born you came out of this belly. Remember the pain I suffered for you for many a long day. Remember, my son, this body from which the Creator, who created you when you were still unborn, made you issue. Remember and trust me. Lay down the arms you are holding, you who come from foreign lands, leading foreign troops in order to destroy your own domains. Are you bringing such joy to your friends, whom you have not seen for a long time, because of the advantages God has bestowed on you? Do you bear us such friendship that you are coming here to kill your brother?

(2750–84) 'Take a rest and assuage your anger. You will never have another sister or brother. You have no father, and your mother is old. Ought you to be coming back here and exiling your impoverished kinsmen? You ought to be bringing your fine possessions to give to us, thus demonstrating to us your great wealth and boasting of your noble status. You ought to have come in peace and offered us your fine possessions,* yet you come to take them away from us, you who ought to be supporting us. If you wish to grieve for your brother, bring this folly to a close. First of all, I shall have given you as a result of judgement what is rightly yours. If you state that he pursued you and that he drove you out of your land, you are wrong, and what you say is unreasonable, for no one other than yourself drove you away. You were completely in the wrong when you created this wickedness. Whatever anyone says, he who inaugurates treachery is in the wrong. Everyone knows you started all this, you who crossed over to Norway and took a wife there. You did not ask his leave for this, and you induced the Norwegians to drive him away but in this you failed, and if you had not challenged him he would not have denied you your rights. You would have disinherited him or killed him, as people know, if you had been able to do so.

(2785–816) 'Belin, who at that time was duke, did not drive you away, rather did he send you to Burgundy to acquire as much or more than he had. You should not get angry with him, as it was he who made you master of Burgundy. From your lowly status he made you powerful, and from poverty he has brought you to riches. You have had your part of the kingdom, and you do well to surrender it to him. Still, if it pleased you, Northumbria would be yours. You abandoned it in order to get something better. You should be grateful to your brother, through whom you had the opportunity to visit another region in order to receive the great domain over which the Lord God has made you lord. You have one brother, and you should love him. But he ought to place great blame on you, for you have done great wrong by him in gathering these forces to fight him for the purpose of disinheriting your kinsmen, and to lay waste our land, forces who would do the same to you if they had the upper hand. Fair son, Brenne, what are you thinking of? Put down your lance and your shield. Take your mother's advice and make peace with your brother. Abandon your anger against him, and let him do the same with regard to you.'

(2817–78) Brenne heard what his mother said, and he took pity on her and trusted her. He took off his sword, removed his shield, and laid aside his hauberk. He darted on to the battlefield before his men, and Belin on his side did the same. Their mother brought them together and ordered them to embrace. As soon as she had given the order, there was nothing more to be said. They went and embraced each other and kissed each other tenderly. Thus, the war was over, and the anger of the brothers was at an end. From there they came to London and held a council. This was the end of the deliberations, and they all said that they would cross over the sea to France and conquer the whole of it. Then Belin summoned his Britons and Brenne took his Burgundians. At the time they proposed, they came to the port and went on board the ships. They crossed the sea to France. The people there were very frightened, and they all felt great fear that in the end they might be destroyed. At that time there were numerous kings in France, who were masters over the French people. They all gathered together for a general council and came to an agreement. They fought the two brothers, but were defeated by them. They were unable to defend themselves, rather were they forced to surrender. There was no one, however powerful, who waited for them. They captured the castles and cities, and in less than a year they had conquered France. Faced with them, everyone trembled. Then the two brothers held a discussion, saying that they would go to Rome and that right up until they reached it they would never leave behind anyone holding a city or a castle who had not become their liegeman. Then they gathered their forces together again and brought their troops together. Leading as many men as they could, they crossed Montgieu and Mont Cenis and took Turin and Ivrea, all the cities of Lombardy,

Vercelli, Pavia, Cremona, Milan, Piacenza, and Bologna. They crossed the river Taro and then Mount Bardon. They conquered and pillaged Tuscany, which was a land of ill-repute. When they continued to occupy more land and got closer to Rome, the inhabitants of Rome, who heard the news of what was happening, became all the more agitated.

(2879–918) In the year I am talking about here, the Romans had established two counts to take charge of wars and keep hold of their lands; one was called Porsenna and the other Gabius. They spoke to the senators, asking their advice about how they should act, whether they should do battle with the brothers, hand over the city to them, or do homage to them for their fiefs. They were terrified and stated in the Senate that they would not fight under any circumstances. The brothers were strong and they had a large number of men, but if they could make peace with them, through promises and gifts, they would do so. They would give them so much gold and silver that they would never want for more. In addition to this they would promise to provide them with a tribute each year and get them to go back home rather than have their city laid waste or their region destroyed. Why should I give you a lengthy account of this? Having received counsel, the counts came to the brothers, bringing them a great deal of money, which they gave to them. To gain their friendship, they promised and granted them each year a tribute from Rome. The brothers accepted the money. They retained hostages from Rome to secure the tributes and the agreements, twenty-four children from amongst the strongest and the wealthiest. Thus, the friendship was secured, but it did not last for long.

(2919–64) The two brothers returned home, crossing Lombardy. They attacked the Germans because of a tribute that was demanded of them, but the Romans, who broke the agreement they had with them, impeded them. Again they abandoned their hostages, who were from their lineages, and they had damaged the friendship. It had only been upheld for a very short time. For as soon as Belin was some a distance away, and Brenne had left Rome, they forgot all the fear they had felt and regained their courage. Thus, of their knights they took I do not know how many hundreds or thousands. They were well armed and prepared, and they sent them in amongst the enemy to defeat and attack them, and to ambush them at the passing-places in the hills. They chose another section of their troops and sent them to Germany so that they would join up with them, expand their forces, and watch over the mountain passes, so that the brothers could not cross there without harm. They sent these forces because they thought that, if they failed in their task, in the great mountain passes with the throng created by so many divisions of men, the brothers would be so surrounded, with the Romans behind them and the Germans in front of them, and thus they would all be killed. For the way was not straight, rather was it twisted, long, and narrow. Anyone who was encountered on such a path would be easily impeded. A small number of men could very easily defeat a whole army. When Belin and Brenne knew this, they took such advice as they could: Brenne would return and do battle with the Romans and, if he could, he would take vengeance for the oath that had been broken.

(2965–96) Belin would pass through the mountains and defeat the Germans. The first brother to win a victory would assist the other. Brenne took warriors from France and Burgundy on his mission, and Belin led his own troops, the Welsh, the Scots, and the Britons. But when those who were in Germany realized that Brenne had turned round and gone to Rome, they took counsel and decided to go and help the Romans. Taking a path they knew, they got ahead of Brenne and his men. Belin found out through a spy what path this division was taking. He knew the time fixed for their return and which way they were to go. He used the peasants as his guides, taking on oath I do not know how many of them. By as direct a path as they could find, they would take him to where the enemy was returning. They entered the spurs of Montgieu, and day and night he strove so hard that he came to a valley where the Romans were to pass, and from which they could not retreat. Belin lay in wait and forbade the host from making any noise or sound.

(2997–3026) The weather was as fine as in summer. The night was clear, there was no breeze, and a clear moon shone brightly. Belin hid himself in the valley and the Romans maintained their route with confidence and without fear. In the light of the moon, which was shining brightly, they were moving along at top speed when they stumbled upon those who were lying in wait. In the moonlight they saw helmets shining and also saddles and shields. Lo, they were suddenly all overwhelmed, and those who had been waiting for them struck them straightaway. As soon as Belin shouted out his battle-cry, not even a coward was faint-hearted. They attacked them on all sides. Their opponents fled, abandoning the battlefield. But they could not flee, nor did they have anywhere to hide. The Britons disembowelled them, mutilated them, and cracked their skulls. They decapitated many of them, killing them just like beasts. The slaughter never finished from morning, when the day broke, to the evening, when it went dark, and the blackness separated them. All those survivors set off in the direction of the valleys.

(3025–72) Next day, very early in the morning, Belin started out on the road. He followed his brother towards Rome. Brenne was aware of this and waited for him. When the brothers got together, they travelled onwards with greater ferocity and greater confidence. They came to Rome and besieged the city. They laid siege to it on many sides. They used stone-throwers, catapults, battering-rams,* and devices of many kinds in order to demolish the walls and break them into pieces. Those in Rome waited on the walls and defended themselves remarkably well. With slings and crossbows, which were all at the ready, they hurled stones and shot arrows. In no way were they shown any pity.* They threw darts and hurled balls of lead, knocking down many men and killing many. They caused the assaults to cease without the wall being pierced or knocked down. For a long time, as all the assaults were being made, the brothers had the worst of it. Many men were injured, and many were harmed. But, to avenge themselves, they erected gallows. In view of those inside, and in the sight of their friends and parents, they brought forward the hostages and raised high on the gallows twenty-four sons of Romans, from amongst the most arrogant citizens. Friends and kinsmen were all very distressed by this. None of them could do anything other than become angry. But they were stronger and fiercer, and they said and swore that they would never be at peace with them. They possessed great power, and they had great hope in Gabius and Porsenna, who had gone some time ago, through Lombardy and through Apulia, in search of support and assistance.

(3073–98) Those in Rome waited for them. On the precise day that they knew the counts would be arriving with the assistance they were bringing, they became very fierce and bold, and they attacked their adversaries in the host. They emerged when they pleased and fought very hard. The counts arrived, and then you would have heard a great hubbub. The Romans, who were on one side, and the Apulians and Lombards, who were on the other, slaughtered a large number of the Burgundians.

'Sons of whores,' they said, 'cowards, did you come here to receive a tribute? You are going to go without it for a long time. We shall make you drink your own blood in order to spare the water in the Tiber. Did you come from the direction of Montgieu to issue a challenge for this land of ours? We do not take this lightly in any way, for Rome as a fief is ours. You acted wrongly and sinfully when you hanged our hostages. You followed shameful advice, but, if it pleases God, you came here at an evil hour for you.'

(3099–124) The Romans tormented them and fought against them violently, delivering great blows against them, harming them, and threatening to do worse. They made them all withdraw and caused them to cry out and bawl. Each one struck his opponent well with no quarter given. Belin and Brenne became very angry that the Romans were making them weaken and were toppling and knocking down their men. They pushed and struck, killed and vanquished. No one was so strong that he did not grieve. They withdrew to one side and had a brief discussion, after which they were emboldened once more. They reassured their men, restrained their horses, armed their men, and arranged their men in squadrons of a thousand, fifty, and a hundred. The boldest and the most able-bodied they made masters and constables for each squadron individually, so that they could maintain them in battle order. The boldest fighters were placed at the front, amongst the fighting men.

(3125–54) Beside them they placed to the right and to the left crossbowmen and archers. The finest and the best of their men were made to get down off their horses, and they stood in the midst of the battlefield, in orderly and well-arranged fashion. They cut their lances in half and abandoned their cognizances. They would travel slowly in order to launch a communal strike against the great throng. None of them would ever break ranks, nor would they be forced by anyone else to evade the battle. Then they blew their bugles and their horns and launched an attack once more. They came back to the fray very swiftly. Then you would have heard arms crunching, broken chunks of lances flying about, and men falling to the ground and thrashing about. I do not know what more I can tell you. A great number of men died on both sides. But the Romans were defeated. Things had come to a very sorry pass, for Gabius was killed there and Porsenna, the count, was captured. The brothers entered Rome by force, and they found there an abundance of riches. They did whatever they pleased and anyone who wanted money found it.

(3155–84) When they had captured the city and conquered the whole of the land, Brenne, who was lord of Rome, stayed in Lombardy. Then he committed a large number of cruel acts as someone who possessed a very ferocious temperament. Belin left and went back to England. He reinforced his old cities and rebuilt the walls that had fallen down. He restored the old cities and erected new towns. One city he had founded in Wales he named Kaerusc because it was situated on the river Usk, a river that ran nearby; afterwards, it was called Karlion [Caerleon].* Hear now how this came about. A long time after Belin's death, and also after Brenne had come to his end, it happened in this way that the Romans had England under their control. In order to keep it within their own domain, they suffered many hardships over a long period of time and endured many burdens and many expenses. They had constantly created from their forces two legions, or three or four, in order to do battle with foreign peoples. At that time the Romans were highly thought of. Six thousand six hundred and sixty-six men made up one legion and that is how it is explained.

(3185–240) When the legions were taking a rest and not fighting with anyone, in winter each year they were at Kaerusc in Glamorgan, because of the ease and plenty they enjoyed in this city. Because of the legions I am referring to, which were residing there, and on account of the customs and the usage, they called it Kaerlion, that is the 'City of Legions'. In this way a good many names have been changed. Through Kaerusc there came Kaerlion, and the rightful name was Kaerlegion. But foreign peoples have their name abridged by subtraction. From Legion Liun was made, and Kaer was cut back. Thus, by shortening it, they made the whole name Karlion, and in this way they made the name smaller. When Belin had built Kaerusc and attracted a huge number of people to it, in London, his finest city and the one in which he spent most time, he constructed a remarkable gate on the river that carries fleets of ships. In English 'porte' is called 'gate' and this gate is called Bilingsgate. The gate was over the Thames, and it was constructed with remarkable ingenuity. The English call it Billingsgate, but the rightful name is Belinsgate because Belin built it. I do not know any other explanation for it. On the gate he placed a tower that was very large in both breadth and height. He revived his father's laws and confirmed them ceremoniously. He was a very fine dispenser of justice and a loyal and upright king. In his time there had been such great plenty that there had never been greater, and there never would be greater in terms of things to eat or drink. Until he became old, Belin reigned and lived from a position of strength. When he died, he was in London. O God! How the people mourned him. His body was burnt, and his ashes were taken and placed in a gold barrel that had been taken from his treasury. Then the barrel was raised, tightly sealed, and closed, and placed outside on top of the tower; there was no other form of burial for the body. It was as a mark of esteem and honour that the body was placed in such a lofty position.

(3241–80) After Belin, one of his sons named Gurguint ruled the land. His full name was Gurguint Bertruc and he was very thoughtful, wise, and possessed of great understanding of things. He loved peace and justice, and in the way he upheld and maintained peace he could be said to resemble his father. His father was a good ruler and so was he. No one did him any harm, except for the Danes, who rejected him as lord and denied him the tribute that Gudlac paid to Belin when he freed his beloved and himself. Gurguint well knew that he was in the right with regard to the lands his father had ruled. He summoned his men, went on board the ships, and had the sails and masts raised. He forced his way into Denmark. There was no city, castle, or borderland that he did not take by force if it were not surrendered peacefully. Many harsh battles were fought, and he killed the king as a result. Then he restored his tribute, just as his father had received it. From the barons he took homage, fealty, and hostages as surety. When Gurguint returned home, he sailed by Orkney. He found there thirty ships gathered together in a company, laden with men and women and very well prepared. Pantalous was in charge of them; he was their lord and he directed them. Gurguint asked what people they were, where they were going, and what they were seeking. Pantalous bowed low and asked him for peace and a truce.

(3281–334) When the king had granted this, and given him permission to speak, he said:

'I am being driven out of Spain, both myself and the whole of this company. We are travelling by sea to seek together some land where we can live. We have journeyed for a year and a half, experiencing hunger, thirst, and foul weather. We have not yet found anywhere we can retain as a fief, or where we can dwell permanently. This is very distressing for us. We have sailed for so long that we are all weary as a result. But if it were pleasing to you to retain us and to decide on a portion of land that you would give us, we would serve you willingly and become your vassals. Gurguint did not want to let them acquire any land in his kingdom, yet he did give them good advice. He sent them to Ireland, recommending that they should go there and cultivate that land. Ireland was not yet populated or occupied by anyone. They sailed on towards it, and as escort King Gurguint gave them some of his sailors, who took them there and handed Ireland over to them. They sailed and travelled swiftly until they reached Ireland, a land that was still wild. There was no dwelling or lodging there, and no other cultivatable land, but it was lovely and well provided for, with rivers, woodlands, mountains, arable meadows, and plains. Then they built shelters and bowers and took possession of the lands. The number of people grew and multiplied. He who was able to do so took the most land. Pantelous was in charge of them; he was their lord and ruled over them. Gurguint, who had sent them there, went back to England. He ruled his kingdom peacefully until his death. When he had completed his allotted time, he died in Karlion on the Usk, and when he reached his end the domain passed to Guincelin.

(3335–88) Guincelin led a good life, and his wife was called Marcia. She was well educated, and a wise woman, highly esteemed, and worthy. She devoted all her ingenuity and attention to learning and to writing. She knew a great deal and studied a great deal. She wrote down and invented a law: it was called the Marçian law according to the British language. King Alfred, it is said, translated and inscribed the law. When he had translated it into English, he called it the Marcenelaga. The queen, who knew so much, had a child by Guincelin, who was called Sisillius. But they never had any more children. Sisillius was not yet grown up when his father began to approach his end. When his father died, he was only seven years old, and he could do neither right nor wrong. After his father had become mortally ill, and died, his mother, on behalf of her son, ruled the kingdom very well in peace and great tranquillity. When the son was of the age at which he was able to govern the land, the mother had him crowned. He was still in his prime when his last day arrived. Then his son Rummarus was king, and after him Damus, his brother. He had a son with a concubine who, through his bravery, became king. Morpidus was his name, and he was a very fierce, bold, and strong knight.

He was praised for his great courage, but he was of very cruel disposition. He could become exceedingly angry, and he was constantly keen to kill someone. As soon as he became angry, he was incapable of sparing anyone. At once, he would strike him with his sword, and he was never prevented from doing this by any affection for him. He always killed his opponent at once, whether rightly or wrongly, yet as long as he was not angry he did whatever anyone wanted him to do. In the whole kingdom, which was large, there was no one as powerful as he. His face was handsome and his body noble. He bestowed great gifts very frequently. He was exceedingly generous and had no interest in accumulating wealth.

(3389–428) At the time that Morpidus reigned, the duke of Moriane sailed along the shores, laying them waste, taking prisoners, and holding people to ransom. He had a large number of armed men with him, and people dreaded and feared him very much. He arrived in Northumbria and began to ravage it. Morpidus was very distressed by this, and with the Britons he had assembled he attacked Moriane and fought with him, defeating and conquering him. People said this in truth, but I do not know how it was proven, that Morpidus conquered more, and killed more, men with his own hand than did the whole of the assembled army. When he had conquered the entire battlefield, he did not capture a single man alive without disembowelling him or beheading him with his sword. He created a great pile of dead bodies, and when he was tired of killing he had them flayed alive to be put on to the pyres, and burnt, in order to satisfy his great rage, which he could not control. When he was in his prime, and his temperament was at its most ferocious, there came over to the sea from the direction of Ireland an exceedingly large beast, a sea monster, a horrible beast with a horrible body and a horrible head. It was a wild sea monster; never had such a huge creature been seen. Through the towns, along the shores, it created much sorrow and harm, devouring men and women and eating the beasts in the fields.

(3429–64) The people took flight, abandoning their homes and towns. They fled into the woods and the high mountains, but they still feared dying there. Morpidus, who had a very ferocious temperament, heard their lamentation. He trusted so much in his own strength that he went to face the monster head-to-head. He attacked it completely on his own, not wishing to have any assistance. An excess of audacity is folly, and he is a fool who trusts in himself too much. Morpidus in his audacity approached the monster very fiercely, shooting arrows, hurling darts, and wounding it in a number of places. When he did not have anything left to hurl, pitch, or throw, he ran towards it with nothing but his sword. But his sword was broken by the great blow it had struck, and the beast opened its mouth, devoured him, and swallowed him up. Because of his folly the king was killed. But the beast did not survive, for the king had beaten him so much, and wounded and struck him so hard that he immediately died on the spot. There was no peasant who did not display joy. The monster that fell down dead was a comfort for the death of the king. They felt great sorrow for the king, but the swift death of the beast provided them with consolation. Then they felt so much joy between them that they had forgotten the king entirely, and they brought all the grief they had experienced for him to an end.

(3465–96) The king had fathered five sons. Gorbonian was the firstborn, then Argal, then Elidur, then Jugenes, and finally Peredur. Gorbonian, who was the first, was a loyal and upright king. Never has any king ruled such a land or people in such a kindly way. He never knowingly told a lie, nor did he do any harm to any man. His behaviour was never excessive, and he tried to do right by everyone. He was loyal and he continued to act in this way until the end of his life. His tomb was in London; it had been prepared with great care. Argal, who was the next to be born, was then raised to the rank of king, but, unfortunately, things were different in his case, and he was not like Gorbonian. He diminished the status of noblemen and raised that of those who were not noble. If anyone had any wealth, he took it away from them, and when he should have told the truth he lied. He accumulated a remarkable amount of treasure and he was avaricious and covetous. He never liked anyone who was loyal, and he constantly took delight in evil. Argan lived such a life constantly, and his wickedness lasted for such a long time that the nobles joined forces and threw him out of the land.

(3487–552) Then they brought Elidur forward, the third brother, and crowned him. He was an extremely friendly man, full of tenderness and compassion. After he had been deposed, Argal travelled throughout many lands, seeking assistance, begging for help in order to have his domain restored to him. He never managed to achieve so much, seek so much, and beg so much that he found or encountered anyone who would promise to help him to restore his loss. Because of outright necessity and poverty, after five years he came to his brother within the wood of Calatere. Argal met with Elidur, and he sought mercy and found mercy. Seeing his impoverished brother, the king was filled with pity and he showed him mercy. He embraced him, hugged him, and kissed him many times. He took him to Aclud, a nearby city, and lodged him secretly in his private chamber. O God! Whoever saw such compassion, such love, such fraternity! The king pretended to be ill and to be afraid of dying from the illness. He summoned all his barons to come and visit him. He had no hope of living, so they should all come and see him. When they had all assembled on the day he had arranged and were to speak to him, he asked them secretly to help him by requesting them to come quietly and peacefully, without crying out or making any noise. Each one would enter the chamber alone, and each one would speak to him alone, for he had a bad headache, and a lot of noise was harmful to him. They did his bidding and would not have entered in any other way. Just as each of them entered and thought he was speaking to the king, the king himself grabbed him and had his men-at-arms, who were holding naked swords, hold on to him and constrain him tightly, so that he did homage to his brother. Not one of them was of such lineage that he was spared, otherwise he would be killed there immediately.

(3553–90) When he had had them all attend and become Argal's vassals, and when they had all sworn an oath of fealty to him, he took him to York, removed the crown from his own head and crowned his brother Argal with it. He re-established him in his kingdom and gave it back to him in its entirety. For the sake of honour and pity, for advantage and friendship, which he showed to his brother when he was in need of it, his name was forever associated with mercy. Argal behaved in a measured fashion and abandoned his evil ways. There had never before been such a sensible king, or one who was so peaceful or so honourable. He reigned for ten years in a position of strength, then he fell into a state of sickness. Death was unavoidable, it could not be otherwise, for this pleased the Celestial King. Then Elidur was made king once more, just as he had been before. He was restored to his authority. If earlier he had been a very good king, later he was considered even better. But his two younger brothers joined forces and launched a war on him together. One day they did battle, and as he had very few troops they defeated him. I do not know by what ruse they captured him and put him in a secure place. Elidur spent many a day in a great tower in London. His brothers divided the kingdom between them. From the Humber southwards, and right down towards the west, Jugenes ruled the land freely.

(3591–610) Peredur had the other part of the kingdom. Then he had the whole of the lordship, for afterwards Jugenes only lived for seven years and then died. Peredur took possession of the domain, but he did not enjoy it for long, for sudden death brought about his demise. He lived wickedly and died wickedly. Then Elidur was made king for the third time, and that was right. He was brought out of the Tower of London and made king for the third time. He restored everything that his brother had damaged. Once more his status, which his brothers had damaged, was raised. He was a model of justice, compassion, and freedom for all those who succeeded him and who ruled the land after him. He was never blamed for anything, and he lived well and died well.

(3611–38) After him, a nephew of his ruled the domain, son of his elder brother, the noble king Gorbonian. The next king was Margan, son of Argal. This Margan was a man of very good character, and he strove to act well. He made his people love him and wanted to honour everyone. His brother, whose name was Eumannus, ruled the region after him. He was a very different heir, and he never managed to make a friend. This is something he never succeeded in doing, as the people hated him so much. He himself hated all the people and did to them whatever harm he could. Even his servants hated him. They served him very reluctantly, as they had found him to be so cruel. But they never dared to do otherwise. He maintained his tyranny, cruelty, and unreasonable behaviour for six years.

(3639–66) Then together all the inhabitants of the country drove him away from the kingdom. He was chased away, and he fled, never to return. Then Iwallo, son of Jugenes, was elected king. Iwallo was capable of very hard work. He could travel a great deal and stay awake a long time. For prowess and good character he was just like his fine ancestors. But he did not rule for long, and this filled his people with sorrow. But there is no consolation for death. Then after him Runo, the son of Peredur, was king of England, then it was Geronces, son of Elidur, then it was his son Catullus. After Catullus, it was Coillus, then Porreus and then Cherim. Cherim was a wine drinker. He turned his attention to good beverages and used up his entire youth in drinking and intoxication. He never performed any other act of prowess, and God endowed him with such good fortune that no one ever waged war against him. He had three sons with his wife and one after the other they ruled the kingdom; their names were Fulgenius, Eldadus, and Andragius. All three of them ruled England one after the other, and each on his own. But their reigns were rather brief. They came to their end in a very short time.

(3667–93) One son of Andragius, Urian, reigned after his father for a year. After Urian, Eliud ruled the kingdom very peaceably. After Eliud came Cledaucus, then Doten, then Gurgustius, then Merian, who was very handsome and knew a great deal about dogs and birds, and also about hawking by the river and hunting. He had the choice of whatever he wanted. He had no interest in any other pursuit, and this one gave him a great deal of pleasure. He was highly desired by ladies, and much sought after and loved. But he had no interest in women, except for his own wife. Bledudo reigned after him; he was his son and was very much like him. But he was more generous in the gifts he gave. He could not refuse anything, or hold on to anything, for his own use without him wanting to give his people generous gifts; he was a very noble lord. After this generous gift-giver, Cap was king and then Oenus, and after him Sillius. But he only lived for a very short time.

(3694–738) After him reigned Blegabret, who understood the nature of song. Never has anyone known more, or as much. He had a mastery over all instruments, and he knew about all forms of song. He knew about lays and about notes,* about viols and about rotes, about harps and chorons, about the lyre and the psalterion. Because he had such knowledge of song, people said in his day that he was the god of minstrels and the god of all singers. The king knew how to enjoy himself very much. Everyone served him joyfully, and he was always filled with joy. He was never cruel or angry. Archinal, his brother, ruled the kingdom after him, and he did so in peace. After him came his son Eldol, who was thought of as very foolish because he was lustful, with a great desire for women. There was never a noble woman, however high her lineage, whether she was a wife or an unmarried maiden, providing he found her beautiful, with whom he did not want to have relations. He caused himself to be hated by many people. Redion came after Eldol, and then Rederch ruled the kingdom. After him, Famu Penissel was king, then Pir, who had a handsome head of hair. Nature had endowed him exceedingly well with a fine head and fine hair. Caporus reigned after Pir, and then his son Eliguellus. He conducted himself very wisely and with great restraint. Heli, his son, who then reigned, lived for a full forty years as king. This Heli fathered three sons: the first was called Lud, then Cassibellan was born, and after him Nennius.

(3740–90) After Heli, Lud, who was very brave and skilled in warfare, ruled the land. He was an outstanding knight and a remarkable host. Willingly, he gave a great deal away, and he honoured knights greatly. He built cities and castles, fortifying old ones and erecting new ones, and he completely surrounded London, the city he liked best, with walls. From the old wall he built the great enclosure, which still survives. There Lud created for the citizens and the barons large houses so that it could be said that in that vicinity there was no city that was so well prepared, nor one so splendidly equipped with dwellings. Until his time and a long time before, London was called Trinovant, but because of Lud, who greatly honoured it and who stayed there and spent much time there, it was called Kaerlu. Then foreigners came who did not know the language, and they used Londoin instead of Lud. Then came the Angles* and the Saxons, who altered the name again, naming Londoin Londene; they used Lundene for a long time. Then the Normans came and the French, who were not able to speak English, and who could not pronounce Londene, but they did their best to do so. They named Lundene Londres, and thus they preserved it in their own language. Through alterations and changes brought about by the languages of these foreigners, who frequently conquered the land, the city was often lost and often captured. The names of the towns were often changed by them, either made longer or cut down. As I understand and hear it said, one could find very few towns that had maintained entirely the names they had in the first place. When Lud, the good king, came to his end, he was buried in London, next to a gate whose name derives from Porlud in the British language. The English changed the word and they called it Ludgate.

(3791–826) Lud left behind two children, but at that time they were scarcely grown. The eldest of them was Androgeus, and next was Tenuancius. Cassibellan was their uncle, a nobleman who was their father's brother. He ruled the domain on behalf of his nephews and he had himself called king over everyone. He successfully protected the land and was a good knight and good at bestowing gifts.

He was good at defending land, and also a good knight and a generous giver of gifts. He was very skilled at upholding land, and he knew how to have himself served. When the nephews had enough wisdom, and had reached such an age that they could rule over land, he made them take possession of two counties. To Androgeus, the older one, for whom he had the greatest love, he gave London and also Kent, so that he could hold them from him freely. He made the inhabitants of Cornwall submit to Tenuancius, who was the younger one. Each one had his own county and they were both called counts. But they recognized their uncle as having lordship over them and all the rest of the kingdom in his possession. As long as they were in agreement, they had power and strength. But later there arose a dispute—as Master Wace, who has composed this narrative in French, bears witness to and records—that caused harm to the whole race. As a result, the Romans obtained a tribute from them that they had never been able to achieve before.

CAESAR ARRIVES IN BRITAIN, DEMANDING TRIBUTE; AT FIRST VICTORIOUS, THE BRITONS FINALLY CAPITULATE AND PAY THE TRIBUTE; THE ROMANS DEPART

(3827–68) SIXTY years before Jesus Christ was born of the Virgin Mary, Julius Caesar started out. He came from Rome to France in order to conquer the regions to the west that were a long distance away. He was brave, strong, and worthy, and he was the conqueror who did so much, was capable of so much, and who conquered and ruled over the whole world. Never before or since has any man, of whom we know, conquered so much. Caesar was emperor of Rome, and he was a very wise and generous man. He was esteemed for his great chivalry, and he was well trained in letters and a man of great learning. When those from Rome had conquered* the whole area round them, Caesar took leave of them in order to go and conquer far-off peoples. He put together the finest group of young warriors and passed through Lombardy and Montgieu. First, he conquered Burgundy, then France, then Auvergne, then Gascony, Poitou, Normandy, and Brittany. Then he turned his men towards Germany, and in a number of places he built castles, cities, and new strongholds. He took advantage of this period of need, entering Flanders and

Boulogne. From there he looked far across the sea, saw an island, and asked what land it was that he could see, whether any people lived there and what kind they were. The peasants told him that what he could see there was a large island that Brutus was the very first to inhabit. He had brought people to it from Troy. From his own name he had called it Britain, and he made himself king and chieftain over it. His descendants ruled the kingdom after him.

(3869–92) Caesar's reply was:

'I know', he said, 'who Brutus was. He and I were of the same lineage. Our kinsfolk originated in Rome, but since the great destruction the barons left and captured many a region. From this island of Britain came Belin and Brenne, who thrived until they took the city of Rome and destroyed our Senate. We certainly must make them aware that Rome's power is now very different. Fortune's wheel has turned, and Rome is once more reinvigorated. Henceforth, it is right that they should submit to us and pay a tribute to Rome. They should restore to us the tribute they used to render a long time ago. I shall summon them by letter and find out what response they wish to make. I would never have any desire to cross the sea if they were willing to accept in peace that they would render tribute to Rome and hold their lands from us.'

(3893–960) Then he had his letters composed and taken across the sea to Cassibellan, demanding that he should hold his lands from him and render him a tribute. Cassibellan, who took offence at this, sent a letter in reply. He refused to include greetings in it, rather did he inform him angrily:

'Caesar, we on our side are amazed, and in our amazement we have disdain for the Romans and for their presumption, which lasts so long and stretches and extends so far. Their greed cannot tolerate that anyone apart from themselves should be free. They want to bring all the gold and all the silver in the world under their sway, as well as the kings, counts, and other people; nothing can bring them satisfaction. They want to get their hands on the whole of the wealth. What do they intend to do with it all? The Romans do not intend to neglect us, we who live on the edge of the world, on an island that we rule. Rather do they demand a tribute from us. Lord Caesar, you are testing us, and you are demanding a tribute from us and want to turn us into tributaries. But you will have very little success in this, as we have always lived freely and have always ruled freely. We must live freely, as the Romans did, and rightly so, for we are of one root, coming from one race and from one origin. Caesar, if you give this some thought, and pay attention to what is reasonable, you are acting in a remarkably shameful way when you seek a tribute from us and want to place us in servitude, we who are of your lineage. We should be equal to the Romans, as we all descend from one people. How dare you, you being such a wise man and such a noble lord as you are, say that we ought to become serfs, we who have not learned to serve, nor, if it pleases God, shall we, as you know, learn how to do so. Do you think we could do this? We have always been so free that never has anyone from our kin known, or will know, how one should live in servitude. We do not know, unless someone tells us, how a serf lives in servitude. We are free and we wish to remain free. Even if the celestial gods themselves wanted to debase us, we would make the greatest effort to ensure that no one would cause us to lose what we have held for such a long time. Now you can know, we do not conceal it, that as long as we are alive, and can protect ourselves, we shall defend our freedom. We want to live freely and with honour, as did our ancestors.'

(3961–4020) When Caesar had seen the letter, he clearly understood that he would have to go across the sea, or otherwise he would have nothing. Then he had large ships built and great barges, eighty of them so large that never had any so large existed. They were to convey a large number of men and heavy loads, and they were in addition to the other small ships that had come from many other places. When Caesar had made everything ready, and the weather was good and the breeze right, he had the cry go up: 'The ships! The ships!' The men went on board and raised the sails. They had a favourable wind and sailed quickly. They reached the harbour and docked. Scarcely had they made land, where the sea meets the Thames, when, lo, news of their arrival spread throughout the country. Cassibellan, who was well aware that these troops would be coming, gathered together his barons, whom he had summoned from all sides. He had many barons and vassals, and Belin, his seneschal, was there. He was his close counsellor and his principal justiciar under him. Next to him he had his two nephews, whom he trusted above all: on one side was Androgeus and on the other Tenuancius. Androgeus led the men from London and Tenuancius those from Cornwall. Nennius of Canterbury, the king's younger brother—no one could choose a better man—was positioned next to his two nephews.

In addition to the counts, as many as three kings came to the host, and each one had with him a large number of troops. Eridious led the Scots, Britael the North Welsh, and Guertaet those from South Welsh. Each man came willingly in order to defend his freedom. They all gave their advice to the king, advising him that the best thing would be to go and attack the Romans, not to let them get off the shore and make themselves secure on land, or to build dwellings or strongholds. As a result of this advice, they all armed themselves. When they were ready, and each one had prepared his equipment, they went to strike the Romans in close array and without disorder. Caesar, who had seen them coming, cried out to his men:

'Arm yourselves. You will soon see them coming to attack us!'

(4021–87) The battle, which that day was very frightening, was soon joined. Then you would have seen horses pricked well, lances pierced, saddles emptied, men felled, and wounds bleeding. Knights joined in battle and archers shot their arrows. They made a great effort and tried their very best. Arrows flew like rain. What pleased some of the men upset others. You would have heard many heads clashing and seen the wounded dying. The grass was covered in blood, and this was no surprise, for the living were on top of the dead and they fought on the dead bodies. Caesar had in his company the finest of his knights, and they strove mightily and dealt many blows. They fought hard and suffered much. No one who was on the receiving end of his blows had any protection from death. Androgeus with his troops from Kent, and Nennius, with all his men, withdrew to one side and formed themselves into a squadron. Then they met Caesar and engaged in battle with his men. Nennius spotted this and came towards him and struck him. He was delighted to draw near to such a nobleman as the emperor of Rome. Caesar stretched out his shield and parried Nennius' blow. Caesar was skilful, and he drew forth his sword with which he had dealt many a blow, striking Nennius on the helmet and knocking off a large section of it. He wounded him on one side of his head, and he would soon have sliced it in two, but Nennius, fearing the blow, lowered his head, raised his shield, and buried his sword so deeply in the shield that, however hard he tried, Caeser could not manage to pull it out. Caesar yanked his sword, and Nennius did the same with his shield, with each one holding on firmly to what belonged to him. Nennius tried to pull away, but Caesar stopped him from doing so. I believe that Caesar would have pulled it out and kept both items together, but Nennius' forces grew more numerous and Androgeus ran towards him with a large company of Kentish troops. At once they struck from all sides, and Caesar, who was not able to defend himself, did not dare to wait for them. He abandoned his sword in the shield, and Nennius, with assistance, turned his shield around, grabbed hold of his sword, and then killed many Romans with it. No one who was on the receiving end of his blows had any protection against death. With the emperor's sword, such a strong man, such a noble lord, Nennius performed such valiant deeds.

(4088–110) Before him appeared Labienus, who was the leader of a company and a man who possessed great power in Rome. Nennius gave him such a blow that he severed the head from his body. I do not know how to count all the dead bodies or name the finest warriors. But again and again many of them fell down and they died in abundance. Many more would have died if nightfall had not dispersed them. Night came, daylight gave out, and they parted. The Romans, who were very fearful, went back to their camp. They were weary and frightened, and they had sustained many losses. They decided that they would depart from and abandon this land, for they were not acquainted with the land, nor did they have any stronghold in it. That night they went on board their ships and set off in the direction of Flanders.

(4111–36) Next morning, when the Britons became aware that the Romans had gone away, they rejoiced and were very happy. But afterwards they were vexed, for Nennius, the brave, could not find a cure for the wound he had suffered when he held on to the sword, and on the fifteenth day he died. At the north gate of London, he was buried royally, splendidly, and in courtly fashion, because he was the brother of the king, who loved him as much as he did himself. Next to the body in the grave was placed the emperor's sword, which he had held on to. It was put there as a mark of honour. The sword was very highly praised, and it was marked with letters of gold. Beside the hilt it had written at the top that its name was Crocea Mors. It had this name because nobody who was ever struck by it could ever find a cure that could save him from death.

(4137–74) This tale was soon told to the French. It could not be concealed from them that the Romans had been defeated. They regarded them with contempt and considered themselves to be cowardly for having made peace with them. Their boldness was restored to them, and they were greatly encouraged when they heard that the Romans had fled. If anyone is fleeing, they do not lack pursuers. When someone issues threats, they are in fact experiencing fear, and those who pursue do not have much to hold them back. They threatened the Romans greatly and scorned them, saying that they would be cowards if they ever ruled any of their land. They would gladly kill them all if they could catch up with them. They hated having them as lords and feared their wickedness. This caused them to become bolder, and they frequently gave them the news that the Britons would cross the sea and do battle with the Romans. But the arrogance of the French came to an end as soon as Caesar spoke to them. Caesar knew how to overcome villains, to restrain the arrogant, and to appease the covetous and make them change their minds. He also knew how to show pity when force was not necessary. He saw that the French were scornful of him and that they had the strength to fight with him vigorously. He saw that his men were wounded and that all of them were weary from fighting.

(4175–224) He preferred to give his wealth away than to enter into battle with a doubtful outcome. To the dukes and to the most powerful barons he made great gifts of gold and silver. He distributed wealth to them so that each man had as much as he wanted, and he promised them a lot more if he conquered the Britons. To the poor he gave their freedom, delivering them from service. To all those who had been exiled and driven away from their heritage he promised to provide them with an inheritance and to restore their losses. As soon as they had seen the wealth, and some of them had received it, each man changed his opinion. Wealth, you have great power! You have soon inspired a war, and soon made one appear needless. Those who hated Caesar earlier and wanted to kill him changed their minds because of the gold. Each man paid homage to him and agreed to whatever he asked of them, even to be taken to Britain. When Caesar had made peace with them and assuaged them all, he had a skilled engineer build a tower on the sea. It was in Boulogne and called Ordre. I do not know another one of its kind. It was curiously shaped, for at its lowest part it was broad, then it got narrower and narrower as it rose up. A single stone covered the highest room. It had many storeys and many galleries, and each one had many windows. There he had his treasures watched over and his valuable possessions gathered together. When he was afraid of treachery, he himself slept inside it.

He spent two years in France, readying his tower Ordre, and throughout the cities and throughout the region he established bailiffs who were to collect tributes and then send them to Ordre.

(4225–63) In these two years he made his preparations and assembled six hundred great ships, saying that he would try again to see if he could defeat the British. He could have no regard for what he had done if in this way he were to leave them in peace. When he had procured his fleet and prepared his entire journey, he loaded his six hundred ships with everything he needed. They rowed and sailed until they entered the Thames. They had thought and decided—but their plans did not work out—that they would go up the river and dock in London. Then they would disembark for the first time and do battle with the Britons. The Britons for their part made preparations to defend themselves. I do not know how they had heard about what was happening. Throughout the Thames they placed stakes covered with iron, well fixed and well set, so that no ship could enter there without perishing ignominiously. When the ships had reached the Thames and started on their route upstream, they had scarcely begun to sail in that direction when they struck the great stakes. Then you would have seen ships breaking up as they sank, taking in water and foundering, one ship banging against another, masts falling and sails tumbling, stitching breaking and ships' sides cracking, one ship smashing into another. They could not reach port or shore, and they had difficulty sailing and rowing.

(4264–90) Caesar saw the damage that had been done, and he also saw the peril and the stakes. He feared that things would be the same everywhere, so he had the ships turn round and everyone get on to land and disembark. Then he set up camp and had his tents readied. Lo, Cassibellan came spurring up, and he did not intend to spare them, nor did his nephews, his kinsmen, and all his barons together. As soon as the king sounded his battle-cry, there was no coward who showed a lack of courage. They went to strike them in their camp. Then you would have heard weapons crunching. The Romans waited for them in their tents and defended themselves remarkably well, with their boldness acting as a wall of defence. They responded with a very tough combat. They held out well at first and withstood the enemy boldly, making them all withdraw some distance away and killing many of them. Later the Britons held out firmly and their men kept on coming. They estimated the number of strong and warlike knights at three times more than Caesar had brought with him. They spurred their horses and attacked them, causing a large number of them to retreat. Then they killed many of the Romans.

(4291–310) Caesar, the brave and the bold, who was never dismayed, saw that the Britons had such forces and that his own men could not withstand them, for they fought furiously and feared no weapon's blow. He placed all his men before him, and he himself remained behind in battle formation. He withstood the Britons so well that his men suffered no harm. He had the ships drawn up close to land and made all his men go on board. He was the last to embark. The weather was good, and the breeze and the wind were good. He reached Ordre, his tower. He stayed there for a long time in order to take care of his wounded men and to give the others a rest. Whilst he was spending time there, he summoned all the barons in the country.

(4311–48) Having been freed from the Romans, Cassibellan was filled with joy. He had defended his kingdom twice and been victorious over Caesar twice. As a result of the joy and the glory he had experienced from this double victory, he promised all the gods that he would hold a very solemn festival and render vows and sacrifices to them. He fixed a day for this service, summoning and sending for his noblemen and his vassals. He told them they should come to this festival in London and partake in it with him. Let none of them be held back by matters of business. They all came joyously, and with their wives, their children, and their other kinsfolk they made their preparations in celebratory mood. The festival was celebrated handsomely, and the assembly was a very fine one. Each person, as was appropriate for him, made his sacrifice in his own fashion. Forty thousand fully grown cows and thirty thousand wild beasts were tracked down in many different ways, and the date for the sacrifice was established. Next there were a hundred thousand ewes and a remarkable number of fowl. When they had sacrificed and eaten in abundance, as the occasion required in accordance with the custom of the time, the day was given over to amusements. The knights jousted and the youths fenced, hurled stones, wrestled, and jumped.

(4349–82) When the games were over and they had all split up, they all fenced together. Hirelgas, who was the king's nephew, a youth of great nobility, and Evelin, Androgeus' nephew, who found favour with everyone in the region, came together to fence. Their fencing lasted until their pride and enthusiasm transformed their playfulness into anger and they began to utter foolish words. The words became so heated that they ended up with naked swords. Straightaway, through misfortune, Hirelgas was killed, and then the whole court was in an uproar. When the king heard what had happened, he was grief-stricken for his nephew, and he was wicked and angry. He had brought him up and had a great affection for him. He would very much like to have avenged him. He asked for Androgeus and demanded that, as the terms of his fief dictated, he should bring him or send him his nephew Evelin at once, before he left to face, rightly, the judgement of his court. Androgeus thought about this. If he handed him over to him, he would kill him. The king knew him to be a rogue, and he feared the judgement of his court. So he said he would not bring him there, for he was a nobleman with his own court. Anyone wishing to make a challenge to Evelin should come to his court, where he would do right by him.

(4383–420) The king, whose heart was swollen with anger, challenged Androgeus. Everything he owned, he said, he would take from him, and if he could he would kill him. They parted on bad terms and hated each other greatly. The king laid waste, burnt, destroyed, and pillaged his lands. Androgeus saw what great losses he had sustained, and he was aware that the king was acting in earnest. He sent his messengers to him, begging and beseeching him not to lay waste his land. He was his nephew, so they should come to an agreement. The king was wicked and angry, and did not wish to offer a truce or peace. Androgeus, knowing how cruel the king was, could not do otherwise. He abandoned his open spaces and fortified his strongholds. He could not find anyone to assist him, nor anyone who could rescue him from the king. He did not want to flee quietly, or to sacrifice what he could hold on to. He would, he said, be filled with anguish if he did not shatter the king's arrogance. Doing what is wrong in order to prevent things from getting worse is something that peasants consider to be a given. One should certainly suffer something bad to protect oneself from something worse, and to destroy one's enemy one must do oneself some harm. Androgeus made up his mind to do very serious damage to the king's land, and to his own, before he could free himself from the king. He would prefer to create problems for himself rather than fail to deflate the king's arrogance.

(4421–72) Privately and secretly, he had a letter written and sealed, and he had it sent to Caesar. The content of the letter was as follows:

'To Caesar, the brave and the strong, after having desired his death, Androgeus, who is lord and duke of London, sends him greetings. Caesar, one has often seen that people conceive great hatred for one another, but they end up loving each other and being good friends. After anger comes great love, and after great shame comes great honour. This happens to many people who are accustomed to hate each other. When you and I did battle, we tried to kill each other. I do not know why I should fail to say this: each one of us wanted to kill the other. But it happened to us in this case that neither of us was killed there. From now on, I believe, I shall provide help to you, and you will be able to do the same for me. Twice you have fought with us, and twice you have been beaten. But now you should certainly know, and I tell you in truth, that you would not have needed to leave our ports if I had not been there with my forces. You could have come in safety, and you would not have been vanquished by the king. But, through me and my assistance, Cassibellan was victorious in the battle. Through me Cassibellan was the winner, and through me he robbed you of the land. You lost our land because of me, and because of my troops you took flight. But I am sorry for the harm I have done you through acting towards you in a hostile way. I am the one who will bring you back, and who will restore the land to you. I am upset that I caused you harm and that I was there along with the king. For he has since gone much too far and become very arrogant. Never at any time did he love me, nor did he ever leave me in peace. He has deprived me of all my land, robbing and driving out the people. He wanted to throw me out and deprive me of my fief.

(4473–510) 'I swear by God and tell you in truth that I have not deserved this, unless one describes as deserving it rescuing my nephew from death and, if I had given him the chance, preventing him from condemning him to death. The occasion for our quarrel, and the reason why it had arisen and become so serious, I wish to demonstrate for your consideration, so that you will know the truth. For the honour that we received from conquering you we summoned our allies and our people and gathered in London. We made our vows to all our gods and made a sacrifice to them. When we had conducted our services, offered our vows and made our sacrifices, boys and young knights all gathered together for a variety of different games. One of my nephews, who accompanied me, and another of the king's nephews, joined in the sport. They fenced and amused themselves until my nephew had defeated the other youth. The king's nephew became angry and threatened to strike him. He drew his sword, intending to strike him, and my nephew ran forward to grab hold of it. He held on to his wrist, where he was holding his sword, and tried to retain him in order to stop him from striking blows. I do not know how, but he staggered and toppled over on to the sword. Falling on it and injuring himself, he died and never got up. He was not touched by any other weapon, and he was not wounded in any other way.

(4511–59) 'The king found out about this and he summoned me, telling me that, as the holder of a fief, I should bring my nephew to him and hand him over to justice. I was well aware of what the king would do: because of the one youth who was killed he would kill the other. I told him that I had my own court, and therefore I would do justice in this matter in my own court. Because I resisted him, and did not do his bidding, he is destroying my lands, driving me away from them and threatening to kill me. My lord Caesar, for this reason I summon you to come to me with the agreement that you will have Britain through me and that I would be rescued by you. May you not suspect that I am speaking treacherously. I would not do this to save my life, but come soon, my lord, and help me. Help me and I shall help you to hand over Britain to you. One can be defeated at first and then return later.'

Caesar heard what was asked of him and he took advice immediately. When he had spoken about it to his own people, he sent a reply through his messenger, saying that he could not believe what he had said, and that on the basis of what he had said he would not come. But if he sent him hostages he would come as requested. Androgeus was afraid of the king, who was keen to besiege London. He took his son, who was called Scena, and sent him as a hostage along with thirty very noble youths, all born of his close kin. Caesar took them all to be guarded in Ordre, his tower. As soon as he could, he went on board the ships. He crossed over the sea and docked, coming secretly and quite unexpectedly to Dover. Androgeus came to him there and the two of them spoke together, confirming their agreement and discussing their affair.

(4560–94) Cassibellan assembled his host with the intention of besieging London. Rumour, which flies everywhere, and turns something small into something greatly exaggerated, came to the king and announced to him that the Romans had returned and were camped in Dover. They would soon either kill or banish him if he did not take advice quickly. The king regarded it as a marvel that they had come back there. He was not expecting to have any more dealings with them. He summoned his host, called upon his barons, and hastened to Dover. When Caesar, who was waiting at Dover, found out that he was coming, he left the town on the advice of Androgeus. He placed his men, fully armed, in a valley, very close by. He prepared his divisions and arranged his squadrons, determining what those in front would do first, then those in the centre, and then those at the back. When Caesar had arranged everything, he told them, and forbade them, saying that whatever they might see they should not break ranks. No one is so brave that he cannot break ranks, and no one is so cowardly that he cannot show bravery. Let them stick closely together until the enemy comes right up to attack them. But anyone who approaches them and launches an attack on them, may they be received with the iron tips of lances, in their faces, their chests, and their bellies.

(4595–626) Androgeus secretly went into hiding in a wood with five thousand armed men, all eager to capture the king. When the king reached Dover, he looked down from a mountain into the valley that lay ahead. He saw the Romans with their helmets laced on them, all of them ready to do battle. He arranged his troops once more and made them ready to do battle. Then he approached the enemy and made his men draw their bows and hurl missiles. For a long time they had been crying out, drawing their bows, throwing and hurling missiles when Androgeus, who had come out of his hiding place, cried out. The king heard the noise behind him, and he saw the great clouds of dust rising. He could not force his way through the Romans, and he did not dare to wait for those behind. He began to escape laterally with the intention of getting back to a mound. It was no great surprise that they all hated him and that they all wanted his death. He regarded himself as dead and betrayed, as did all the Britons. Each man was concerned with protecting himself by departing swiftly and taking flight. It is better to flee than to wait foolishly, so they concentrated their minds on taking flight swiftly. I do not know of any other form of protection for people who have no way of defending themselves.

(4627–64) Beside them, there was a mountain that was somewhat round at the top. It was completely covered by bushes, rocks, and hazel thickets. They fled and spurred on until they had climbed up the hill. But as they climbed up and scaled the maintain, you would have seen many men knocked down. But once they had climbed up and gathered together in the bushes, they were as secure as if they had been surrounded by a wall. Then the Romans had no strength left, so well had they defended themselves. Caesar surrounded them, periodically attacking them, and when he saw that their opponents were so high up that they could not be taken by assault he laid siege to them all round the hill. They would not be going anywhere unless it was through his men. At the exit points and the footpaths he placed extensive troops of knights, and he positioned great tree trunks across them to prevent them from crossing. He often reproved them, not forgetting that they had insulted him a great deal and twice driven him away from the land. The Britons were proven warriors, bold, strong, and tough, who had twice fought with and twice vanquished the man who had conquered the whole world. Also, where they were being besieged, and where they could not expect any assistance, they still withstood the enemy and defended themselves, not wanting to let themselves be defeated by those who were accustomed to conquering and banishing their opponents.

(4665–90) But Fortune has a different complexion, and her wheel had turned. Those who had been down below now came up to the top. The Britons, who were besieged, were surrounded by their enemies and they lacked food and drink and any opportunity to make purchases elsewhere. They did not fear weapons, attacks, or any form of trickery. But of what concern was this when hunger and thirst grasped them all so tightly that, without weapons being used against them, they would be overcome? You will never see a fortress, however many men of great prowess it may contain, that is so strong and difficult to capture that famine will not force it to surrender. As soon as a lack of supplies develops, there is no need for any other opponent to attack a fortress. Cassibellan was filled with anguish. He did not know how he would be rescued from there. He saw all round him the Romans, who were expecting to get their hands on him shortly. He did not have the wherewithal to fight. For great hunger was defeating his men, and he greatly feared Caesar's power. Their great hunger dismayed him.

(4691–716) Either he would make peace with the emperor, or else he would die of hunger on the hill. Before seeking and offering peace, he suffered for two days and into the third. Then the king took a messenger; I do not know whether it was a man-at-arms or a knight.

He entrusted him with his message and sent him to his nephew Androgeus, who was in the siege and whose anger greatly upset him. He asked him not to shame him, and if he could save him let him do so. He had not deserved this of him, and he had not done him sufficient harm for him to have a mortal hatred for him, even if he had done battle with him. One should not mortally hate one's kinsman just because some slight wrong has been inflicted. They could still be reconciled and redress the wrong they had done. But as soon as one loses one's kinsman, there can no longer be any rectification. There has been war between many people, with goods captured and land taken, without them having any desire to kill each other, whatever they had lost.

(4717–66) Now may Androgeus behave in a courtly fashion and provide assistance for him. He does not know anyone in whom he trusts so much. He should take his message to Caesar and, if he can, get an agreement with him that he would not disinherit him, or dishonour him with regard to his person. The nephew could gain no honour from anything that shamed his uncle. Androgeus replied to him:

'What has befallen my lord the king? He has soon changed his mind. Not much time has passed since he wanted to banish me and to chase me away from the whole of this country. He used to threaten to kill me, but his anger was soon assuaged. When someone displays very great ferocity, that is regarded as cruelty. A lord is not praised who in a time of peace acts in a harsh and violent manner. When it comes to war and to combat, he is like a frightened hare. When the king defeated a lord, such as a powerful emperor, he should not have thought, or said, that he was solely responsible for the victory, because he never fought him alone, and he was not the only one involved in defeating him. It was through myself and through his other vassals—and we were wounded many times as a result—that Cassibellan won the victory from which he later achieved such glory. The barons and the knights are partners in this glory. As each man makes every effort to win better victories in battle, to improve his valour, and to strike better, thus he should have his fair share of chivalry's fame. One should definitely let the king know that, if he does not have assistance from others, he cannot win a victory through his own efforts. Anyone who thought that was a fool. But I have avenged myself on him well, since he has humbled himself so deeply as to ask me and beg me to have mercy and pity on him. I shall not respond to evil with evil, as if it were to my mortal enemy. He is my uncle, and I shall not fail him. I have done him harm, but now I shall do right by him.'

(4767–806) Speaking in this way, Androgeus quickly went to look for Caesar. He went down on his knees, beseeching him very tenderly:

'Caesar, you have defeated and vanquished Cassibellan and his country. He will come, my lord, and ask you for mercy, and he will hold his fief from the Romans. Take his tribute, take his homage, and let him have Britain by way of heritage. Let him have mercy, let him be. What more of him could you ask other than that he should become your vassal and hold his lands from the Romans? Pity given by a lord is of great value, better than any other form of goodness.'

Caesar moved on. He turned a deaf ear to what he said and ignored him. Androgeus came up to him again; it seemed that he was being scorned. He said to him:

'Stay there, Caesar. Do not go any further! I have kept your agreement. I have placed Britain in your power. You can have the lordship over it. I did not promise you anything else, and I did not make any other promise to you except that I would make every effort to hand over Britain to you. You can have it. What more do you want? May God above forbid that my uncle should be in prison, or in close confinement in any way. It is not easy for him to be killed, as long as I am alive and well. He is my uncle and he raised me. When he seeks help from me, I am his vassal and cannot fail him. If you are not willing to accept that I shall do what I say, I shall withdraw from you and challenge you.'

(4807–34) As a result of this, Caesar was then appeased, and he granted what Cassibellan sought. They asked for hostages, and they were provided on both sides. They fixed the amount of the tribute and the Britons agreed to it: three thousand pounds a year. Then Cassibellan came forward, as did Caesar, and they met each other, embracing and becoming reconciled. I have not been able to find it in writing, and I have never heard anyone mention it, that England paid a tribute until it was conquered by Caesar. When the discussion was over, and the agreement was granted, each man returned to his region, and the assembly broke up. People say, and it may well be true, that Caesar built Exeter, which is so called because it was constructed on the river Exe. Caesar remained there the whole winter, but when summer arrived he left. Through friendship and affection he brought

Androgeus along with him, and from England he took hostages, who came from all the most noble families.

(4835–77) Cassibellan lived for seven years after Caesar departed. The payment of the tribute survived for seven years. I do not know whether or not he had a wife or children. His body was buried in York, where he had died. Tenuancius of Cornwall ruled the kingdom after him. He was his nephew and he took possession of it; he was the brother of Androgeus. After his death the domain passed to his oldest son Kimbelin, who was a brave and courtly man. The emperor Augustus Caesar had made him a knight in Rome. In his time the Saviour was born, Jesus the son of God, who came from heaven. He was God, but he became a man because of us, and for our redemption he suffered death upon the Cross. In Britain there was a soothsayer called Teleusin. He was regarded as a good prophet and was trusted by everyone. On the occasion of a festival they were celebrating, for which the Britons had all gathered together, the king begged and requested him to tell him something about the time that lay ahead. He replied to him, saying:

'Man, do not be sorrowful. We have waited night and day. Jesus Christ, the one who has been awaited and is to save us, has come down to earth from heaven.' The prophecy that was made was noted by the Britons and not forgotten for a long time. He had told the truth and not lied. At that time Jesus Christ was born. When they heard talk of Christ, for this reason the Britons soon became believers.

(4878–906) Kimbelin was greatly honoured, and he was a very close adviser to the Romans. He could have retained their tribute, and he would never have been asked for it, yet he handed it over in full, keeping no part of it back. He had two sons: Wider was the elder and Arviragus the younger. He was king for ten years, then he died. His son Wider was his heir. He was a remarkable knight, but he was very cruel and arrogant. He was not interested in making peace with the Romans, or in doing right by them. He dispossessed them of Britain and took the tribute off them. He was not willing to pay heed to them in any respect, and he refused to render the tribute to them. This made Claudius very angry. He was the emperor and he swore on oath that he would get the tribute back and disinherit Wider. By common accord of the entire Senate he rode and travelled until, with the large host that he had assembled, he crossed the sea to England. He reached the harbour and disembarked at Portchester, but then there followed a day he would have preferred to avoid. Portchester was the name of the place at that time, but later it was burnt to the ground and laid waste.

(4907–42) The emperor besieged Portchester, but he was to suffer distress before it was taken. He had stone prepared and mortar brought there. Then he had a wall built in front of the gates so that no one from outside could enter and no one who was inside could escape. In this way he thought he could starve them out; otherwise, he could not do them any harm. But Wider, who arrived with more than a thousand knights, came to their rescue along with Arviragus. Claudius was not able to withstand them. With most of his troops he made his way to the ships; very few remained on the battlefield. Nevertheless, they all repeatedly did their very best. They repeatedly engaged in fighting. With him Claudius had Hamon, who was his counsellor and his baron. He had complete faith in him, for he was a man of great valour. He saw Wider fighting, striking Romans and knocking them down. He arranged his troops wisely and led them in orderly fashion, clearly seeing that as long as he was alive Britain would never be captured. He went over in his mind in how many ways he could kill him. He found one of the Britons dead and secretly removed his armour. He armed himself with the Briton's armour and intermingled with the Britons. He stayed together with the Britons, spurred on his horse with the Britons, moved round with the Britons, and engaged in conversation with the Britons.

(4943–78) The armour deceived everyone. Hamon spoke their language, for amongst the hostages in Rome he had learnt many languages. Hamon was able speak the British language well and he knew the names of many of the Britons. He moved round so much, up and down, that he came up against King Wider and was side by side with him. When the king turned round, Hamon withdrew his sword and killed him. Hiding first behind one person and then behind another, he got back to his men. Arviragus, who noticed that the king was lying dead on the ground, was the first to find him. But he stopped there very briefly as this was not a spot at which to dwell, nor one for crying or lamenting. Without delay he took the king's armour and emblem. Secretly, he armed himself with them and got back on his horse. Then you would have seen knights spurring their horses, often wheeling round and often coming to blows. They sounded the king's battle-cry and encouraged the Britons. No one could have realized that this man was not King Wider. The Romans fled in disarray, unable to support each other. He made them divide themselves into two parts, but they were unable to stay together. One section of them turned towards the ships, and the quickest to get on board did so.

(4979–5016) Claudius went along with these men, and he boarded the ships with them. Those in the other section, who were unable to make their way back to the fleet, went into the woods. Hamon fled together with them and Arviragus pursued them. He was told, and he believed it, that it was Claudius who was on the move there. They galloped through woods and over plains until they reached a port where there were ships. Hamon dismounted. He wanted to go on board one of the ships belonging to merchants, who had come there for the market. Arviragus chased him and separated the head from his body. Because Hamon died there, was killed there, and lay there, this place was later, and throughout the region, called Southampton, that is to say, it seems to me, that it was the city where Hamon was killed. In this way surnames often derive from a tiny source. From an insignificant happening comes a surname that lasts for a long time. Arviragus had killed Hamon, leaving his body lying in the harbour. Whilst this was happening, Claudius came back to land. He assembled all his ships and they returned to Portchester. He knocked down and smashed the walls, banished all the men, and burnt and destroyed the city. Never again did it have the merit, the prestige, and the worth that it had that day.

(5017–44) When Claudius had destroyed Portchester, he came to Winchester with as many men as he could muster. He besieged Arviragus, who was inside the city with the majority of his kinsmen. He had devices built and he raised them up high, in order to break down and shatter the walls. This caused Arviragus great sorrow, and it seemed to him to be very humiliating to be so closely hemmed in. He emerged from the city and organized his knights into squadrons, placing his archers on two sides. The infantry stayed together at the back, all armed according to their fashion. They were on the point of coming together in battle, and of hurling and throwing missiles, when the old and the wise men moved to one side. They were afraid of losing their troops, so they sought out the emperor in order to ask him what he would do, and whether he would like peace or conflict. He replied in a friendly fashion that he had no desire for combat, rather he wanted peace and friendship, provided that Rome was granted deference in this matter. He had no interest in any other outcome except that Rome should have what was its due.

(5045–98) He would honour Arviragus. He had a daughter, whom he would give to him if he were willing to become his vassal and to hold his fief from Rome. Arviragus accepted this, and it was agreed between them. They set up camp in Winchester, became allies and became better acquainted with each other. From there they sent to Rome men who were ready to bring back Genois, whom Claudius was to grant in marriage. In the meantime, he conquered Orkney through the assistance of Arviragus, and also other surrounding islands whose names I do not know. The messengers set out on their journey, and in early summer they came back. They brought with them Genois, who possessed a noble body and a beautiful face. To give the maiden in marriage, and to secure their agreement, the barons of the land, from both Wales and England, were there in a valley on the Severn that was very rich and fertile. So that this assembly would be remembered, they honoured the place to such an extent that they constructed a city there and called it Gloucester. The town had this name because Claudius built it. Others mention a different source that seems very reasonable. A son was fathered there by Claudius, and he was called Glois, who was lord of Gloucester and duke of Wales, I have heard it said. Because Glois was born there, and was called the lord of this place, it was called Gloucester after him. I find this source in writing; Gloucester is Glois's city. I do not know of any more correct explanation. When Genois was married, she was crowned at the wedding ceremony. It was after the ceremony was over that Claudius went back to Rome. At that time, as I find in writing, St Peter was preaching. He had been in Antioch and established Christianity there. He had recently arrived in Rome, and there he was performing wonders.

(5099–152) When Claudius had departed, Arviragus ruled Britain. But he thought remarkably highly of himself and was remarkably arrogant. He refused to pay tribute to the Romans and did not deign to hold anything from them. The Romans unwillingly lost whatever they used to have by right. They sent Vespasian there with I do not know how many knights. He set sail, making for Dover, but the king, who was aware of his arrival, defended the land against him. He spread his sails, since he could not dock at Dover. He sailed along the coast, keeping close to land. He docked at Totnes and did not find anyone to defend it against him. Intending to enter it unawares, he went spurring to Exeter. But the men there were equipped, and he besieged it for seven days without being able to penetrate it. As soon as ever he could, Arviragus, who soon found out about this siege, came to the city's assistance with his knights and his host. He could not have done so more quickly. From the early morning, when the sun was rising, to the evening when night was falling, they did battle without there being any victors on either side. They separated at nightfall, but many men were weary and wounded. When they had rearmed themselves the next day, and were about to do battle again, they were reconciled by the queen, Genois, who was suffering a great deal from this. She was of very high lineage, for she was born of Roman nobility. In order to honour her kin, she gave them so much advice on both sides that she caused the barons to make peace with each other, adopt peace, and grant peace to each other. Vespasian remained in Britain until the summer. Then he went back to Rome, filled with joy and delight. For the rest of his life Arviragus maintained the agreement with the Romans and he never let them down in any way, rather did he serve and honour them through his friendship with the queen, who was born of their people.

(5153–98) Marius, his son with his wife, then had the kingdom to rule over. He possessed great wisdom and remarkable eloquence. When his father was alive, he was brought up in Rome with his mother's kinsfolk. He made sure he was splendidly attended to and that he knew how to behave well. At the time, when Marius reigned, Rodric landed in Scotland. He was king of the Picts and he came from Scythia. He was full of malice and had a predilection for robbing people. He had come to pillage Scotland, and he had already done so for so much of the land when Marius, who had no truck with bad neighbours, discovered him, defeated him, and brought about his demise. In the spot where he had vanquished the Picts and had killed and decapitated Rodric, he had a huge stone raised. One can find it there still; its aim was to demonstrate his prowess. In order to ensure that the event would be remembered, he had an inscription placed on the stone, which, as far as I know, is still there and still bearing witness to what happened and recording the defeat in the place where Marius killed Rodric. This was the reason he put the stone there. It is still there, as I have heard said, and it is called Vestinaire. The Picts, whom the king vanquished, were retained in his land. He had handed over to them a large section of land to populate that was still wasteland and permanently left as uninhabited. The Picts took up lodging there and they ploughed and tilled. They sought wives from Britain, but the Britons refused them, so he crossed over to Ireland and brought wives over from there. They settled throughout the land and soon grew and increased in number.

THE BRITONS ARE CONVERTED TO CHRISTIANITY, FOLLOWING THEIR KING LUCES

(5198–242) MARIUS lived for a long time, and after his death Coil, who was his son, ruled. He was brought up with the Romans and profited from their counsel; they found him to be loyal. He mastered Roman laws as well as their skills and many forms of arts. He conducted himself splendidly and made sure he was looked after sumptuously. After Coil, his son was king. His name was Luces and he was very courtly. Luces was a very honourable man, and it was through him that England first discovered Christianity. I shall tell you how this happened. Luces heard about Jesus Christ, the miracles and marvels he performed, and the signs that he made that converted the people. He sent a message to Eleutere, who was pope, and asked him to send him someone to baptize him and teach him about the faith. When the pope heard this, he gave thanks to God and glorified him. He sent Dunian to the king, and also one of his companions named Fagan; both were exceedingly good scholars and learned bishops. They came to the king and baptized him, teaching him the law of God. After the king his household and all his people were baptized. They did whatever the king did, following his example. The two bishops travelled round the country and preached. Through the king and with his consent, as was customary and right, they established bishoprics and, above these, archbishoprics. In the bishoprics they placed bishops and in the archbishoprics archbishops.

(5243–72) They arranged the bishoprics and divided up the parishes. The temples, where the gods in whom the pagans believed dwelt, they sanctified and purified, dedicating them to the service of God. The fiefs, incomes, dwellings, and other possessions were retained for use by those who were to serve in the temples; they were all donated by the king to the bishops and the clergy. When Britain was converted and had received the law of God, King Luces was very pleased to see the people baptized and devoted to the service of God. He granted exemptions to the churches and provided them with fiefs from his lands, granting them large domains. He served God willingly, ruling in peace and coming to his end in peace. His body lay in Gloucester. He died one hundred and fifty-six years after God was born for our redemption. At the time he died, the king had no wife or child, and no close relative who could rule over his heritage.

SEVER IS SENT TO BRITAIN, AND HE REBUILDS HADRIAN'S WALL*

(5273–316) WHEN it came to the attention of the Romans that the king had died without an heir, they prepared two legions and sent them to Britain, along with one of their senators named Sever (Septimius Severus), in order to retain the land for their own purpose. Sever came with two legions, but he found the Britons to be villainous. Nevertheless, he fought so intensely, made so many promises, and gave so many presents, that part of the people submitted to him, and through them he conquered most of the others. The remainder, who were very indignant, retreated far over the river Humber, and Sever pursued them until he drove them into Scotland. They made Fulgene, a proven warrior, their lord. Joining forces with the Picts and allying themselves with them, they launched many attacks, both openly and secretly, in a region over towards Scotland, which used to be called Deira. When Sever had withdrawn and gone back to London, Fulgene, who ruled the Picts, the Scots, and the fugitives, took a great deal of booty and many prisoners, for whom he received great ransoms. When Sever heard about this, he hoped to be able to find them. They had fled into Scotland and were scattered over many different places. Fulgene did this repeatedly, and this lasted such a long time that Sever had a dyke dug across the entire width of the country, and on the dyke he constructed, from one sea to the other, a tall, dense fence made up of stakes that were closely linked together; this was to close off and protect the land. Thus, he shut out all his enemies.

(5317–52) For a long time there was no one who would have dared to cross the palisade, in order to steal or to pillage. When Deira was so well closed off that Fulgene did not dare to enter it, he took advice from the Picts and from his own men about travelling to Scythia, which he did. He spoke to the Picts who were there. He promised them so much, and beseeched them so much, that he brought with him a great fleet and landed in England. He came to York, besieged it, and took control of the surrounding land. Then he summoned the very powerful kinsmen he had in the country. For love of him, they and many others left the emperor and attached themselves to him. He promised them a great deal. Sever took the other Britons and assembled his legions. Then he went to relieve York and to help those in the city. He joined battle with those in the siege, and Fulgene rearmed himself. They attacked each other violently, and he who could fight better struck better. The battle consisted of fine blows and many a soul departed from its body. Fulgene was mortally wounded, and he did not live long afterwards. Sever was also killed there, as were a huge number of his allies. But at the request of the Romans, amongst whom were many of his kinsmen, he was taken into York and buried with great honour.

(5353–72) Sever had two sons, one was named Bassian and the other they called Getan. Getan's mother was a Roman woman, who was related to the leaders of the Senate. Bassian was born of a British woman, but she was very well connected. The Romans took Getan and raised him to the rank of elected king, and the Britons took Bassian and promised him the kingdom. Each of them had a close relationship with their parent and also with the closest of their people. The Romans loved their Roman and the Britons loved their closely related Briton. Thus, there was, because of this election, great strife between the brothers, but Getan was soon killed, I do not know how. Then the war was over and Bassian conquered the land.

(5373–5402) In Britain there was a youth; we have heard him called Carais. He was very bold and adventure-loving, and physically he was very strong. He had proven himself in many critical situations, and he was brave and highly praised. He was of very low rank and his heritage was very poor, but he conducted himself much better than his income required of him. He was skilled at bearing a great burden, and he preferred war to peace. At that time some people sailed round, robbing others. No one dared to occupy the shores because of pirates and raiders from the sea. I do not know what Carais had in mind, but he came to the Senate in Rome and said that, if he were granted permission, he would guard the sea and look after the shores so that no pirate could make his way there, and he would restore their tribute so that nothing would be lacking. The Romans had a desire for what was advantageous to them, and they gave him what he wanted. They handed over letters and charters to him and, lo, Carais set off from there. He showed his letters throughout the land and made every effort to acquire what he could. He gathered ships and sailors and sought men-at-arms and good archers.

(5403–44) The disinherited, the fugitives, the robbers and the rebels, those lacking land and those who wanted to live off other people, young knights who were bold and brave, and pirates were all summoned. He had a huge company of men, who were born and raised in wickedness. When Carais had brought together his fleet, he sailed round many lands. He passed them, from one island to another, taking prisoners and laying waste lands. From knights and peasants, neighbours and those some distance away, he took everything he could, knowing no restraint. If the pirates had behaved wretchedly, Carais did worse, for he left nothing behind. The man whose task it was to protect people left nothing he could remove. He who was to protect them did them harm, and his household continued to grow constantly. There was no thief or robber, no criminal or traitor, who did not want to accompany Carais. No one who came to him was refused. The more men he had the more arrogance he assumed, and the more he took the more he desired. He destroyed castles and towns, seizing everything and stealing everything. He was a man of great presumption with a great desire for power. In Britain he spoke to the Britons, and he sent one of his messengers to them. He made many extravagant promises and told them in private that they were being wrongly and foolishly advised, as they did not make him king. For he would drive out the Romans and take them off their hands.

(5445–74) In secret, he also spoke to the Picts, of whom there was a large number in the land and who were very close advisers of the king. They promised him that if he engaged in battle with the king they would make sure that without fail he won it, and that they would desert the king on the battlefield and ensure his defeat. Carais challenged Bassian, threatened him, and made war against him. They threatened each other so intensely that they were brought closer to doing battle. In the place where the combat was at its height, and where they fought best and fell in battle, the Picts, who were traitors, left their lord. The king trusted them more than any of his other men. The more he believed in them, the more he trusted them, and the more generous were the gifts he made to them. Yet they abandoned him in this time of need. It is at such a time that one sees one's true ally, and at this time they abandoned their lord. They were traitors and they betrayed him. Carais killed the king and then conquered the entire kingdom. He sent the Picts to Scotland and gave them towns and lands. From that time onwards the Picts have all been merged with the Scots.

(5475–526) As soon as the inhabitants of Rome had heard how Carais had behaved, they sent three legions and two of their best barons. One of them, Allec, was very knowledgeable, and also very bold and very brave. Livius Gallus was with him and they were both good knights. They did battle with Carais, defeating and conquering him. He was killed, as was also a large portion of the men who were supporting him. Then Allec waged war against them and frequently harmed those who had caused damage to the Romans and trusted Carais's advice. The Britons, who refused to hand over the tribute, intended to defend themselves. As king they elected a baron named Asclepiodot, who was lord of Cornwall; there was no Briton who could match him. Then the Britons gathered together and prepared themselves for action. They went on assembling men and urging each other to fight until they found him in London on the day a high festival was to be held. He was at a service, where he intended to make a sacrifice. When he heard the noise and the uproar, he emerged on to the fields with his armed men and did battle with the Britons. But his men dispersed too soon, wanting to take flight. But he could not protect himself in this way, as the Britons captured him as he fled. He could not save himself from death. Gallus would have met the same fate if he had not forced his way into London. He had the Romans enter with him and close and secure the gates. He made the armed men take over the walls in order to be able to hurl missiles and defend themselves. Asclepiodot besieged them and sent messengers everywhere, telling the barons and requesting them to come and help him with the siege. If they were willing to help him, they would be freed from the Romans, who were accustomed to doing them harm. He wanted to cleanse the whole land of them so that they could not establish themselves there again.

(5527–68) At Asclepiodot's command the Welsh came, and also Scots and Britons from all parts and all those who were closest to them. Then they made their crossbowmen shoot their arrows, and they raised their belfries and constructed their catapults. They shattered and broke down the walls, forcing their way in. Then you would have seen Romans dying and blood pouring from the wounded, who lay strewn upon the ground. Never would you have seen so many men slaughtered. Many of those who saw the walls being shattered withdrew into the fortresses. The Britons captured the bourgs and attacked the Romans in the towers. They oppressed Gallus, who was within, so much that he told them that he would surrender if they allowed him to escape alive, to take away his companions alive, and to depart from England alive, with no loss of life or limb. There was only one legion of men left who would beg to be pardoned in this way. Agreement was soon reached, and the tribute was taken and bestowed. The Romans had surrendered, and they descended from the parapets when the troops from Scotland arrived, and those from Wales with their large forces. They found them in the heart of the city, captured them all, and beheaded them. On a river running through the city they captured and decapitated Gallus; they separated his head from his body. Both body and head were thrown into the depths of the river. The river where Gallus fell and lay took on the name Galli; the Britons called it Nentgallin and the English and Saxons call it Gualebroc. The names have a different sound, but they mean the same thing.

(5569–614) Asclepiodot, who was not wicked or stupid, was made king. He held a festival and had himself crowned. He reigned for ten years very peacefully, getting rid of thieves and robbers and hating all evildoers greatly. But that time there was slaughter and great persecution of those who served the Lord God and who believed in Jesus Christ. This was done by Diocletian, who out of cruelty and injustice dispatched Maximian to destroy all the Christians who had dwelt beyond Montgieu, towards the west. Throughout almost every land attacks were made on Christians. Satan had a great deal of power. At that time St Alban was martyred, and also St Julius and St Aaron, two citizens who came from Caerleon. All the bishops and the clergy were captured and slaughtered; not a single cleric or priest remained. Choel,* a count from Gloucester, who came from a very good family and had a very fierce disposition, made war on Asclepiodot. The war grew and increased so much that they all fought and inflicted great damage on each other. Choel was the stronger, and he won the battle, killing the king and taking possession of the land. Whoever was upset or pleased by it, he became king of England. He raised a daughter,

Eleine, who was skilled in the arts and in learning. She was to be the king's only heir, as he had no other son or daughter. The maiden was well educated and greatly praised for her beauty. Choel had her very well taught, and he had teachers devote careful attention to her, so that when the king died she would be able to rule the kingdom.

(5615–44) When the Senate in Rome found out that Asclepiodot was dead, there was not a single Roman who was not happy about this, for he had tormented them greatly, often robbing them of their knights, their dues, and their tribute. They sent a senator there named Constanz, whom they admired greatly. He had already conquered Spain and placed it under Roman rule. At that time no one knew of anyone with his prestige and his worth. When Constanz entered Britain, he was accompanied by a large number of men. He was feared, and so were his men. Choel, who heard of Constanz's arrival, did not dare to do battle with him, as he was a man of great prestige and he feared him greatly. He sent his messengers to him, offering and promising him that he would hold Britain from him and that he would hand over the designated tribute. He had not, he said, done him any harm and he had killed Asclepiodot, who had held on to their tribute for a long time and killed Romans wickedly. Then as a result of invasion, he ruled their lands. They ought to be grateful to him for having freed the country.

FOUNDING OF THE HOUSE OF CONSTANTINE

(5645–67) CONSTANZ was fully aware that what he was saying was correct, and that he was seeking nothing other than what was right. He granted him the kingdom and they became allies. After that, a month passed and a second month was beginning, when Choel felt unwell and fell ill. A week later he passed away. Constanz married Choel's daughter Eleine and ruled the land in her name. In her day no one knew of a woman of her worth and her intelligence, nor of any maiden with her reputation. Constanz married her and made her queen. They hoped for a son and God gave them one: his name was Constantine. They loved him greatly and strove to bring him up well. He was eleven years old, or a little more, and was growing up and getting bigger when Constanz's health began to decline. Even a doctor could not help him. This was the end; death was inevitable.

(5668–710) Constantine grew bigger and matured. The barons, who loved him in true faith, raised him to the rank of king, and his mother educated him. She who loved him the best trained him the best. As soon as he reached the age when he was able to take charge of a body of men, he befriended a large number of knights and gladly gave them generous gifts. If Constanz was a man of great goodness, Constantine surpassed his goodness and his fame. He never rested until he had made his neighbours entirely subject to his command. He was very kindly, and very fond of true justice. In his youth he behaved just like others would do in their mature years. Because of his mother he loved the Britons, and because of his father he loved the Romans, for he was born of these two people and had kinsmen on both sides. He loved his whole family. At that time Maxenz was in Rome. He was a very arrogant emperor of Rome and a very evil man, filled with malice. He laid waste lands belonging to Rome, diminished its status, and brought low this noble race. He abolished the authority of the Senate and destroyed its authority. There were those who hated him greatly and who abandoned their fiefs and their dwellings because they did not wish to remain with him. They went to make their complaint to Constantine because he was the most powerful and the wisest man of their lineage. Through him they thought they could regain what they had possessed if he were willing to strive with them. They discussed the matter with him and begged him so much, and his own people advised him so much, that he made preparations to go to Rome, taking with him archers and knights.

(5711–58) Out of affection Constantine took to Rome three of his mother's uncles, whom he loved and trusted very much, and he gave them the rank of senator. One was called Joelin, one Trahern, and the third Marin. He eradicated Maxenz's audacity and took away his power. Then Constantine was emperor. Eleine, his good mother, journeyed to Jerusalem and assembled all the old Jews. It was through her that the Cross, which had been hidden for a long time, was found. Joelin, Eleine's uncle, was given a wife of high lineage, a Roman lady of high repute, who was from a very good family. They had a son, whom they brought up well, and they gave him the name Maximien. Those who were responsible for protecting Britain, and had been placed there by Constantine, were captured by Octavius and beheaded. He made himself king and crowned himself. He was a count from Wales, and he claimed authority within Britain. He killed the provost and the counts, and also the bailiffs and sheriffs.* Constantine remained in Rome and occupied himself with very important matters. He sent an uncle of Eleine by the name of Trahern, in whom he trusted greatly, giving him two legions with which to free England. Trahern made his way to Portchester and spent two full days there. Then the city was handed over to him; it could not hold out any longer. From there he went to Winchester, expecting to take it by force. But Octavius had got there first, and he did not intend to give him a warm welcome. On a field named Maisure the battle between them was very intense. But the Britons had the greater force, and the Romans could not withstand them. They were forced to go back to the ports.

(5759–800) Trahern had the ships loaded. He sailed over the sea and travelled until he reached the coast of Scotland. He did a great deal of harm and damage there, pillaging, burning, destroying, and laying waste all the towns. Octavius heard the news, which was later confirmed as the truth, that Trahern was laying waste Scotland and leaving no possessions or booty behind. He summoned his men and was very keen to get there. He thought and said that Trahern would not wait for him. But Trahern did not take flight, rather did he attack him and defeat him. He who was the first to win was later defeated. Octavius, who was initially conquered, fled to Norway to King Compert, asking for help against Trahern, if he could provide it. In secret, he had requested that all his allies he had left behind should do battle to the best of their ability and kill Trahern for him. Trahern felt entirely secure, and he was proclaimed king everywhere. One day he had left London, but people were well aware of where he was going. He was passing through a wooded valley with confidence and experiencing no fear, when a count, who had hated him because of Octavius, jumped out of a hiding place. He had a hundred good knights with him, and he killed Trahern in the midst of his men. Then he had Octavius come back and take over the kingdom. He did not leave a single Roman behind who was not dead or banished. He ruled the kingdom in peace for a long time.

MAXIMIEN TAKES BRITAIN FROM CUNAN, GIVING HIM BRITTANY AND MAKING BRITTANY ONLY FOR THE BRITONS

(5801–41) WHEN he had come to the end of his days, and had become very old, he wondered what he should do, to whom he should leave

England, and about who would have the country after his death without giving rise to any discord. He had a daughter and was keen that she should have the kingdom after him. He spoke to his allies about this and some of them asked him to send word to one of the noble Romans and give his daughter to him along with the domain. There were those who loved Cunan,* the king's nephew, and they recommended that he should inherit everything, and that he should marry off his daughter elsewhere, giving all his possessions to Cunan and making him his heir. There was a noble count there, Caraduec from Cornwall, who said that he would never grant this and never advise the king to make Cunan his heir; rather he should send for Maximien. He was the son of Joelin and the cousin of Eleine and Constantine and he was in Rome. He was born a Briton on his father's side and a Roman on his mother's side. On both sides he was of high lineage, and he was regarded as brave and wise. Then the king should grant him his daughter as his wife and make him the heir to his kingdom. His daughter would thus be queen and the land would be entirely subject to her. For if he had given Cunan the heritage and married his daughter elsewhere, her husband would want to challenge him and say that he should have the inheritance.

'If you do not act in this way,' he said, 'we shall never have peace in our lifetime.' The king adhered to this advice.

(5842–86) Then there was great agitation at court, for Cunan was very angry with Caraduec, whose advice this was. He uttered insulting and foolish words to him, and if he had dared to do so he would have done more. But Caraduec had little regard for his wrath and for everything he said. Through the king, and with his permission, he sent his son Mauric to talk to Maximien and take him to Britain. Mauric found Rome in turmoil. A great quarrel had developed there between Maximien, on the one hand, and Valentin and Gratian, on the other hand, two brothers who possessed very great power, to prevent Maximien from having any part of it or any power over it. They wanted to rule over the kingdom. Maximien found Mauric, and in secret he explained who he was and where he came from, what his name was and what he was seeking. When he heard that he had been summoned, Maximien was filled with great joy. If he was delighted, I am not surprised. He did not dwell on his preparations, and he came to the king who had summoned him. The king honoured him greatly, giving him his daughter as his wife and England as his heritage.

Cunan had departed angrily, and he joined forces with the Scots. He defied his uncle and his men and waged war on Maximien. The latter, to whom the king had given possession of everything, defended himself. On many occasions he was the winner and on many occasions the loser. This is what happens in such circumstances, that one loses and then recovers. In the end they came together, and the wise men reconciled them. Maximien promised to make him a rich man, and he did so.

(5887–914) In three years he assembled treasure and a large amount of goods, and he boasted that he would cross over the sea to France, do battle with the French, and wage war against the Romans, because of the two brothers, whom he hated and who ruled Rome in opposition to him without any attempt to make peace with him. He had a large number of men, carried with him a great amount of possessions, and displayed great arrogance. Towards the west, at the upper end of France, he reached the region called Armorica. Humbauz, who was lord of that country, summoned his men and his allies. He wanted to take the land away from them by force and to drive them out of his fief, but the Britons had greater strength and killed many of his men. They could not resist effectively, so they were forced to turn and flee. Maximien pursued them, killing a remarkable number. A good fifteen thousand of them died, and neither castle nor town could protect them. Maximien turned back and returned to camp. Taking Cunan to one side, he smiled at him.

(5915–48) Smiling, Maximien spoke privately to him:

'Cunan,' he said with a smile, 'this region is very fine, and it seems to me to be very profitable, very fertile and delightful. I can see how abundant these lands are, and also these rivers and forests. There is a large amount of fish and also of venison; I have never seen such a fine country. I have tried to obtain it for your use. Britain was given to you, and it would have been well served by you, but you have lost it because of me, and you are, I believe, displeased with me. But now pardon me for this, and I shall offer you a great reward for it. Take possession of the whole of this kingdom and rule the land I have conquered. I shall conquer the rest for you. I shall make you king and lord of it. We shall get rid of the peasants and populate the land with Britons, and when it is populated it will be called Lesser Britain. I do not want other people to live here, for it will be Britain for us Britons.'

Cunan received the gift and was very grateful for it. He bowed low and thanked him humbly. Then he promised him that for the rest of his life he would maintain faith with him.

(5949–90) At that time, and for that reason, Armorica lost its name. It then acquired, and still has, the name Brittany. It will never, I believe, lose it. From there they went to Rennes and besieged the city. It was swiftly surrendered to them without any resistance. The men had fled and abandoned everything, leaving it unguarded. Many people told them that no one would be found there who would not die a painful death and be tortured in great shame. For that reason all the peasants fled, each vying to outdo the other. In this way, the land was evacuated and left for the Britons. Maximien took everything and placed his guards in the castles. No one was left who could cultivate the fields or who could till the land. Maximien, who was very knowledgeable and who wanted to populate the land, brought a hundred thousand peasants from England, all selected to work the land. He also took thirty thousand knights who would support the peasants and protect them from other people. Then he had Cunan crowned and the strongholds handed over to him. Not wanting to tarry at that time, he advanced towards France. He conquered France and Lorraine, and he made Trèves the capital of his kingdom. But he still could not tolerate it if Rome was not under his control. So he set off towards Gratian and Valentin in Rome. He conquered Lombardy and Rome, driving one of the two away and killing the other.

(5991–6026) He had England handed over to Dionot, one of his vassals and a noble and loyal man, whom he trusted to rule over it. Dionot was the younger brother of Caraduec, who, like his son, had participated in this diplomatic mission. But Caraduec was already dead and Dionot had the inheritance. He had a very beautiful daughter, who was called Ursula.* The French, who were heartened by this, engaged in battle with Cunan, but he defended himself very well and was never defeated by them. To take advantage of his land, to populate and provide it with occupants, and to give his men more protection, he wanted to give wives to the men. But he did not want them to marry French women, through the use of force or for costly gifts, to merge their lineage, or to join their lands together. Rather did he ask Dionot, who had England under his protection, to grant him Ursula, his daughter, and to send her to him with the as yet unmarried daughters of vavasours. He should also send daughters of the peasants, and of the poor and the rich, as many as he could. He would marry them off well. Each one would marry according to the order of her lineage. Dionot gave him his daughter, and with her he sent a large amount of riches.

(6027–76) He asked for the maidens who were available to be married, and he gathered together eleven thousand of them, all born of noblemen. Likewise, he also took sixty thousand peasant girls all together, some young, some fully grown, all well adorned and arrayed. They were put on ships in London along with those who were to keep them safe. They sailed down the Thames until they came to the sea. They crossed over the deep sea, expecting to encounter joy and well-being. But, lo, there was a remarkable storm, and then there arose a rain cloud that caused the wind to turn towards them, the air to turn black, and the day to become dim. I have never heard of a storm or a tempest that came about so suddenly. The sky darkened and the air turned black. There was a high wind and the sea became agitated. Waves began to swell and to crash on top of each other. In a very short time the waves caused the ships to drift, flood, founder, and capsize. The helmsmen were of no use and no one could provide any further assistance. Whoever would have heard the maidens crying, women's voices raised, palms being beaten, hair being torn out, fathers and mothers being called upon, great cries emitted, great lamentations and the invoking of God and his saints—and whoever would have seen how the women died and how they held on to each other—could never have had a heart so wicked that they would have had no compassion. Never at any time of danger have I ever heard of women being so devastated, for there were so many ships in such peril there, and maidens drowning sorrowfully. The few who escaped and found themselves amongst pagans were killed, sold, or retained in servitude. Eleven thousand were taken away and beheaded in Cologne. Ursula was captured along with them, and she was killed together with them.

(6077–116) Wanis and Melga found many of them in the sea, disoriented. Wanis was king of Hungary. He was sailing over the sea with a large number of ships. Melga was lord of Scythia. Many of the maidens with whom they wished to have relations, but who refused to give their consent, they had killed; they did not kill them for any other reason. These cruel men were pagans, and they all gathered together. They were told and knew very well that England was weakened and devoid of good knights. A number of them, led by Maximien, went to Rome, and Cunan had the remainder. Thus the land was not being defended. These two kings coveted it, and they invaded through Scotland. They destroyed and pillaged everything, not sparing any of the inhabitants. After this, they crossed the Humber and laid waste the entire country. There was no one there, apart from the peasantry, who had no interest in fighting. The outlaws killed them, and the wretches bawled and yelled. How could a land be defended that was devoid of good knights? In so far as there were barons there, they could hold on to the towers and to the keeps. They sent a message to Maximien, and he sent Gratian to them, a very helpful knight, who was in command of two legions. He brought succour to the besieged and defeated all the pirates. He threw them all out of England and pursued them into Ireland.

(6117–40) Meanwhile, Valentin's kinsmen and his noble relatives arrived. Through Theodosien, a king of great power from the east, they captured Maximien in Aquileia by force and they killed him. Of the Britons who had followed him some were killed and some fled. Valentin recovered what Maximien had taken from him. Gratian, who had control over England, did not need to do anything more. Displaying great haughtiness, he made himself chieftain and king. In him there was a very cruel tyrant, one who inflicted great harm on the poor. He honoured the nobility and drove out the peasants. The latter joined forces, and in great throngs they took revenge, tearing him apart like an enraged wolf treats a dog. His men departed and returned to their lands.

THE ROMANS ARE NO LONGER ABLE TO HELP DEFEND THE BRITONS AGAINST INVADERS, AND THEY LEAVE BRITAIN

(6141–78) WHEN Wanis and Melga heard what the peasants had done with Gratian, they assembled the men from Gotland, the Norwegians and the Danes, and those from Scotland and Ireland, and they took possession of Northumbria. With their large number of troops they crossed the Humber, destroying castles and towns. The Britons saw the grief and the massacre of their men, and once more they sent word to the senators through messengers and letters, asking whether they could provide assistance at this time of need, as the people in whom they trusted the most. They would never deviate from their advice, and they would serve them for all time. The Romans had not forgotten the treachery and the deceit they had often used against them. They only sent one legion from amongst their men. They came swiftly, freeing England and driving away the outlaws. They chased them into Scotland, killing a number of them and cutting them to pieces. Collecting mortar and stone, they built a wall on a bank of soil.* There was not a crenel to speak of separating those in Scotland and those in Deira, for those who destroyed the land often came from that direction. In numerous locations they placed guards, who, as a reward, received very large fiefs. When they had completely finished building the wall, they instituted talks in London with the most powerful men in the country.

(6179–212) Then they said that they would be leaving them and going back to their lands. They would display courage, seek arms, and defend themselves vigorously. They [the Romans] could not support the costs of coming and going. There was a wise man who spoke there; he was the first to do so:

'My lords,' he said, 'some of our fine ancestors have suffered huge losses and many great hardships, and we for our part have also done so because of our love for you. You have given us your truce, but we have paid a good deal for it. It has scarcely been of any benefit to us, for we have spent it on matters concerning yourselves. If we had the truce for one year, two years later we had lost it. For never, as soon as you dared, did you show us any faith or love. You repeatedly found opportunities to deny us our rights. Many of our men died there, and they have suffered much pain and many wrongs. You seek help from us when you need it, and you promise us faith and peace, but when you have escaped and the crises are behind you, then you show scarcely any interest in us. Thus, we have found you to be very arrogant. You take away our tribute again, or you resent having to pay it. It is better for us to abandon the tribute than to do service for it in this way over a long period of time.

(6213–58) 'Since you are frequently in need of help, there is a great cost if we remain at a distance from you. We cannot attend so many times. Do the best you can. If we can go to Rome, we shall never come back for anyone, rather we shall leave everything to you. We do not wish to support you any longer. If you can, support yourselves and defend yourselves. With regard to your ancestors, we know that they were strong and proud. As far as Rome, no land remained for them to conquer. They conducted themselves ferociously. But in your case things are very different. I do not know the meaning of it, or how it comes about, that any people could attack you without destroying your land and putting you to flight. It is out of evil, it seems to me, that you have all betrayed your ancestors. Be more rigorous, remember the prowess that the barons who conquered great lands used to show. Since you are unable to defend your fiefs, you will have difficulty conquering others. Defend yourselves against hostile peoples who pass through here so frequently. If you have men who can guard the wall, we have shielded you on one side. Build great towers and strong castles on the shores, and in the ports through which outlaws force their way in and attack you so often. Maintain your freedom well, and rid yourself of service to others. This will correspond to our wishes.'

There was much sorrow when they heard these words. They felt great distress and shed many tears, some out of pity, some out of fear. Then they said farewell, and the Romans departed. As they spoke, they made it clear that they did not intend to return.

(6259–90) Wanis and Melga had heard the news through their spies that the Romans had finally left. With the Picts and the Danes, the Scots and the Norwegians they entered Northumbria, and went about burning, destroying, and pillaging. As far as the wall, they left nothing behind them without destroying it. The Britons strengthened the wall and those outside attacked it. Then from all sides you would have seen javelins and darts dispatched, bolts and arrows flying round, and stones hurled from catapults. Those who defended the wall fought very fearfully. They donned their armour once more and were attacked vigorously. All they had to do was to reveal so much as a single eye and those outside would force them into hiding. Never did any rain, driven by the wind, fall more densely than the arrows and darts that flew round, along with the stones that they hurled. The Britons abandoned the battlements and vied with each other as they descended. Those outside scaled the wall and demolished it in many places. Afterwards, they flattened everything, and ditches and walls were razed to the ground.

(6291–320) Then they could pass quite freely, because there were no defences left there. They took possession of castles and towns, and many of the Britons were killed. They had free rein to move round in all directions, finding no resistance. I have never found, nor shall I find, that, at any time before or since, so many men, knights, or peasants died together. O God! What destruction and what devastation of good and noble land! In the olden days the Britons were very brave, but now they were so subjugated that they would never recover by themselves without getting help from elsewhere. They sent to the senators for knights and for assurance, but they refused, telling them that they should do the best they could, as they could not suffer such distress and such hardship on their behalf every year. They had plenty of things to see to elsewhere, so they could no longer occupy themselves with the affairs of the Britons. The bishops gathered together. They were sorrowful because they greatly feared that because of this foreign race their Christian faith would be destroyed, and that if this were to continue for a substantial period of time God would not watch over them.

(6321–70) At that time there was a very eloquent archbishop in London. This was Guencelin, a man of very great learning who lived a good life. He first had the diocese of London, and later for a long time he had the archbishopric's see. I do not know for what reason he was transferred to Canterbury. Guencelin, this good archbishop, on the advice of his bishops, crossed over into Armorica, which Cunan populated with Britons and which we now call Brittany. It has lost the name of Armorica. Aldroen, who ruled the domain, was the fourth king after Cunan. The population increased considerably, and the land was well settled. The archbishop travelled so far that he found King Aldroen. The king honoured him greatly, for he had heard him widely praised. He asked him what he was seeking, since he had come to him from such a distance.

'My lord,' he said, 'you can clearly take note, and you have no reason to doubt, that I have come from overseas because great need has driven me here. You were not born so recently, nor do you live so far away, that you have not heard tell of the great hardships and the great wounds that the Britons have repeatedly experienced since the man named Maximien conquered the domain over which you now rule and made Cunan the lord over it. Because of the people who were taken away, and who came and populated these lands of ours, he led our people into decline. We have never since had a single neighbour who has not waged war on us, and who did not aim to defeat us. In the past the British were accustomed to conquering many regions. Now they cannot even defend their land from other people. The inhabitants of Rome used to assist and help us in our times of great need. They have abandoned us, for they live too far away and they complain about the cost and about the journey.

(6369–408) 'We are a very courageous and sizeable people, but we have no prince or king. An evil people, without faith, has conquered our land, and a race taken unawares will never, I fear, be able to recover, unless we have the help of other people. I cannot tell you, for it troubles me greatly to remember it, the sorrow and the misfortune that we have had to endure, and which still continues. For this reason, my lord, I have come to you, who are known for your bravery. You were born of our people, and your kinsfolk came from us. You are Britons and we are Britons. We are related, this we know, and we should be as one and hold all we have in common. One must be rescued by the other, you by us and us by you. We are in need, so help us now and you will gain great honour from it. Because of lineage and justice, you should do this naturally.'

On account of the sad tale he had heard, Aldroen, who was very compassionate, became very distressed and tearful. In tears, he replied to him:

'If I can be of service to you, I shall assist you as much as I can. Take my brother Constantine and make him commander. He is a wonderful knight and very skilled in warfare. I shall give him two thousand armed men, from amongst the most esteemed I possess.'

(6409–23) Then he asked for Constantine and handed him over to the archbishop, who looked at him and made the sign of the Cross with his right hand. Constantine bowed and came forward, and then the archbishop said to him:

'Christ conquers, Christ reigns, Christ conquers and governs.' The king summoned his knights and handed over to him two thousand men. As soon as there was a favourable wind, they were put on board the ships with splendid equipment. He would have gone with them himself, if he had been able to do so, and had been bold enough. But he was at war with the French.

THE BRITONS ELECT CONSTANTINE AS THEIR KING, BUT, AFTER HIS MURDER TWO YEARS LATER VORTIGERN CROWNS CONSTANT

(6424–68) CONSTANTINE came to Totnes along with many good knights. Each man considered he was as worthy as a king. They set off towards London, summoning Britons from all sides. Earlier no one had put in an appearance, but now out of the thickets and the mountains they came forward with huge numbers of men. Why should I give you a lengthy account of this? They fared so well, and accomplished so much, that they defeated the evil people who had destroyed the land. Then they held counsel in Silchester. All the barons were to be there, and they elected Constantine as king. With no objections or delay, they joyfully made him their leader. Afterwards, they gave him a wife who was born of a noble Roman family. He had three sons with her, and they named the eldest of them Constant. They raised him in Winchester and made him a monk there. After him, Aurelius was born; his surname was Ambrosius. Lastly, Uther was born, and he was the one of them who lived the longest. Archbishop Guencelin took charge of the two boys. If Constantine had lived long, he would have enhanced the land. But he died very soon, reigning for only two years. He had one of the Picts in his household, a traitor and an evil villain, who had served him for a long time. But later, and I do not know the reason why, he conceived a hatred for him. He took him into an orchard as if it were his intention to advise him. But when he was giving advice to the king, who had no defence against the evildoer, he had a knife, and he struck him with it, killing him. Then he took flight.

(6469–502) The inhabitants of the land gathered together. They wanted to appoint a king, but they were in doubt about which of the two youths to choose. They were young and lacking in experience. They were still being nursed and knew no malice. They did not dare to withdraw Constant, who was the firstborn and the eldest, from his monastic habit. It seemed to them to be villainy and madness to take him out of the abbey. They had chosen one of the youngsters when Vortigern sprang forward. He was a powerful man, living in Wales, and a very wealthy count. He was supported by a substantial number of kinsmen and he was very shrewd and cunning. He had been scheming well in advance with regard to the plans he intended to put in place.

'Why do you continue to hesitate? Make Constant the monk king. He is the rightful heir, so let us take away his monk's habit, for the others are too young. Do not grant the domain to anyone else. Allow me to accept the entire responsibility for this. I shall bring him forth from the abbey and deliver him to you as king.' There was no one else who wanted the monk to become king. But Vortigern, intent on wickedness, went spurring to Winchester. So determined was he to meet with Constant that with the permission of the prior, he spoke with him in the parlour.

(6503–40) 'Constant,' he said, 'your father is dead. The domain has passed to your brothers. You must, by virtue of inheritance, be first to take possession of the kingdom. If you want to enhance my rights, and if you love me and trust me fully, I shall rid you of your black garments and dress you in royal robes. Then I shall take you away from the monastic life and restore your inheritance to you.' Constant, who had no particular liking for the abbey, was very keen to have this authority. He was totally displeased by life in the monastery and eager to get away from it. He swore and pledged everything that Vortigern asked of him, and he immediately took him away from the abbey. There was no one who would have dared to raise an objection. What use would it have been to do so, since that would not have caused him to abandon his plan? Vortigern took off Constant's monk's garments and dressed him in expensive robes. From there he took him to London. Very few people had gathered and the archbishop who was to anoint the king had died. There was no one else who could do this or who wanted to become involved in this matter. Vortigern took the crown and placed it on Constant's head. There was no blessing other than the one by Vortigern. Constant accepted the crown, abandoning the order he should have maintained. He abandoned God's order wrongly and thus he came to a bad end. A man should not come to a happy end by doing what he ought not to do.

(6541–80) Vortigern had full power over the king and his governance. The king did as he advised, and he took whatever he was to take. Very soon he realized that the king, who had been brought up in a cloister, was largely ignorant of many matters. He saw that the two brothers were very young and also that the barons in the country were dead. In addition, he saw that he was the strongest of those who remained alive and he saw that people were somewhat quarrelsome. He spotted a very convenient time and place, for he wanted to seize the kingdom for himself. Now hear about a man of evil and cunning.

'My lord, I know in truth, and I must inform you of this, that the Danes and the Norwegians from Norway have gathered together. Because you yourself are not a knight, and because of our weakness, they intend to enter this country and to seize and lay waste your castles. You must make preparations to defend your land and yourself.

Strengthen and watch over your towers. I am very much afraid of traitors, so you must hand over your castles to those who can defend them properly.'

'I have', said the king, 'handed over everything, so do what you will with it all. I shall never take responsibility away from you, for you know better than I do. Take all the land under your care so that no one will steal it or burn it. I shall do as you say, so do the very best of which you are capable. Take my cities, take my dwellings, take my treasures, take my possessions.' Vortigern was a very cunning man, skilled in covering up his own desires.

(6581–614) When he had taken over the fortresses, the treasures, and the riches, he said:

'My lord, if it pleases you, it would be my advice and counsel that you send for the Picts from Scotland as mercenaries, and let them be with you at court, whatever happens with regard to our war. You will be able to send the Picts wherever you need them. Through the Picts and their kinsfolk we shall know the situation concerning the foreigners. They will carry messages and go back and forth between us.'

'Do as you please,' said the king, 'and have as many men as you like come here. Give them whatever you wish, and act in the best way possible. Do things to the best of your ability.' When Vortigern had taken possession of everything and assembled all the treasure, he summoned as many Picts as he wanted, and they arrived just as he desired. Vortigern honoured them very much and gave them food and drink in abundance. With great joy he provided them with sustenance, and very often they were drunk. Vortigern gave them so much, and honoured them so greatly, that there was not one of them who failed to say, in the hearing of anyone who wanted to listen, that Vortigern was more courtly, and a much finer man than the king. He was thoroughly worthy of ruling the domain that the king held, even more so.

(6615–52) Vortigern gloried in this and honoured them more and more. One day, when he had given them drink, and they were completely intoxicated, he came amongst them and greeted them, displaying a sad countenance:

'I have held you very dear,' he said, 'and served you very willingly, and I shall continue to do so if I have the means. But this land belongs entirely to the king. I cannot give any gifts, or spend money, without having to account for it. I have very little income in this land, and

I have devoted myself to serving the king. Yet I do not have enough income from him to be able to maintain forty men-at-arms honourably. If I make conquests, you should return, for with your permission I am now departing. I am sorry to be leaving you, but I am poor and can do nothing else. If you hear that things have improved for me, be sure to come back to me.' Then Vortigern left. He was cunning and spoke in a cunning way. Those who had drunk copiously believed the villain completely. They regarded as the truth whatever false words he uttered, and they spoke amongst themselves:

'What would we do if we lost this good lord? Let us kill this foolish king, this monk, and raise Vortigern to the rank of king. He is worthy of honour and power. This foolish monk, what service does he offer us? Why have we tolerated him for so long?'

(6653–86) Then they went into the bedchamber, grabbed the king, and decapitated him. They severed his head from his body and presented it to Vortigern, crying out:

'Have you seen what support we have given you? The king is dead, so retain him with you. Take the crown and become king!' Vortigern recognized the lord's head and he feigned great grief. In his heart he was filled with joy. But he was cunning, and he disguised it. In order to conceal his wickedness, he assembled the Londoners and had the traitors decapitated, not leaving a single one alive. There were many who believed, but they only said so in private, that these men would never have touched the king or adopted an unfavourable view of him. Nor would it ever have entered their heads to do so if Vortigern had not issued the command for it to be done. When those who were raising the two brothers heard about the death of the king, they feared that the perpetrator would do the same to them. For fear of Vortigern, they took Aurelius and Uther. They made their way to Brittany and entrusted them to King Budiz, who welcomed them. He was their kinsman and had brought them up. He cared for them and dubbed them in splendid fashion.

THE ARRIVAL OF HENGIST AND HORSA, AND THUS THE BEGINNING OF THE *ADVENTUS SAXONUM*

(6687–736) VORTIGERN had control of the strongholds, the castles, and the cities. He made himself king and was filled with arrogance.

But he was anxious about two things: on the one hand, the Picts were waging war against him along with multiple threats (they wanted to avenge their kinsmen whose heads he had cut off), and, on the other hand, it troubled him grievously that everyone was announcing to him that the two brothers were armed and would return shortly. The barons would welcome them and do homage for the fiefs they held from them. They would avenge their brother Constant, for they would bring with them a huge number of men. This information was provided by a large number of people. Meanwhile, three ships arrived and docked at a port in Kent,* bringing foreigners with fair countenances and noble bodies. Their leaders were Hengist and Horsa, two brothers of hefty build and foreign speech. The news was soon related to Vortigern, who at that time was staying in Canterbury, that three ships together had arrived there with men from another region. The king ordered that, whoever they were, they should be offered peace and safe-conduct, and that they should speak with him in complete safety and return home likewise. They heard what had been offered to them, and because of this they came in safety. The king looked at the two brothers with their handsome bodies and their fair countenances. They were taller, better looking and more handsome than all the other youths.

'From which land', he said, 'do you come? Where were you born and what are you seeking?' Hengist, who was the older and the first-born, replied for everyone present:

'We come from Saxony,' he said. 'We were born there, and we live there. If you wish to hear the reason why we are travelling across this sea, I shall tell you the truth if you guarantee our safety.'

(6737–66) 'Explain things to us fully,' said the king, 'it would be wrong of you to have any fear of us.'

'Fair king,' said Hengist, 'noble lord, I do not know whether you have heard that our land has more native-born inhabitants, and is more fertile, than any other land you know, or have ever heard about. Our remarkable people thrive, and our children are multiplying greatly. There is a large number of both women and men, and this distresses those of us who are here. When our population is overgrown, the princes who rule the lands have all the youths who are fifteen years old, or older, gather together according to custom and usage. The finest of them, and the strongest, are all banished by lot from the country, and they travel through foreign regions in search of lands and dwellings, in order to break up the profusion of people, which the land cannot sustain. For children are being born there in greater numbers than the beasts are that feed in the fields. Through the lots that fell on us we have abandoned our country. Mercury was our guide. He was a god and he brought us here.'

(6767–816) When the king heard him name the god who acted as his guide, he asked him which god he had and in which god his people believed.

'We have', he said, 'many gods to whom we should build an altar. They are Phoebus, Saturn, Jupiter, and Mercury. We have many other gods according to the religion of our ancestors, but above all with great reverence we honour Mercury himself, who in our language is called Woden. Our ancestors honoured him so much that they devoted the fourth day to him, and it is still called Wodesdai [Wednesday]. In addition to this god, whom I have mentioned to you, we cultivate the goddess Free [Freya}, who is greatly honoured everywhere. The ancients, in order to do honour by her, dedicated the sixth day to her, and with great authority they named the day Freesdai [Friday] from Free.'

'Your beliefs are wrong,' said the king, 'and your gods are wicked. This distresses me, but nevertheless I am pleased that you have come here. You seem to be valiant and brave men, and if you want to serve me I shall retain all of you and make you rich men. Brigands from Scotland are waging war against me, burning my lands and pillaging my towns. If you should wish, and if it pleased God, for this would be of great benefit to me, I want to destroy the Picts and the Scots with the help of God and with your gods. For the Picts, who are destroying my land, come from there and are fleeing back there. With your help I would like to avenge myself by killing and driving them all away. You will receive your provisions, your pay, and your gifts.' Thus, the Saxons remained, and they drew their ships up on to dry ground. The court was soon filled with many noble youths.

(6817–50) It was not long before the Picts entered the king's land very forcibly, burning, destroying, and pillaging. When they were to cross the Humber, the king, who had heard of their arrival, went to face them with his barons, together with the Saxons and the Britons. Then you would have seen a tough battle and a great defeat. The Picts, who were used to frequent conquests, were not at all afraid of them. At first they withstood their opponents, and then they struck boldly. The fighting was remarkable. They withstood the enemy remarkably well. Because they were accustomed to victory, they wanted to maintain their normal habits. But on this occasion they lost what they normally had and the Saxons won the day. Through them and their assistance Vortigern won the victory. He handed over their pay to them and increased their provisions. He gave them fine dwellings in Lindsey and an abundance of property. This situation was maintained for a long time and their friendship lasted well. Hengist saw what he needed to do to further the king's affairs. He started to take care of his own advancement, as everyone should do. He was fully aware that he should stay close to the king and adopt the role of flatterer.

(6851–92) One day, finding the king in a joyful mood, he offered him a piece of advice:

'You have', he said, 'honoured me greatly. You have given me a great many of your possessions. I am serving you and shall continue to serve you. If I have served you well, I shall do so better in the future. But since I have been in your court, and since I have known your people, I have very clearly noticed, heard, and seen that you have no baron who loves you. Each one of them hates you and each one complains about you. I do not know which children they are referring to, who are robbing you of your people's love. These men are their natural lords, and the sons of one of their rightful lords. In a short time they will come from overseas and take this land away from you. All the men wish you ill. They want you to suffer great misfortune, and they wish great evil upon you. They hate you intensely and threaten you greatly. They want harm to come to you, and they are doing you harm. I have been thinking about how I can help you. I want to send to my own land for my wife, my children, and other relatives. Then you will trust me more and I shall serve you all the better. You will no longer encounter anyone who through war will take from you even a full foot of land. I have already served you for a long time, and I have acquired enemies because of you. At night I cannot feel safe unless I have a castle and walls. For this reason, if it were to please you, it would enhance your prestige and be to your advantage, to give me a city, a castle or a stronghold where I could lie and sleep in safety at night. Your enemies would fear me and they would cease doing you harm.'

(6893–924) 'Send for your men,' said the king, 'receive them warmly and equip them well. I shall give you what is needed. But you are not of our religion. You are a pagan and we are Christians. It would not be well thought of if I were to give you a stronghold. Try and find something else.'

'My lord,' said Hengist, 'let me turn one of the manors I possess into a retreat and reinforce it with as much land—I seek no more—as I could extend a hide, covering it all round with the hide. With just a bull's hide I would sleep more securely.'

Vortigern granted him this and Hengist thanked him for it. He got his messenger ready and sent him for his kinsmen. He took a bull's hide and split it in order to pull out a thong from it, and then he surrounded it with a large mound. He sought good workmen and built a castle. He gave it the name Thongcastre in the language of his country. Thongcastre took its name from the hide, and one can call it by a different name, Chastel de Cureie in French and Kaer Carrei in the British language, because it was measured and calculated using the thong.

(6925–70) When Thongcastre had been built, eighteen ships came there, laden with knights and also with household troops, whom Hengist had summoned. They brought his daughter, who was not yet married. Her name was Ronwen and she was a remarkably noble and beautiful maiden. He sent word to the king to come and stay with him on a day he had chosen, in order to enjoy himself eating and drinking, and also viewing his new warriors and his new dwelling. The king, who wanted this to be a private affair, came with just a small retinue. He saw the castle and looked at the workmanship. It was erected very well, and he praised it greatly. Vortigern retained the newly arrived knights as mercenaries. That day many of them ate and drank so much that they became drunk. Then Ronwen emerged from her bedchamber. She was very beautiful and well dressed. She carried a cup of wine and knelt down before the king, bowing to him very humbly and greeting him according to her custom:

'Laverd King, Wesheil!' she said to him. The king, who did not know this language, asked and enquired what the maiden had said to him. Keredic replied first. He was a Briton and a good translator. He was the first of the Britons to know the language of the Saxons:

'Ronwen', he said, 'has greeted you and called you lord king. It is the custom, my lord, in their country, that when friends drink together the man who is about to drink should say "Wesheil", and he who is to receive it should say "Drincheheil". Then he should drink all of it, or just half of it, and, out of joy and friendship, when the cup is received or given there is the custom of the sharing of a kiss.'

VORTIGERN MARRIES THE PAGAN HENGIST'S DAUGHTER, RONWEN, AND GIVES HIM KENT AS A DOWRY

(6971–7018) As soon as he learnt this, the king said 'Drincheheil', and he smiled at her. Ronwen drank, and then gave the cup back to him, and when doing so she kissed the king. It was through these people that it first became customary to start in this country by saying 'Wesheil' and to respond with 'Drincheheil', to drink all, or half, and to exchange kisses. The maiden had a very handsome body, and her face was very beautiful. She was very beautiful and pleasing, and also fair in shape and height. Without a cloak, she stood in front of the king, who gazed at her intensely. He was feeling happy and had drunk a good deal. He had a great desire for her. The Devil, who has driven many a man towards evil, had goaded him into this, and he was burning with love and rage to take Hengist's daughter. O God, what shame! O God, what a sin! The Devil had turned him so far from the rightful path, and he would not refuse marriage to her because she was a pagan, born of pagans. He immediately asked Hengist for her, and Hengist granted her to him, but before doing so he sought advice from his brother and his allies. They were very keen to see this marriage go ahead, and they advised and counselled that they should give her to him at once and ask for Kent as a dowry. He gave her to him, not wishing to do otherwise. Hengist asked for Kent as a dowry. The king desired the maiden, and he loved her and made her queen. She was a pagan, and he made her his wife according to pagan custom. There was no blessing from a priest and no mass or prayer. He fell in love with her during the day and he had her in the evening. He passed over Kent to Hengist, who took it, held it, and ruled it. Gerangon, who had held it as his inheritance, knew nothing about it until he was banished by Hengist.

(7019–50) The king trusted and loved the pagans more than the Christians. The Christians hated him for this. They ignored both him and his counsel. Even his sons hated him, and they deserted him because of the pagans. He had taken a wife, but she had already died and passed away. He had three sons with her, and they were already fully grown. The first was called Vortimer, and then came Paschent and Katiger.

'My lord,' said Hengist to the king, 'you are already hated in some measure because of me, and I in my turn am hated because of you. I am your father, and you are my son. You have taken my daughter and you possess her. I am grateful to you for asking for her. I must rightfully advise you, and you must trust me and help me, for if you wish to reign in safety and cause harm to those who hate you, send for my son Octa and his cousin Ebissa, two remarkable warriors and remarkable fighters. Give them land over towards Scotland, for that is the region where you are constantly being attacked. They will protect you from hostile people and prevent them from getting their hands on anything that is yours. Thus, for the rest of your life you will be able to live in peace on this side of the Humber.'

(7051–130) 'Do what you wish,' said the king, 'summon all those whom you consider to be brave.' Hengist sent word at once, summoning his son and his nephew. They came with three hundred ships. No brave knight who wanted to serve for money remained behind and failed to accompany them. After them, from day to day, others repeatedly came with four ships, with five, with six, with seven, with eight, with nine, and with ten. The pagans had soon mounted their horses and engaged in battle with the Christians. It was scarcely possible to tell who was a Christian and who was not. This greatly vexed the Britons, and they asked and told the king not to trust these foreigners, for they were clearly acting faithlessly. He had brought in too many of these pagans, and this was wickedness and great shame. He should banish them and send them away, all or most of them, by whatever means. The king said he would not do this. They were giving him good service, and he had summoned them. Then the Britons assembled and went to London together. They raised Vortimer, the eldest of the king's three sons, to the rank of king. He challenged the Saxons and banished them from the cities. For love of his wife, the king kept the Saxons with him, refusing to abandon them. The son drove them away repeatedly and routed them repeatedly. He was brave and received good support. The battle fought between Vortimer and the Britons against his father and the Saxons was very harsh. He did battle with them on four occasions, and each time he defeated them. The first combat was above Derwent Water. Then they fought with them at a ford near Epiford. There Katiger, the king's son, and Horsa came together in single combat. Each one wounded the other fatally, as each aimed to do. On a river on the Kent shore, near their ships and at a crossing point, was the third great battle. When they had taken flight over the Humber as far as Kent, there was a great rout there. Then they fled to Thanet, a small island in the sea. The Britons attacked them there and routed them all day long, with arrows and bolts from skiffs and small boats. They killed them on one side, and on the other side they died of starvation. When they saw that they would not survive unless they abandoned the land, they sent a message to King Vortigern so that he would beseech his son Vortimer to let them go peacefully without causing things to get worse. The king was with them the whole time, and on no occasion did he leave them. Whilst he was on the move and attempting to arrange this truce, the Saxons went on board their ships. They sailed and rowed hard in order to get as far away as possible, leaving behind their sons and their wives. They escaped in great fear and went back to their own regions.

(7131–86) When they had escaped, the Britons felt safer, and Vortigern handed over to everyone what each one of them had lost because of the Saxons. In order to rebuild the churches and to proclaim their faith in God, which had been poorly upheld because of Hengist, who had corrupted it, St Germain came to Britain. He was sent there by St Romain, who had the authority of the archbishopric of Rome. St Lupus of Troyes came with him. They were both bishops, one from Auxerre and one from Troyes, and they knew the ways to reach God. Through them, faith was recovered, and people were returned to it. Through them, many people knew salvation. For the two of them God performed and displayed many miracles and many wonders. As a result the whole of England was enhanced. When the law of God was re-established and Britain was reconverted, hear how an act of devilry was performed. Through great hatred and envy, Ronwen, as an evil stepmother, poisoned her stepson Vortimer, whom she hated because of Hengist, whom he had banished. When Vortimer realized that he was dying and that no doctor could cure him, he summoned all his barons and handed over to them the great amount of treasure he had collected. Hear what he asked of them:

'Retain knights,' he said, 'and give them pay and gifts. Maintain your land and yourselves, and defend yourselves from the Saxons so that you never bring them back to fight against you. Avenge my torment and your own. In order to frighten them, have my body buried on the shore and a tomb raised such that it will last for a long time, and be seen for some distance over the sea in their direction. The place where they know that my body is buried they will never approach, dead or alive.' The noble lord spoke to them in this way, and thus he died and came to his end. The body was taken to London and buried in London. But they did not bury the body where he had commanded them to do so.

THE SAXONS' TREACHERY AT THE 'NIGHT OF THE LONG KNIVES'

(7187–234) THEN Vortigern was made king again, as he had been before. His wife begged him to send for Hengist, his father-in-law, and he did so. He sent word to him that he should return, but only bringing with him a small number of men, so that the Britons would not be frightened and become embroiled in fighting once more. Vortimer, his son, was dead, so there was no need for extensive troops. Hengist came back gladly, but he did bring with him three hundred thousand armed men. He was afraid of the Britons, and he would act differently from the way in which he had behaved earlier. When the king knew that he was returning and bringing so many men, he was very fearful and did not know how to respond. The Britons were very angry, and they said that they would do battle with them and drive them out of the country. Hengist, who had a wicked disposition, sent word treacherously to the king, asking to be given peace and safe-conduct whilst parleying with them. They loved peace and wanted peace. They desired peace and sought peace. They did not want war, or to remain there by force. The Britons should retain those they would choose, and the remainder would go. The Britons agreed to this truce, and it was accepted on both sides. Who would have imagined treachery? They fixed a day for the meeting, and the king sent word to Hengist to come with few companions. Hengist agreed to this and sent word back that no weapon would be carried there in case a conflict should break out. On the broad Salisbury Plain, near Amesbury Abbey, both sides arrived to discuss this matter on the day of the Kalends of May.* Hengist had all his companions well trained, and he called upon them urgently to carry double-edged knives in their boots, so that they could strike from both sides.

(7235–76) When they were speaking to the Britons and were all intermingling, he would cry out 'Nim eur sexes!' ('Grab hold of your knives') for none of the Britons would understand this. Each man would then take out his knife and strike the Briton who was closest to him. Hengist, who was close to the king, pulled him towards him by the mantle and let the massacre take place. Those holding the knives made their blades pass right through their cloaks, mantles, chests, and innards. They fell on to their backs or on to their fronts. At once, there were four hundred and sixty men dead on the spot, the wealthiest and the most powerful. Some of them fled, using stones with which to defend themselves. Eldulf, a count from Gloucester, held a large pike in his right hand, which he had found lying at his feet; I do not know who had been carrying it. He defended himself with the pike, killing and knocking down many men. The count, who was brave and highly esteemed, killed a good seventy men. He dispersed the throng in such a way that no one could harm him directly. They hurled a large number of knives at him, but they did not touch him. On his horse, which was fine and swift-moving, he rode across the battlefield. He fled to Gloucester and strengthened his city and his keep.

IN EXCHANGE FOR HIS LIFE VORTIGERN GIVES THE SAXONS WINCHESTER, LINCOLN, YORK, AND CHICHESTER, AND FLEES ACROSS THE SEVERN INTO WALES

(7277–308) THE Saxons wanted to kill the king, but Hengist began to shout out to them:

'Leave the king alone. He has done me a great deal of good and suffered much torment for me. I must protect him as my son-in-law. But, if he wishes to preserve his life, let him hand over his cities to us and surrender his strongholds.' In this way they ceased attempting to kill the king, rather they put him in chains. They bound him and constricted him so much that he swore that he would hand over everything. He surrendered London and Winchester, Lincoln, York, and Chichester. To be free of ransom and escape from prison, he granted them Sussex as a fief and the whole of Essex and Middlesex, because they were close to Ken, which Hengist had been the first to hold. To commemorate the treachery of the knives, this became the counties' names, deriving from 'sexes', as the English say. There are many types of knife in French, but those who do not know what the words mean vary the names to some extent. The English heard themselves admonished for the treachery they had committed, and they took away the end of the word and turned round the names of the knives in order to wipe away the shameful act committed by their ancestors.

(7309–54) Vortigern surrendered everything to them and fled beyond the Severn. He crossed far into Wales, and once he was there he stayed there. He had his soothsayers come forward, and also the finest of his men. He asked for advice about what he should do and in which way he should conduct himself. If stronger opponents attacked him, how would he defend himself? His counsellors advised him to build a tower, such that it could not be taken by force or captured by any human trickery. When it was provisioned, he should remain inside it, so that no hostile adversary could kill him. Then he set about choosing and guarding a suitable location to build a tower. A satisfactory and pleasing location turned out to be on Mount Erir [Snowdon]. He sought the best masons he knew and had them get to work as soon as they could. They began to work and to arrange stone and mortar, but whatever they worked on during the day the earth swallowed up at night. The higher up they went the more the building was swallowed up in the foundations. Thus, many days of work collapsed into the ground. When the king found out and became aware that, as things were going, his construction would not develop otherwise, he asked for advice from his soothsayers:

'In faith,' he said, 'I am wondering about the outcome of this building. The ground cannot support it. Examine it, take a look at what is happening, and find out how the ground can bear the weight.' They made their surmises and predictions, but it is possible that they lied, saying that if he could find a man who was born without a father he should kill him, take his blood, and sprinkle it in with the mortar. In that way he could make his work more enduring.

(7355–84) Then the king sent messengers throughout the whole of Wales in order to make sure that if such a man were to be discovered he would be brought to him. Many men set out throughout many regions. Two of them, who were travelling along the same route, reached Kaermerdin together. Before the city, at the entrance, there was a large group of children, who had come there to play. The messengers began to look at them. Amongst the others who were playing there were two youths who were quarrelling. They were Merlin and Dinabuz, and one of them was angry with the other. One of them was clashing with the other and insulting his lineage:

'Be quiet, Merlin,' said Dinabuz, 'I am of a good deal higher rank than you, so you should keep quiet and calm down. Do you not know who you are, you evil creature? You ought not to quarrel with me or to insult my lineage, since I am born of kings and counts. But, if you examine your kinsmen, you will never be able to name your father, for you do not know him, and you will never do so. You never knew your father, and you never had a father.'

(7385–434) When the messengers, who were seeking just such a man, listened to the youths and heard the quarrel, they came to those who lived nearby to enquire about who it was who had never had a father. They replied that he had no father, nor did his mother who had carried him know who had sired him. They knew nothing about his father, but he did have a mother whom they knew. She was the daughter of the king of Demetia, which was part of Wales. She was a nun who lived a very good life in an abbey in the town. Then they went to the provost,* and asked that, on behalf of the king, Merlin, who had never had a father, should be brought to the king, along with his mother. The provost had no wish to refuse, and he had them both taken to the king. The king received them warmly and spoke to them in pleasing fashion:

'My lady,' said the king, 'tell me the truth. I cannot know, except through you, who sired your son Merlin. The nun bowed her head, and when she had thought for a short while she said:

'So help me God, I never knew, or saw, who sired this youth. I never heard, and never knew, whether it was a man with whom I had him. But I did know in truth, and I know it now, and in truth I will confess it, that when I was fairly well grown—I do not know if it was a vision—something would often come and embrace me tightly. I heard him speak like a man and I felt him as a man. He communicated with me many times without ever revealing himself to me. He approached me so often in this way and went on embracing me so frequently and for so long, that he lay with me and I conceived. I have never known another man. I had this youth and I still have him. There was nothing more to it, so I shall say nothing more.'

(7435–78) Then the king had Marcie come forward, who was a very learned cleric, and he asked him whether what the nun had described was feasible.

'We have found in writing', he said, 'that a type of spirit exists between the moon and the earth. For those enquiring about their nature, it is in part human and in part supernatural. They have the name 'incubi'.* They have their own realm throughout the air, and they have their own abode on earth. They cannot do a great deal of evil. They cannot create a great deal of harm, except for mockery and derision. They easily take on human shape, and their nature is very suitable for this purpose. They have deceived many a maiden and violated her like this. Merlin could have been born in this way and sired in this way.'

'King,' said Merlin, 'you have summoned me. What do you want with me, and why have you done this?'

'Merlin,' said the king, 'you shall soon know this. You wish to hear it, and you will do so. I have started to build a tower and I have put in place stone and mortar. But whatever work I have done during the day is swallowed up in the ground and it sinks down inside. I do not know whether you have heard of this, but I cannot do enough work during the day without it being swallowed up during the night. I have already wasted a great deal of my own money. My soothsayers say that, because you were born without a father, I shall never complete my tower unless your blood is placed inside it.'

'May it never please God', said Merlin, 'that your tower should remain upright because of my blood. If you bring before me all those who have made prophecies with regard to my blood, I shall prove them to be liars. They were liars and they lied.'

(7479–506) The king sent for them and had them come to Merlin. When he had looked at them, he said:

'My lords, you who are doing the prophesying, say what is happening, and why it comes about that this construction is not holding firm. If you cannot reply to me and say why the tower sinks, how can you prophesy that it could remain standing because of my blood? Say what there is in the foundations that explains why the tower collapses so often, and then say what it will take to make it hold firm. If you do not provide an explanation of why the tower falls, how will it be credible that because of my blood it will be more stable? Tell the king what the obstruction is, and then explain what needs to be done about it.' All the soothsayers fell silent, not knowing what to say to him.

'Lord king,' said Merlin, 'listen. Beneath the tower, in the foundations, there is a large, broad pool through which your tower sinks into the ground. So that you are absolutely clear about what I am saying, have the ground excavated and see.'

(7507–42) The king had this done, and he found the pool that Merlin referred to.

'My lords,' said Merlin, 'listen. You who had me sought out in order to mingle my blood in the mortar, say what is in this pool.' They were all silent and dumb. They did not say anything at all, good or bad. Merlin turned to the king and called upon him in the hearing of his men:

MERLIN PROPHESIES TO VORTIGERN (BUT WACE DECLINES TO INCLUDE THE BULK OF THE PROPHECIES)

HAVE this pool drained', he said, 'and emptied through channels. At the bottom there are two sleeping dragons, who are lying in two hollow stones. One of the dragons is completely white, and the other is as red as blood.' When the water was dispersed and had completely flowed through the channels, two dragons sprang out of the depths and attacked each other ferociously. They fought with one another with great ferocity, so that all the barons could see them. You would have easily seen them foaming at the mouth and with flames spewing from their jaws. The king sat down next to the pool. He begged Merlin to tell him the meaning of the dragons, who were fighting each other so angrily. Then Merlin told him about the prophecies you have heard, I believe, concerning the kings who were to come and who were to rule the land. I do not intend to translate his book since I cannot interpret it. I would not wish to say anything that was not the way it would come about.

(7543–82) The king praised Merlin warmly and regarded him as a fine soothsayer. He asked him when he himself would die and what sort of death it would be, because he was frightened of how he would end up.

'Beware,' said Merlin, 'beware of the fire coming from the children of Constantine, for through their fire you will meet your end. They have already set off from Armorica and are sailing with great vigour over the sea. I can make you certain of this: they will reach Totnes tomorrow. You have done harm to them and they will do harm to you. They will exact severe vengeance on you. Your act of wickedness was to betray their brother. Your wickedness made you king, and your wickedness brought pagans and Saxons to this country. Misfortunes await you on both sides. I do not know which of the two you should guard against first. On one side the Saxons, who would gladly destroy you, are making war against you. On the other side come the heirs who want to possess this kingdom. They want to make a claim for Britain and to avenge their brother Constant. So if you can flee, then flee, for both of these brothers are on their way. Aurelius will be the first to be king, and he will be the first to die, through poison. Uther Pendragon, his brother, will rule the region next. But very soon he will fall ill and be poisoned by your heirs. His son, who is from Cornwall and is as fierce as a boar in battle, will annihilate the traitors and destroy all your kinsmen. He will be valiant and brave, and he will defeat all his enemies.'*

THE BRITONS MAKE AURELIUS AMBROSIUS THEIR KING

(7583–640) MERLIN finished speaking and Vortigern left. Next day, with no delay, the brothers' fleet arrived with knights and equipment in Dartmouth at Totnes. Lo, the Britons, reinforced by these newcomers, were happy and joyful. They were now gathered together, whereas hitherto they had been widely dispersed. Hengist had made these men hide and flee into woods and mountains, destroying them with knives and by using trickery. The Britons gathered together, and they made Aurelius their king and lord. Vortigern, who heard about this situation, was in Wales and he equipped himself. In a castle named Genoire he went to seek protection with his most valiant men. Genoire was near the Wye, a swift-flowing river; the locals call it Wye and the region is called Hergrin. It was on top of a mountain, named Cloart;* that is what those who live there call it. Vortigern equipped himself greatly with arms, provisions, and men. If by so doing he could have escaped, this would have been very successful. The brothers took their men and went in search of Vortigern until they besieged him in a castle, where they shot many arrows and darts at him. They were keen to capture him, for they had a profound hatred for him. If the brothers hated him, Vortigern had richly deserved this. He had killed their brother Constant, and before that their father Constantine, through the use of trickery, and not through his own bare hands, in such a way that everyone knew this to be the case. Eldulf, the count of Gloucester, who had a thorough knowledge of the Welsh, became a vassal of Aurelius and he accompanied him into the host.

'Eldulf,' said Aurelius, 'in God's name, have you already forgotten my father, who raised you and gave you a fief, and my brother, who loved you very much? They both honoured you, trusted you deeply and loved you greatly. Through the ruse employed by this scoundrel, this perjurer, this tyrant, they were killed. They would still be living if they had not perished because of his deceit. If these men caused you sorrow, take vengeance on Vortigern.'

(7641–78) As a result of this advice alone, they all armed themselves at the same time. They brought and gathered together materials and wood with which they filled a large ditch. Then they set fire to the material they had assembled. The fire caught hold of the castle, from where it spread to the tower and the surrounding dwellings. Then the castle could have been seen burning, flames shooting into the air, and dwellings toppling. The king was burnt, as were those who were accompanying them and had sought refuge with him. When the new king had been victorious and taken the country for himself, he said he would attack the pagans and liberate the land. Hengist was aware of this and he was very fearful. He made his way towards Scotland, abandoning the whole of the remaining territory and fleeing beyond the Humber. For those in Scotland should provide him with succour, help, and reinforcements. If a serious crisis developed, he could make his way into Scotland. Day after day the king led his troops in that direction, and the Britons constantly increased in number and came to him with such density that no one could count them any more than the sand on the shore. The king found the land completely ravaged, and he saw that no one was working it. He saw castles and cities destroyed, towns burnt, and churches pillaged. The pagans had been driven out and not in any way spared. He promised everyone compensation, providing that he returned safe and sound.

(7679–702) Hengist knew that the king was coming and that he would not turn away without doing battle. He wanted to comfort his companions and inspire courage in them:

'Barons,' he said, 'do not fear this wretched company of men. You know very well that they are Britons and that they will never withstand you. If you can hold out against them a little, you will never again see them oppose you. On many occasions you have conquered and destroyed them with very few men. If they have a large number of troops, why does this matter to you? The number of their troops is of no consequence. A company that has a feeble and foolish commander is scarcely to be feared. One has no need to be afraid of a miserable race of people with no lord to lead them. Their leader is a child who cannot yet bear arms, whereas we are good fighters and are proven in many a battle. Let us lay down our lives to defend ourselves, for there is no other form of ransom.'

(7703–36) Hengist ceased his exhortation. He had all his knights armed, and swiftly and secretly he rode to attack the Britons. He expected to find them unarmed, and he thought he would defeat them all. But the Britons, who feared the pagans, were armed day and night. When the king [Aurelius] knew that they were coming, and that they intended to enter into combat, he led his men and drew them up into a field that seemed appropriate and organized them. Over to one side, he had mount their horses three thousand armed knights, whom he had brought from overseas and who were all considered to be excellent vassals. From the Welsh he created two companies. One of them he had position itself in the mountains, so that the pagans could not climb up and reach it, however great their need. He had the other company take up position in the woods, guarding the entrance to them, so that the pagans could not force their way in without being killed by the Welsh. The remainder of the troops he made come down into the battlefield and take up their position there and defend themselves well. When he had made all his preparations, according to the advice he had been given, he took up his position with those he knew to be the most loyal to him. He fixed his standard next to him, and his men came close to it and clung on to it. Count Eldulf was at his side, as well as a good many of the other barons.

(7737–74) 'O God,' said Eldulf, 'I would be so delighted if I could see the time when I could get to Hengist. Then I could have a clear memory that near to Amesbury he killed the entire flower of our kingdom, on the first day of May, when I only just managed to escape.'

At these words spoken by Eldulf, who was lamenting about what Hengist had done, lo, Hengist suddenly arrived in the camp and occupied a large amount of it. They did not delay long before engaging in battle. As soon as they had set eyes on each other, they charged at one another. Then you would have seen men fighting and assailing each other, with one side attacking and the other defending. Great blows were being received and great blows were dealt, with some knocking others down and the living striding over the dead. Shields were shattered and lances smashed, the wounded were falling down and the fallen were dying. The pagans fought very well, but the Christians fought a good deal better. The pagans called upon their false gods, and the Christians invoked God. They made their troops disperse and caused them to abandon the field. Receiving huge and hefty blows, they were forced to turn their backs. When Hengist saw his men turning round and exposing their backs to the blows, he came spurring up to Conisbrough, thinking he could find support there. But the king continued to pursue him, yelling out to his men 'Forward! Forward!'

(7775–824) When Hengist saw that they were pursuing him, and that they would be besieging him in the castle, he preferred to fight outside and take a risk with his own person rather than letting them besiege him in the castle, since he had no hope of succour there. He withdrew his men and reorganized them, sending them back to the fight. Lo, the battle began anew. It was a harsh combat and a grievous battle. The pagans had turned round, and each emboldened the other. The Christians thus experienced losses and the pagans captured a large number of them, because the Christians fought in disorderly fashion. But the three thousand men on horseback arrived in battle order, and they helped and supported them. The pagans fought very fiercely, and no wonder for they well knew that they would not escape with their lives unless they could defend themselves. Eldulf saw Hengist and recognized him. He hated him, and had good cause to do so. He saw at once the time and opportunity to fulfil his desire, and with his sword drawn he ran forward and attacked him. But Hengist was strong and he withstood the blow. Suddenly, the two men were joined in battle with their swords bare and their shields raised. You could have very clearly seen their blows increasing, and sparks flying, from the steel of their swords. Gorlois, the count of Cornwall, entered the battle like a brave man. Eldulf saw him approach and he became more confident and more fearsome. Like a truly courageous man, he ran to grab Hengist by the nosepiece. Pulling him towards him, and making him fall forward, he led him away forcibly.

'Knights,' he said, 'thanks be to God, I have fulfilled my desire. We have captured and conquered the man who has inflicted much harm on us. Kill this mad dog, who never showed us any pity. He was the cause of the war that has ravaged our land. Once you have killed this man, you hold victory in your hands.'

(7825–76) Then Hengist's punishment was administered. Bound and in chains, he was handed over to King Aurelius. He was confined and closely guarded. His son Octa, who was on the battlefield, together with his cousin Ebissa, only just managed to escape. They entered York and fortified the inside of the city, deploying as many men as they had available. Many others took flight, some going into the woods, some on to the plain, and some into the valleys or mountains. The king was delighted by this glorious victory that God had given him. He went into Conisbrough and stayed there for three full days in order to have the wounded taken care of and to allow the weary to rest. Meanwhile, he spoke to the barons and asked them all what they wanted him to do with the traitor Hengist, whether he should hold on to him or kill him. Eldadus, the younger brother of Count Eldulf, got to his feet. He was a devout bishop and very knowledgeable in letters:

'I want', he said, 'to do to Hengist, this traitor, this enemy, what Samuel did long ago to King Agag, when he was captured. Agag was very arrogant and a vainglorious king of the Amalekites. He was constantly waging war on the Jews, doing them harm and acting maliciously against them. He plundered and burnt their lands, very frequently killing them. Agag, to his misfortune, was captured and defeated. He was taken before Saul, who was at that time the crowned king. When Saul asked what he should do with Agag, who had been handed over to him, Samuel, a holy prophet of Israel, stood up. Never had anyone in his lifetime been known to be of greater holiness. This Samuel seized Agag and tore him to pieces. He completely tore him to shreds and scattered his body throughout the region. Do you know what Samuel was saying when he was tearing Agag apart?

(7877–94) '"Agag, you have harassed many men, you have killed many, and you have banished many. You have drawn many souls out of their bodies, brought grief to many mothers and turned many children into orphans. But you have now come to your end. I am going to make your mother childless, and I shall separate the soul from your body." You ought to do with this man what Samuel did with that one.'

In view of the example Eldadus had given, Eldulf darted forward and took hold of Hengist. He took him outside the town and withdrawing his sword he beheaded him. The king had the body prepared, buried, and placed in the ground in the same way as those who maintained the pagan faith used to do.

(7895–928) The king behaved decisively and did not remain there for long. He came to York with a large host and surrounded the enemy closely. Hengist's son Octa was inside, along with a group of his kinsmen. Octa saw that he would have no assistance and would not be able to defend himself. He made up his mind to surrender. He would venture forth and beg him for mercy very humbly. If he was granted it, he would be happy. He did as he had decided, and his kinsmen praised him. He emerged from the city on foot, as did all his men. Octa, who was the first to come to the king, was holding an iron chain.

'My lord,' he said, 'mercy, mercy! All the gods in whom we trusted have failed us. Your god has greater power. He works miracles and great wonders that through you have defeated us all. I am defeated and I come to ask for mercy. Take this chain that I am holding, and with me do whatever you wish, and likewise with my men. We have placed our lives and our limbs at your pleasure. But if you were to spare our lives, you would have great service from us. We shall serve you loyally and become your vassals.'

(7929–62) The king was a man of great compassion. He looked round him to find out what the barons had to say and what advice they would give him. Like a wise man, Eldadus, the good clergyman, spoke:

'It is right,' he said, 'and it was right, and it will be right, that he who seeks mercy should have mercy, for he who does not grant mercy to someone else will not himself receive mercy from God. These men are seeking mercy from you. They want mercy and should have mercy. Britain, which is long and broad, is deserted in many places. Have a section of it handed over to them and make them plough it and work it. Then they will live off their own cultivation of the land. But, first, take some good hostages, who will serve you with loyalty and fight loyally. Long ago, when the Jews conquered them, the Gibeonites sought mercy. They sought it and found it, and the Jews set them free. We ought not to act in a fashion that is worse than what the Jews did in those days. They begged for mercy and received mercy. Henceforth, let them not die.' As Eldadud advised him, the king gave them land to work, near to Scotland. Thus, they went to reside there, but first they handed over hostages, who were children of their finest families.

(7963–89) He then stayed in the town for fifteen days. He summoned his men and held council. He summoned his barons, his clerics, his abbots, and his bishops. He gave them back their fiefs and their jurisdiction. Then he ordered and established that the churches the pagans had destroyed would be rebuilt. He broke up his army and created sheriffs and stewards, who would restore his domains to him and look after his revenues. He had masons sought, and carpenters, who rebuilt the churches. Throughout the land, the king had the churches restored that had been destroyed in the war in order that they could serve and worship God. From there he set off for London, where he was greatly desired. He saw that the city had deteriorated immensely and that it was bereft of good citizens. Its dwellings had been laid waste and its churches had collapsed. He grieved over this many a time and had the churches rebuilt and the clerics and townspeople brought back home, to live according to the customs as they used to be.

(7990–8024) Then the king came to Winchester. As he had done earlier, he rebuilt churches, dwellings, and towers. Then he went to Amesbury to visit the graves in which those who had been killed by knives had been buried. He summoned a large number of masons, skilled engineers, and carpenters. He wanted the spot that marked the slaughter that Hengist had perpetrated so treacherously to be honoured by a monument that would survive forever. Tremorius, a wise man, who was archbishop of Caerleon, asked him to summon Merlin and to carry out the work according to his counsel. No one would give him better advice concerning what he wished to do, for no one could find his equal with regard to deeds or to prophecy. The king was very keen to see Merlin, and he wanted to listen to his wise words. He had him summoned from Labanes, a fountain in Wales that was a good distance away; I do not know where it is because I have never visited it. He came to the king, who had summoned him, and the king honoured him greatly. He received him with great dignity, honouring him greatly and cherishing him greatly. He begged him and beseeched him fervently to indicate to him and tell him about the time that was to come. He was very anxious to hear this through him.

(8025–78) 'My lord,' said Merlin, 'I shall not do this. I shall not open my mouth unless it is absolutely necessary, and then only with great humility. If I were to speak boastfully, scornfully, or arrogantly, the spirit I possess, through whom I know what I know, would depart from my mouth, and my knowledge would go with it. My mouth would no longer utter any more than anyone else's. Leave the divine mysteries alone and think about what you are obliged to do. If you wish to build something that will last, something that is very beautiful and appropriate, and something that people will talk about forever, have brought here the Dance that the giants created* in Ireland. This is a remarkable and extensive structure, with stones arranged in a ring and placed one on top of the other. Such are the stones, so numerous are they and so enormous and heavy, that no man alive is strong enough to lift any of them.'

'Merlin,' said the king, laughing, 'seeing that the stones weigh so much that no one could move them, who could bring them here to me? As if we had in this kingdom a lack of stones!'

'King,' said Merlin, 'do you not know that ingenuity surpasses strength? Force is good, but ingenuity is better. Ingenuity works where force fails. Ingenuity and skill accomplish many things in which force does not dare to begin. Ingenuity can move the stones, and through ingenuity you can have them. They were brought from Africa; that is where they were first fashioned. Giants, who carried them from there, brought them to Ireland. They were very efficacious and very helpful to the sick. People used to wash them and pour the water into their baths. Those who were sick, and suffering from some infirmity, created baths out of the cleansing waters. They bathed themselves and were cured. Whatever the infirmity they were experiencing, they never looked for any other medicine.'

AURELIUS WANTS TO BUILD A MONUMENT; UTHER HIS BROTHER AND MERLIN GO TO IRELAND TO BRING BACK THE STONES

(8079–124) WHEN the king and the Britons knew that the stones were worth so much, they were all delighted, and everyone had a great desire to go and fetch the Dance, of which Merlin had spoken so highly. Together they selected Uther, as he had offered to go to Ireland, taking there fifteen thousand armed men, who would do battle with the Irish if they denied them the stones. Merlin would go along with them and devise a plan to move the stones. When Uther had summoned his men, they crossed the sea to Ireland. Gilloman, who was king, summoned his men and his Irish troops. He began to threaten the Britons, as he wanted to drive them out of the country. When he found out what they wanted, that they had come for the stones, he repeatedly mocked them, saying that those who had crossed the sea to another land in search of stones were acting foolishly. They would never have a single stone, he said, and would never take one away. He could easily pour scorn on them, but they were hard to defeat. He scorned, threatened, and sought them out until he found them. They clashed immediately and dealt blows against each other. The Irish were not well armed, nor were they accustomed to fighting. They had scorned the Britons, but the Britons defeated them. The king took flight, going from town to town. When the Britons had disarmed and had had a thorough rest, Merlin, who was in the company, led them to a mountain, where the Giants' Dance, which they had been looking for, was situated.

(8125–50) The mountain was called Killomar and the Dance was situated at the top. They looked at the stones and frequently went round them. They said to each other that they had never seen such a structure.

'How were these stones raised up, and how could they be removed?'

'My lords,' said Merlin, 'see if, using the strength you have, you can move these stones, and if you can carry them.' They took hold of the stones, behind, in front, and laterally. They shoved hard, thrust hard, and pushed hard without ever succeeding through strength in making them budge to the slightest extent.

'Get up,' said Merlin, 'strength will not improve things. Now you will see ingenuity and skill superseding bodily strength.' Then he moved forward and sat down. He looked round and moved his lips, like a man who was saying a prayer. I do not know whether or not this was what he was doing.

(8151–78) Then he called to the Britons:

'Come forward,' he said, 'come forward. Now you can take hold of the stones, carry them and load them on to your ships.' As Merlin indicated, stated, and devised, the Britons took hold of the stones, carried them to the ships and placed them inside.

They took them to England, carrying them to Amesbury and putting them into the countryside nearby. The king came there at

Pentecost and summoned all his bishops, abbots, and barons. He also gathered together there many other troops, and he held a celebration and was crowned. For three days he held a great celebration, and after careful consideration on the fourth day he handed over crosses to St Dubric of Caerleon and St Samson of York. Both were men of great learning, and both lived a very holy life. Merlin lifted the stones and arranged them in order. The Britons are used to calling them in the British language the Giants' Dance. In English they have the name Stonehenge, and in French they are called Pierres Pendues [Hanging Stones].

(8179–214) When the great celebration was over, the king's court dispersed. Paschent, one of Vortigern's sons, fled towards Germany for fear of Ambrosius and Uther, abandoning Wales and Britain. He sought men and ships, but he did not have a large company. He arrived in the north of Britain, destroyed towns and laid lands waste, yet he did not dare stay there for long, for the king came and drove him away. When Paschent was at sea, he did not dare to go back to where he had come from. He went on sailing and rowing until he landed in Ireland. He spoke to the king of that land, explaining his situation and his needs. Paschent begged the king so much, and they discussed the matter so much, that they agreed to cross the sea and do battle with the Britons. Paschent did this in order to avenge his father and claim his inheritance, and the king so that he could seek vengeance over those who had recently defeated him, robbed his people, and taken away the Dance. They both made a pact to seek vengeance for the two of them. With all the forces they could muster they crossed the sea when the wind was favourable Arriving in Wales, they all entered Menevia. At that time this was a beautiful city, and it is now called Saint David's.

(8215–50) King Ambrosius was lying sick. He was in Winchester, where he was languishing in bed. He was ill and lay for a long time without either getting better or dying. When he heard about Paschent, and also about the king of Ireland, who had arrived in Wales intending to lay waste his land, he sent his brother Uther there. He was not able to go himself, and this distressed him. He told Uther that he should find them and do battle with them. Uther summoned his barons and all his knights. Partly because of the length of the journey, and partly because of the time it took to gather the men, he was considerably delayed and took a long time to reach Wales. While he was tarrying, Eappas spoke to Paschent. Born in Saxony, he was a very wise pagan. He knew a great deal about medicines and was able to speak many languages. But he was also wicked and of bad faith.

'Paschent,' he said to him in private, 'you have hated the king for a long time. What will you give me if I kill him?'

'I shall give you a thousand pounds,' he said, 'and I shall never let you down if you do what you say, and the king is killed by you.'

'I do not ask for anything more,' he said. Thus, they made their agreement: Paschent to give him a thousand pounds, and he to poison the king.

(8251–84) Eappas was very skilful, and he longed for the money. He dressed in monkish clothes, had his head shaved, and gave himself the tonsure. Shaven and tonsured, he dressed like a monk, and with a monkish demeanour he went to the royal court. He was a trickster and pretended he was a doctor. He spoke to the king and promised to make him well again in a short time, if he were willing to put himself in his hands. He felt the king's pulse and examined his urine, saying that he knew what the problem was and what medicine to give him. Who would have doubted such a man? The noble king wanted to get better, as we would all wish to do. Not suspecting any treason, he placed himself in this wicked man's hands. He gave him a potion mixed with poison. Then he had him wrapped up warm, and he made him lie down peacefully and go to sleep. As soon as the king warmed up, the poison entered his body. O God, what pain! All he could do was to die. But when he knew that he was going to die, he told his men, who were taking care of him, in accordance with the true love they had for him, to take him to Stonehenge and bury him there. There he died. There he came to his end. The traitor fled.

(8285–320) Uther had gone into Wales, where he came across the Irish at Menevia. Then a star appeared that was observed by many people. According to the clergy, it was called a comet, and it signified a change of king. It was remarkably bright, but it cast out just one ray. A flame that emerged from this ray had the shape of a dragon, and from its mouth there appeared two rays. One of them stretched over the whole of France, and it shone as far as Montgieu. The other was projected towards Ireland, and it was separated out into seven rays that shone clearly over land and sea. When they saw such a sign, the people were very agitated. Uther wondered at it, and he was exceedingly troubled by it. He begged Merlin to tell him the meaning of such a sign. But Merlin was greatly disturbed. There was sorrow in his heart, and he did not utter a word. When he got his breath back, he lamented greatly and sighed deeply:

'O God,' he said, 'what great sorrow, what great harm, what a great outpouring of tears has befallen Britain today, which has lost its fine leader. The king is dead, the good vassal who has freed this land from sorrow and great harm. He liberated it from the hands of the pagans.'

(8321–44) When Uther heard what had happened to his brother, the good lord, who had come to his end, he was greatly distressed and dismayed. But Merlin comforted him in these terms:

'Uther,' he said, 'do not be dismayed. There is no escape from death. Accomplish what you have set out to do and do battle with your enemies. Victory over the king of Ireland, and over Paschent, awaits you tomorrow. Fight tomorrow and you will win and become king of Britain. For us the sign of the dragon signifies you, who are brave and bold. One of the rays is a son you will have, who will possess great power and conquer all the land beyond France. Through the other ray, which diverged here and separated into seven rays, a daughter is signified. She will be married in Scotland. Many good heirs will be born from her, and they will conquer lands and seas.'

(8345–86) That night, when Uther had heard Merlin's comforting words, he had his men rest, and in the morning he armed them. He wanted to attack the city, but the Irish, who saw him coming, took up their arms, made their preparations, and emerged to do battle. They fought fiercely, but they were very soon defeated, for the Britons killed Paschent, and also the king of Ireland. Those who remained alive on the battlefield turned round and fled towards their ships. Uther, who came up behind them, forced them to die unshriven. There were some who escaped from there and who fled to their ships. They dashed out to sea, so that Uther could not get to them. When he had completed his business, he made his way back to Winchester, along with the finest of his men. As he made his way there, he encountered a messenger, who told him truthfully that the king was dead, and he explained how this had happened. The bishops had constructed a tomb with great care inside the Giants' Dance, as he had requested during his lifetime of his men-at-arms and barons. When Uther heard this news, he went spurring to Winchester. The people came to meet him, yelling and crying with one voice:

'Uther, lord, in God's name, have mercy! The man has died who has supported us, and from whom we have benefited greatly. Support us now, take the crown as it is given to you, by right and by inheritance. We, fair lord, beg you to do this, and we want what is advantageous and honourable for you.'

(8387–406) Uther saw that this was to his advantage and that he could not do any better. He was delighted by what they had said, and he immediately did what they wanted him to do. He took the crown and became king, delighting in the honour and protecting the people. In honour and memory of the dragon, which was the sign that he was brave, that he would be king, and that he would have heirs who would be successful conquerors, Uther had two dragons made out of gold on the advice of his barons. He carried one of them in front of him when he was on the point of engaging into battle. The other he gave to the bishop's church in Winchester. Ever since, for this reason, he was called Uther Pendragon. The British name Pendragon is equivalent to Dragon's Head in French.

(8407–54) When Octa, who was Hengist's son, and someone to whom the king had given extensive lands and huge dwellings, both to him and to his companions, heard that the man who had supported a large number of troops was dead, he had little regard for the new king. He was not bound to him by oath or faith. He gathered together allies and kinsmen, along with his cousin Eosa. These two had control over everyone, and they were the bravest of them all. The troops Paschent had brought, who had escaped from Uther, were retained for the help they could offer; they formed a huge body of men. They captured the entire land from one end to the other, broad and long, just where the Humber divides it, up towards Scotland. Then they went to York and launched an attack on it from all sides, but those inside defended themselves so that the pagans took nothing from there. But the enemy had a great many men and they besieged them. Uther wanted to rescue his city and to help his allies who were inside. Summoning his men from all parts, he came at top speed to York. He wanted to make the pagans abandon the siege, so he went to strike them straightaway. The combat was harsh and grievous, and many a soul was separated from its body. The pagans possessed great strength, and they supported each other very well. The Britons could scarcely inflict any harm on them, nor could they force a way in amongst them. They had to pull back and withdraw, and when they wanted to depart those in the siege pursued them, inflicting intense harm on them. Catching up with them from time to time, they followed them to a mountain, and then night caused them to disperse. The name of the mountain was Danien and it was somewhat steep at the top. There were rocks and narrow passages there, with dense hazel-thickets all round.

(8455–504) The Britons reached the mountain, some climbing straight to the top and some tackling it from the sides. They took over the entire hill, and the pagans, who were down on the plain, besieged them. They positioned themselves round the mountain. The king was very frightened, both for his men and for himself, and he was uncertain about what they should do, and about how they could escape. Gorlois, count of Cornwall, who was a very brave, very wise, and very courtly man, was with the king. A man well on in years, he was regarded as very learned. They asked him for advice, handing the responsibility for their situation over to him, for he would not have behaved in a cowardly fashion, even if it had cost him life or limb.

'You ask me for my advice,' he said. 'My advice is, if you want it, that we arm ourselves secretly and go down this hill. Let us go and strike our enemies, who think they are sleeping peacefully. They are not fearful or worried that we could ever launch an attack against them with our lances. They expect to capture us in the morning if we wish to wait for them here. Let us approach them secretly, and all of a sudden strike every single one of them. It will be in vain if they try to maintain order, sound their horns, or let out a battle-cry. Before they are awake, we shall have cut so many of them to pieces that not one of those who survive will ever withstand us again. But first let us promise God that we shall make amends to him, and that we shall seek penance and pardon for the sins we have committed. Let us abandon our wicked deeds, which we have performed all our lives, and pray to the Saviour that he should uphold us and inspire us in our fight against those who do not believe in him and who fight against Christians. Thus, God will be with us and we shall be saved by him. As soon as God is with us, who could possibly defeat us?'

(8505–40) As a result of the advice he gave them, and as he said and recommended, they promised God humbly that they would live better lives. Then they armed themselves, and in secret came down the slope. They found the pagans lying down, unarmed and fast asleep. Then you would have seen a remarkable number of men slaughtered and put to the sword, bellies pierced, chests staved in, heads, feet, and hands flying about. Just as a proud lion that has been hungry for a long time kills sheep and ewes, large and small animals, in the same way the Britons acted, killing the rich and the poor. Throughout the meadows they were slumbering and they were so startled that at no time had they any chance to don their armour or to get away. Since they found them without armour, the Britons slaughtered them. They pierced their bellies and innards, dragging forth bowels and entrails. The lords who had set the war in motion, Octa and Eosa, were captured. They were sent to London and placed in chains in a prison. If anyone escaped from the battlefield, the dark night saved him. Those who could flee fled, without waiting for an ally. But many more were killed than escaped alive.

(8541–78) When Uther had left there, he passed through Northumbria, and from there he went to Scotland, with a large number of household troops and warriors. He surrounded the whole area, from one end to another. All those people who had no one to govern them were all brought into his service. He instilled such a sense of peace throughout the whole kingdom that no one had ever created one so complete. When he had dealt with matters in the north, he set off back to London. Easter Day was approaching on which he wanted to have himself crowned. Dukes, counts, and castellans, the furthest away and the closest, and all his other barons, he summoned by letter and message to be in London with their wedded wives and private households at the celebration, for he wanted to have an extensive celebration. Everyone he summoned came, and those with wives brought them. The festival was celebrated well, and when mass was over the king sat at dinner on a dais at the head of the table. The barons sat all round, each one according to his status. In front of him, clearly visible, sat the count of Cornwall, and beside him was his wife; there was no more beautiful woman in the entire kingdom. She was courtly, beautiful, and wise, and a woman of great breeding. The king had heard talk of her, and he had heard her greatly praised.

(8579–618) Before he gave any sign of it, indeed before he had even seen her, he felt love for her and desired her, for she was exceedingly praised. The king stared at her throughout the meal and turned his attention to her. If she ate, if she drank, if she spoke, he thought about her constantly and looked across at her. As he looked at her, he smiled and made her aware of his love. Through his close advisers he greeted her and had presents sent to her on his behalf. He smiled at her warmly and winked at her, giving her many signs of his affection. In this matter, Ygerne's behaviour was such that she neither accepted nor refused his attentions. With jokes, smiles, and signs, and with greetings and presents, the count fully realized that the king loved his wife, and that he would never be faithful to him if he were able to have her at his pleasure. He jumped up from the table where he was sitting, took his wife, and departed. He called for his companions, went to the horses, and mounted. The king called him back, saying that he was acting in a shameful and wretched fashion in leaving his court without permission. He should do what is right and proper towards him and return. If he failed to do this, he would issue a challenge against him, wherever he might go, and he would never be able to trust in him again. But the count refused to return and left the court without permission. The king threatened him severely, but the count had little regard for these threats. At that time, he did not know what was going to happen next.

(8619–48) The count went back to Cornwall, where he had two castles, and he fortified them. He placed his wife at Tintagel, which had belonged to his brother and his grandfather. Tintagel was easy to defend, and it could not be taken by any ruse, as it was enclosed by cliffs and the sea. Anyone guarding the gate alone would be wrong to have any worries or concerns that the enemy could enter any other way. Thus, Ygerne was confined by the count. There was nowhere else he dared put her in order to prevent her from being taken away or abducted. For that reason he placed her in Tintagel, and he took his men-at-arms and most of his knights to another castle he held, which guarded the majority of his domains. The king was aware that he had been taking on reinforcements and that he would defend himself against him. Partly in order to wage war against the count, and partly to get closer to the countess, he summoned his men from all parts and crossed over the river Tamar. He came to the castle where the count was, with the intention of capturing it, but the count held tight. The king laid siege for a week without being able to capture the castle. Nor was the count willing to surrender, for he was awaiting the king of Ireland, who was to come and assist him.

(8649–80) The king hated the delay and it started to trouble him. Love for Ygerne was pressing hard upon him, for he loved her above all else. Privately he summoned Ulfin, one of his closest barons, saying to him:

'Ulfin, advise me. I am reliant on you for advice. Love for Ygerne has overwhelmed me. It has completely defeated me, it has completely conquered me. I cannot go, I cannot come. I cannot remain awake, I cannot sleep. I cannot get up, I cannot lie down. I cannot drink, and I cannot eat without having her in my thoughts. But I do not know how to get possession of her. I am dead if you do not advise me.'

'What I hear now', said Ulfin, 'is a wonder. You have inflicted harm on the count in war, ravaged his land, and confined him in his castle. Do you believe that this is pleasing to his wife? You are in love with her, and yet you make war on him. I do not know what advice would enable you to have her. I do not know what advice to give you. Ask for Merlin, who is imbued with many arts and has come here to this host. If he does not know what advice to give you, no one can set you on the right road.'

UTHER FALLS HOPELESSLY IN LOVE WITH YGERNE

On Ulfin's advice the king had Merlin summoned and come to him. He explained to him the critical situation, begging him, crying for mercy, asking for his advice, if he could give it, for without comfort he would of necessity die if he did not have his way with Ygerne. He should do his very best to let him have her. If he were willing to do this, he would receive a reward from him, for he was experiencing great harm and great sorrow.

(8681–736) 'My lord,' said Merlin, 'you will have her. Ygerne will never be the cause of your death. I shall bring it about that you can have what you want, and it would be wrong for you to give me any part of your wealth or your possessions. But Ygerne is closely guarded and confined within Tintagel, which is so strong that it will not be captured or taken by any troops. The entrance and the exit can be defended by two good men, but I shall get you inside, using new medicines. I know how to change a man's shape, to change one person into another, to make one person seem like another, and one look like another. The body, the face and the demeanour, and also the speech and the likeness belonging to the count of Cornwall I shall make you assume without fail. Why should I give you a lengthy account of this? I shall make you seem just like the count, and I shall go with you and take on the appearance of Bretel, and Ulfin, who will be with us, will look just like Jordan. The count holds these two men very dear as his close counsellors. In this way you can get into the castle and fulfil all your desires. You will never be recognized or taken for someone else.'

The king trusted Merlin and followed his advice fully. He secretly handed over the responsibility for his men to one of his barons. Merlin cast his spell and changed their faces and clothes. In the evening they entered Tintagel. Those who thought they recognized them welcomed them joyfully and served them with joy. The king lay with Ygerne and that night she conceived the good king, the strong, and dependable one, the one you hear called Arthur.

(8737–80) The king's men realized very quickly that their lord was not with the host. There was not a single baron who was not scared, or who did not want to take action. Fearing a delay, they took up their weapons and armed themselves. Without forming into a squadron and making preparations, they came to the castle impetuously and attacked it from all sides. The count defended himself strenuously, but in doing so he was killed, and the castle was immediately captured. Some of those who managed to escape went to Tintagel in order to announce how badly things had turned out with respect to their count, whom they had lost. Hearing the news being imparted by those who lamented the count's death, the king rose and darted forward:

'Silence,' he said, 'things are not as they seem. I am alive and well, thanks be to God, just as you can see here. This news is not accurate, so do not believe or disbelieve everything. But I shall tell you clearly why my men feared for me. I left the castle without taking leave, so that I spoke to no one. I did not say that I was going to leave, or that I was coming here to you, for I was afraid of treachery. By now they are afraid that I have been killed, because they have not seen me since the king was at the castle. The fact that my men have been killed, and that they have lost the castle, can cause great vexation for us. But for my part it is good that I am still alive. I shall emerge and talk to the king. I shall seek peace and come to an agreement before he besieges the castle, and before worse befalls us. For, if he takes us by surprise here, it will be more shameful to plead our case.'

ARTHUR IS CONCEIVED AS A RESULT OF MERLIN'S RUSE TO DISGUISE UTHER AS GORLOIS

(8781–822) YGERNE, who had always feared the king, praised this advice, and the king then embraced and kissed her when he left. Then he left the castle, having fulfilled all his desires. When the king, Ulfin, and Merlin were outside the castle, and on their way back, each of them regained his appearance so that each of them was in the form he should be in. They came swiftly to the host. The king wanted to find out why the castle had been captured so easily, and if the count were dead. There were many men who were able to relate the truth about both matters. He was, he said, saddened by what had happened to the count, and he would not have wanted this to happen. He mourned him greatly and grieved for him greatly. He was angry with his barons, and it appeared that he was very upset about it. But very few of them believed it. He returned to Tintagel and called to those inside the castle, asking them why they were defending it. The count was dead, so they should hand over the castle, since they could not expect any help from the local area, or from elsewhere. They knew that the king was telling the truth and that they had no hope of being rescued. They opened the gates of the castle and surrendered the fortress to him. The king loved Ygerne passionately and he married her without delay. That night she had conceived a son, and at the due time she gave birth to him. He name was Arthur, and because of his excellence he was later widely talked about. After Arthur, Anna was born, a girl who was given in marriage to a brave and courtly baron, whose name was Loth, from Lothian.

(8783–858) Uther reigned for a good long time, safe and sound, and peacefully. Then his strength declined, and he started to feel ill. His sickness caused him to become weak. He lay in bed for a long time and lost all his strength. The men-at-arms, who were in London in charge of the prison, were vexed by this lengthy period of guard, and as a result of his promises and his gifts, they freed Hengist's son Octa and released him from prison along with his companion Eosa.* They abandoned their custody of the prison and fled along with the prisoners. When these prisoners were back in their own regions and had assembled their forces once more, they delivered severe threats against Uther and acquired a large navy. With great bands of knights, men-at-arms, and archers, they crossed into Scotland, burning the country and laying it waste. Uther, who was sick and could not help himself, handed over the defence of his land and himself to Loth, his son-in-law, and also the responsibility for his host and for paying his knights. He told them that they should pay heed to him and do what he told them. Because he was courtly, generous, very brave, and very wise, Octa waged war against the Britons, and he had a huge number of troops and was possessed of a great deal of arrogance.

(8859–916) Partly because of the king's feebleness, and partly to avenge his father and himself, he created great consternation within Britain and refused to offer a truce or a pledge. Loth did battle with him frequently and often defeated him. Many a time he overcame him, and many a time he destroyed him, for it is customary in such matters for someone to lose and then to win. Maybe Loth could have defeated him and driven him out of the country, but the Britons were filled with arrogance and scorned his commands because they were just as noble as he was. They had just as many, even more, possessions. In this way the war lasted and grew, until the king became aware, and the inhabitants informed him, that the barons were indolent. Just hear about the audacious acts committed by this man! He was not prevented from acting in this way because of his infirmity. He did not want, he said, to fail to act. He wanted to see his men in the host. He had himself transported by horses on a bier, as it were, on a litter. Now he would see, he said, who would follow him and who would remain behind. He had summoned and called upon those who had not deigned to respond either to Loth or to his command, and they came quickly. The king came straight to Verulam, which at the time was a city; St Alban was martyred there. But later the place was ravaged, and the city was completely destroyed. Octa led his men there and positioned them in the city. The king besieged him from outside the city. He had devices built to smash down the walls, but the walls were strong and could not be damaged. Octa and his men, who defended themselves against the devices, were elated. One morning they opened the gate and emerged in order to participate in the fighting. To them it was upsetting and shameful that the gate was closed because of the king, who was fighting from a bier and participating in the battle on a bier. But their downfall was, I believe, their arrogance, and the one who should rightly conquer did so. Octa was defeated and killed, as was his brave cousin Eosa. Many of those who escaped set off towards Scotland, and they made Colgrim, who was an ally of Octa and his cousin, their lord.

(8917–50) Because of the victory and the honour that God gave the king that day he jumped from his bed in joy, as if he were hale and hearty. He began to make every effort to bring cheer to his barons. When he had risen and was standing up, he said to his men with a laugh:

'I prefer to lie on a bier and to languish with a long illness, rather than to be healthy and strong, having been defeated shamefully. It is much better to die honourably than to live dishonourably for a long time. The Saxons held me in contempt because I was lying in my bed. They mocked me extensively and said that I was half dead. But now, it appears to me, the man who is half-dead has conquered the living. Let us follow those who are taking flight and who are destroying my fief and yours.' When the king had been there for a little while and had spoken to his men, he would have gone after those who were fleeing, and he would not have failed to do this because of his illness. But the barons asked him to remain in the city until God brought him relief from his pain, for they were very fearful that he would be harmed. Thus, he did remain there, and he did not follow them. He lay on his sickbed and the host departed. He had dispatched his men, all except his personal retinue.

(8951–9004) When the Saxons who had been driven away had gathered together once more, they wrongly thought that if they had killed the king he would have no heir to harm them, or to take the land away from them. They wanted to bring about his death through poison, through venom, and through treachery, for they were not confident that they could use their weapons to kill him. They chose some evildoers; I cannot tell you who or how many. They promised them money and lands and sent them to the king's court dressed in poor garments, in order to estimate how they could get to the king and quickly murder him. Able to speak many languages, they stole round and got close to the king's court. They watched closely to see how things were in that place. But they were unable to see a way of making contact with the king. But they went to and fro until they heard and saw that the king drank cold water. He did not taste any other drink, for water was safe for his malady. He always drank from one fountain that rose from close to the hall; no other fountain pleased him so much. When those who were out to kill the king, and who wanted to murder him, saw that they would not get to him with their weapons, they poisoned the fountain. Then they fled from the region to avoid being spotted. They waited and listened in order to find out when and how the king would die, for he would soon come to his end. When the king wanted to drink, and did take a drink, he was poisoned; there was no escape from death. He drank some water and then his body swelled up. He was drained of colour and went black; he quickly died. All those who had drunk the water after the king also died, so it was known what had happened and the wicked act was recognized. The common people then gathered together, and the fountain was stopped up. They carried so much earth there that they constructed a mound on top of it.

ARTHUR IS CROWNED BY THE BRITONS AT THE AGE OF FIFTEEN

(9005–32) WHEN King Uther was dead, he was taken to Stonehenge and buried there next to his brother, side by side. The bishops called a meeting and the barons gathered together. They summoned Arthur, Uther's son, and crowned him in Silchester. He was a fifteen-year-old youth and strong and tall for his age. I shall tell you about Arthur's characteristics and not lie to you in any way. He was a very powerful knight, very highly thought of and impressive. Towards the arrogant he was arrogant, but he was tender and compassionate towards the humble. He was strong, bold, and victorious, a generous and liberal giver of gifts. If circumstances required it, and he could manage it, he would have concealed this. He loved fame and he loved glory, and he was very keen for his deeds to be remembered. He had himself served in courtly fashion and conducted himself very nobly. As long as he lived and reigned, he exceeded all other princes in courtliness, nobility, virtue, and largesse.

(9033–58) Shortly after Arthur became king, of his own volition he swore an oath that as long as the Saxons were in his kingdom he would never be at peace with them. They had killed his uncle and his father, and they harried the whole of the country. He summoned his men and sought mercenaries, giving them a great deal and promising them a great deal. He summoned so many men, and travelled so far, that he went well beyond York. Colgrim, who after Octa's death sustained and led the Saxons, was assisted by the Scots, the Picts, and a large company of Saxons. He set out to do battle with Arthur, intending to bring down his arrogance. They met at a pass near to the river Douglas.* As a result of lances, arrows, and darts, many men fell there on both sides, but in the end they were defeated and Colgrim took flight. Arthur, who pursued him, chased him into York. Colgrim entered the city and Arthur besieged him.

(9059–92) Baldulf was Colgrim's brother. On the shore he waited for Cheldric, the king of Germany. When he heard that Arthur had besieged his brother in York and that he had driven him away from the battlefield, he was grief-stricken and filled with sorrow. If he had had his way, he would have been with his brother. He ceased waiting for Cheldric and made his way to a point that was five leagues away from the host, where he lay in ambush in a thicket. Whether it was the men from his lineage, or the foreigners he had brought with him, he was accompanied by six thousand armed men. It was his intention to catch the enemy unawares at night and to make the siege disperse, but someone who spotted them lying in ambush ran to inform the king. Arthur knew that Baldulf was lying in wait, and he took advice from Cador, who was count of Cornwall and who would not have let him down even if it had cost him his life. He handed six hundred knights over to Cador and three thousand foot soldiers, and they were dispatched to where Baldulf was in hiding. The Saxons did not hear a word of this, nor did they hear any cry or noise, until Cador, who was quick to strike, sounded his battle-cry. He killed more than half of them, and he would never have let them get even a foot away from him if the night had not been dark and the wood had not impeded him.

(9093–134) Baldulf turned and fled, hiding in this bush and that. He had lost the best and the greater part of his company. He was at a loss to know how to bring assistance to his brother. He would very gladly have spoken with him if he could have done so, and if he had dared. He went to the siege as a jongleur and pretending to be a harpist. He had learnt to sing and to accompany lays and harmonies on the harp. In order to go and speak with his brother, he had his beard shaved off on one side. He also had one side of his hair cut off and he did the same for one of his side whiskers. He looked just like a scoundrel* or a fool. He put a harp over his shoulder and acted like this for some time without anyone suspecting him. Playing the harp, he went to and fro, until he got so close to the city that the watchmen on the walls recognized him and pulled him up with ropes. They were in a state of despair about how they could take flight or escape, when the news reached the tents that Cheldric had arrived at a port in Scotland with six hundred ships and was coming to the siege vigorously. But he thought and said clearly that Arthur would never wait for him, nor did he. He did not wait for him, for his allies said to him that Cheldric would not wait, nor would he do battle with him. The men with him were awesome and fierce. He should return to London, and if Cheldric followed him there Arthur would do battle with greater confidence, for he would summon his own people, since his men would get more numerous by the day.

(9135–70) Arthur accepted his barons' advice and came with them to London. Then you would have seen a land embroiled in conflict, castles defended, and people fearful. Arthur decided to send for Hoel, his nephew and his sister's son. He was king of Brittany. His kinsmen were there, his cousins, and the finest men in his lineage. He sent letters to Hoel and sought his help through a messenger. He informed him that, if he did not help him, all his land would in the end be lost, and it would bring great shame on his lineage if he lost his inheritance in this way. Aware of the critical situation, Hoel did not seek an excuse or a delay. His barons and his kinsmen swiftly prepared themselves. They quickly readied their ships and equipped them well with men and weapons. They had twelve thousand knights, besides men-at-arms and archers. They had a fair wind and they crossed the sea, docking at the port of Southampton. Arthur received them joyfully and honourably, as he should do. They did not waste any time or spend a long time in pleasant greetings. The king had his foot soldiers summoned and his household knights assembled. Silently and wordlessly, they went to gather at Lincoln, which the wicked Cheldric had besieged. But he had not yet captured it.

THE BATTLE OF LINCOLN

(9171–226) ARTHUR armed his men, and without any blowing of horns or sounding of bugles he made a sudden and swift assault on the enemy. Never did such slaughter, such terrible destruction, such devastation, or such sorrow take place as befell the Saxons on one day.

Casting away weapons and abandoning horses, they fled over mountains and over valleys. They went stumbling through rivers and a large number of them drowned. The Britons who were chasing after them gave them no chance of repose. With their swords they dealt them great blows on their bodies, heads, and shoulders. The Saxons fled as far as the Celidon Wood, withdrawing into it and making it their place of refuge. The Britons watched the wood and surrounded it completely. Arthur feared that they would escape and get out of the wood at night. So, on one side, he cut down the wood and created a very thick fence of intermingled branches, with one trunk crossing over another. He camped on the other side, and thereafter no one went in or out. Those in the wood, who could not eat or drink, were very fearful. There was no one so strong or so knowledgeable, so powerful or so rich, who could have brought into it bread or wine, or meat or corn. They had only been there for three days when they were all overcome by hunger. When they saw that they would starve to death, and that they could not force their way out, they sought advice on what agreement they could come to: they would leave behind their wealth but would retain their ships and provide the king with hostages as a guarantee of permanent loyalty to him. If he were to let them depart with their lives and take their ships away without weapons, they would also hand over to him an annual tribute. Arthur agreed to this and gave them leave to depart. He kept some men behind as hostages to ensure that his agreement would be kept, and he handed over all their ships to them, but retaining their weapons. They set sail without any booty and without any weapons.

(9227–54) When they were a long way out of sight and could no longer see land—I do not know what advice they were given or who it was who gave it to them—between England and Normandy they turned their ships round and rowed and sailed until they came to Dartmouth. They landed at the port of Totnes. Lo, how they destroyed and slaughtered people. They emerged from their ships on to land and spread throughout the whole country, looking for loot and capturing weapons. They burnt dwellings, killed people, and criss-crossed the whole of the country, capturing whatever they came across. They robbed the peasants of their weapons and in the same way killed them. They destroyed and laid waste Devonshire, Somerset, and a large part of Dorset, ravaging and laying everything waste, without finding anyone who could stand in their way. The men who could have done so to a certain degree were with the king in Scotland. As much through the countryside as along the roads, carrying booty and taking away spoils, the Saxons came to Bath, but its inhabitants held out against them.

THE BATTLE OF BATH

(9255–300) WHEN Arthur, who was in Scotland, destroying those who lived there because they had waged war against him and helped Cheldric, found out what the pagans, who were laying siege to Bath, were doing, he immediately had the hostages hanged. He had no wish to hold on to them further or to delay any longer. He left Hoel of Brittany, whom he considered to be in a sorry plight and who was lying in the city of Aclud and suffering from I know not what illness. With as many men as he had he came to Bath as soon as he could, intending to break up the siege and save his men inside. Near some woods, on a wide open plain, Arthur armed his troops. He divided up and ordered his men, then he armed himself. He had put on iron leggings, handsome and ready for purpose, and he wore a fine and well-positioned hauberk, such as was fitting for such a king. He had his sword Caliburn girt about him; it was very long and very broad, and it had been made on the isle of Avalon. Anyone who held this bare sword rejoiced greatly. On his head he had his helmet that shone so brightly. Its nosepiece at the front was made of gold, as was the circle round the helmet. It had a dragon portrayed upon it, and in the helmet were many bright stones; it had belonged to his father Uther. He rode a very fine mount that was strong, spirited, and swift, and he had his shield called Pridwen round his neck. He did not seem like a coward or a fool. Within the shield there was, skilfully placed, a portrait and likeness of the Virgin Mary in honour and remembrance of her. He had a sturdy lance called Run; at the top the iron was sharp. It was rather long and somewhat broad, and it was greatly feared when it was needed in action.

(9301–36) When Arthur had armed his men and organized his troops, he made them move along slowly. He did not want ranks to be broken until they were in a position to strike. But the Saxons could not maintain this pace. They turned towards a hill nearby and vied with each other to reach the top. There they resisted, and protected themselves very well, as if they had been surrounded by a wall. But they did not stay safe for long, since Arthur, who hated them being so close, attacked them there. He followed them up the hill and urged on his men:

'See before you', he said, 'the treacherous and the arrogant, who have entirely destroyed and driven away your kinsmen and your cousins, your allies, and your neighbours, and they have done harm to yourselves as well. Avenge your allies, your kinsmen. Avenge the losses and the torments they have inflicted on you so many times. I shall avenge their wicked acts, and I shall avenge the perjurers, and I shall avenge my ancestors, their pains and their sorrows. I shall avenge their return to Dartmouth. If we could penetrate them and knock them down from this hill, they would never hold their position against us, and they would not have any defence against us.'

(9337–404) At these words, Arthur spurred his horse, bringing his shield up to his breast. I do not know which of the Saxons he struck, thrusting him down dead on the ground. He went on past him and cried out:

'God help us, Holy Mary,' he said. 'My blow is the first. I alone have given this man his reward.' Then you would have seen the Britons joining in the combat, knocking down Saxons and smashing them to pieces. They surrounded them on all sides, hurled weapons at them, shoved them, and delivered blows against them. Arthur was a man of great ardour, of great vigour, and of great courage. With his shield raised and his sword drawn, he pushed his way upwards. He completely smashed through the throng, killing many men to the right and to the left. He himself killed four hundred of them, more than all his own men did together. He caused them to come to a sorry end. Baldulf was killed, as was Colgrim. Cheldric, along with the others, took flight, descending a slope. They wanted to get back to their ships, to board them, and to defend themselves. Arthur heard that they were fleeing and that they intended to return to their ships. He took Cador of Cornwall and sent him after the fugitives with ten thousand knights, the finest and the most agile of the men. Arthur turned towards Scotland, for a messenger came to him, informing him that the inhabitants of Scotland had besieged Hoel and almost captured him. Cheldric was fleeing in the direction of the ships, but Cador was a man of great cunning. Using a path he knew, in order to get straight to Totnes, he outstripped Cheldric and his men. He came to the ships and positioned men to guard them. He placed villeins and peasants there, and then he set off after those who were fleeing. In twos and threes they fled in order to make quicker progress. To move more nimbly, and get away more swiftly, they had cast away their weapons and they took with them only their swords. They made their way to the ships as fast as they could, for they thought that thanks to them they could escape. As they were crossing over the river Teign, Cador came towards them, shouting out his battle-cry. Lo, the Saxons, in a state of confusion, scattered in all directions. Cheldric was caught and killed as he was climbing up the mountain of Teignwic. As they arrived, the others were killed by the sword in great pain. Those who were able to escape fled on all sides to the ships, and those in the ships fired arrows at them, sending them tumbling into the sea. There were some who surrendered and there were those who killed themselves. In large groups they hid throughout the woodland and the mountains. They hid and remained there until they died of hunger and thirst.

ARTHUR HEADS TO LOCH LOMOND; THE SCOTS BEG FOR MERCY, WHICH ARTHUR GRANTS

(9405–65) WHEN Cador had finished this slaughter and made all the land peaceful, he followed Arthur and did not stop until he reached Scotland. He found Arthur at Aclud; he had been helping his nephew there. He found Hoel safe and sound, and cured of his illness. The Scots left the siege when they heard of Arthur's arrival. They fled far off to Moray and sought protection in the city.* They decided to await Arthur there and to defend themselves. Arthur knew that his opponents were assembling and joining forces against him. He followed them as far as Moray, but they had fled further on. In the lake of Lumonoi [Loch Lomond]* they dispersed throughout the islands. There are sixty islands in the lake, which provide a great refuge for birds. On each island there is a rock where eagles build their nests and establish their eyries. As I have heard tell, when evil people were accustomed to come with the intention of laying waste Scotland, all the eagles would gather together, fight, and cry out. For a day or two, or three or four, you would have seen them fighting with each other, which was a sign of great destruction. The lake was large and deep, for sixty rivers entered it from the valleys and the hills. With one exception they all stayed there, as there was just one way out. The Scots plunged into the water and dispersed throughout the islands. Arthur followed them quickly, gathering together small boats, barges, and larger ships. He attacked them so much, watched them so much, and assailed and starved them so much that in their twenties, in their hundreds, and in their thousands they fell down dead on the shore. Gillomar, an Irish king, who came to aid the Scots, landed very close to Arthur. Arthur attacked and fought with him, defeating him very easily. He caused him and his men to flee and go back to Ireland. Then Arthur returned to the lake where the Scots had been left.

(9466–502) Lo, bishops and abbots were there, and monks and people in holy orders, carrying holy bodies and relics and asking for mercy on the Scots. Then suddenly there were also the women from the regions, all barefoot and dishevelled, with their clothing torn and their flesh scratched, and with babes in their arms. They prostrated themselves at Arthur's feet, weeping, bawling, and crying for mercy:

'My lord, have mercy,' they all said. 'Why have you destroyed this country? May you have mercy on those who are in a predicament, and whom you are, my lord, starving to death. If you do not have mercy on the fathers, look at these children and at these mothers. Look at their sons, look at their daughters, look at their people, whom you are devastating. Give their fathers back to the little boys and give their husbands back to the womenfolk. Give their lords back to these ladies, and the brothers to their sisters. We have paid the price for the Saxons passing here. We did not want them to pass through our country, and it is distressing to us that they came this way. They have inflicted great harm on us and wearied us greatly. If we accommodated them, they harmed us all the more by taking our land, eating our goods and chattel, and sending them off to their own lands. We had no one to defend us, or to safeguard us against them. If we served them, we did so unwillingly.

(9503–26) 'The advantage lay with them, and expecting no assistance we just went on suffering. The Saxons were pagans, and we were Christians. Because of this, they inflicted harm on us all the more, and they treated us all the more shamefully. They treated us badly, but you are doing worse to us. Killing people who are seeking mercy and who are starving to death amongst those rocks, will provide you with neither honour nor fame. You have defeated us, but let us live. Wherever it may be, hand over some land to us! If you wish, make us and all our lineage live in servitude. Have mercy on Christians. We follow the faith that you follow. Christianity will be diminished if this land is ravaged. Already most of it is destroyed.' Arthur was now victorious, and he took pity on this wretched people, on the holy relics, and on the clergy. He granted them life and limb, took homage from them, and departed.

(9527–86) Hoel looked at the lake and spoke to his men about it. He was astonished by its size, both its length and its breadth. He was also amazed by the number of islands it contained and that its rocks were so numerous, with so many eagles and so many nests, and all the noise and the cries. He considered everything he saw there to be a marvel.

'Hoel,' said Arthur, 'fair nephew, you are marvelling at this lake. You will marvel all the more at another lake you will see near here in this region. Square-shaped, it is twenty feet long by twenty feet broad, with a depth of five feet. In the angles of the four corners there are four types of fish. Those in one corner will never cross over into the other, even though there is no separation or obstacle of any sort that one could detect, either by touching it or by seeing it. I do not know whether it was created by man or whether Nature arranged it. I shall tell you about another lake that will also astonish you. It is situated near the river Severn in Wales. The water comes rushing into it when the tide rises, but the sea never rises so high, no matter how much water enters the lake, that it floods, nor does the tide start to overflow the banks. But when the sea round it retreats, and the tide reverses, then you would see the water rising, covering the banks and swamping the ground. Then it will fly up with great whirlwinds, soaking and watering the fields. If anyone born in that country goes to visit it, with their face turned towards it, the water will swiftly rise up high and burst over him and his clothing. No matter what degree of strength he may have, he cannot but fall into it. In this way, many people have tumbled in, and many have drowned. But if someone turns his back on it when approaching it, with his heels turned round, he can stand on the riverbank and remain standing as long as he wants, and they will never be touched by the water, neither affected nor soaked.'

'This is a great wonder,' said Hoel, 'and God who has created it is also wonderful.'

(9587–624) Then Arthur had his horns blown and his trumpets and his bugles sounded. This was a signal to return. He gave his men leave to return to their dwellings, except for his closest advisers. They all set off home, filled with joy and extolling Arthur their king. They said that in Britain there had never been such a valiant chief. Arthur returned to York, staying there until Christmas. He celebrated the feast of Christmas Day there. He saw that the city was impoverished, degraded, and enfeebled, and he saw churches that were totally deserted and devastated, and dwellings that were in ruins. To Piram, a wise chaplain, who had not served him in vain, he gave the archbishopric, in order to have the churches maintained and the monasteries restored that the pagans had destroyed. Then the king brought about peace by proclamation, and he set the peasants to work in the fields. From all over his kingdom he summoned the free men, who had been disinherited, giving them back their inheritances and granting them fiefs and enhanced incomes. There were three brothers there of very noble birth and royal lineage: Loth, Agusel, and Urien. They were from a well-connected family that had followed their ancestors, and they ruled by right, as long as the peace lasted, the land to the north of the Humber. They did no harm to anyone. Arthur gave them back their fiefs and enhanced their heritages.

ARTHUR RESTORES HIS KINGDOM AND MARRIES GUINEVERE; FOREIGN CONQUESTS

(9625–58) IN the first instance he restored Moray to Urien without there being any charge or payment accruing. He asked him to be king again, so the man who was lord over the people of Moray was once again king at that time. He gave Scotland to Agusel, who claimed it as his fief. To Loth, who had been married to his sister and had ruled it for a long time, the king gave the whole of Lothian, and also other fiefs in addition. Gawain, Loth's son, was still a young boy and small in stature. When Arthur had established his kingdom, created justice throughout it, and restored the whole of his kingdom to its former authority, he married Guinevere, an intelligent and noble maiden, and made her queen. She was beautiful, courtly, and noble in appearance, and she was related to Roman nobility. For a long time, Cador had raised her splendidly in Cornwall, as his close cousin; her mother was Roman. She had been very well brought up, and her demeanour was most gracious. She was generous and eloquent, and Arthur loved her greatly and held her dear. But they never produced an heir between them and could not have children.

(9659–702) When winter had passed, summer had returned with its heat, and the sea was calm for sailing, Arthur had his fleet of ships prepared. He would go to Ireland, he said, and conquer the whole of it. He did not delay for long, summoning his finest young knights, those who were most skilled in war, and the richest and poorest throughout his land. When they had crossed to Ireland, throughout the land they seized victuals, cows, and oxen, and whatever they could make use of for food. Gillomar, the king of that land, was aware that Arthur was in search of such provisions. He knew from the disturbance, and from what people were saying, from the laments and the arguments, what the peasants were doing, and what they had lost in the way of cattle. He went to do battle with Arthur, but he did not have much success, as his men were lacking in armour. They had no hauberks and no shields. They knew nothing about arrows and had no skills when it came to archery. The Britons, who had bows, shot arrows at them repeatedly. They did not dare expose their eyes, nor did they know where to hide. You would have seen a great exodus of men, hiding next to each other, dashing into the woods and the bushes, into towns and dwellings, all attempting to find some way of escaping with their lives. But they were defeated and discomfited. The king wanted to escape into the wood, but he was caught and could not escape. Arthur sought him out and pursued him until he overtook him and captured him. He paid homage to Arthur and took back his inheritance from him. He granted him hostages permanently, to make sure that he would receive his annual tribute.

(9703–30) When Arthur had conquered Ireland, he crossed over to Iceland. He captured and conquered the whole land and made it submit completely to him; he wanted to have lordship over it all. Gonvais, who was king of Orkney, Doldani, king of Gotland, and Rummaret of Wenelande soon heard news of all this (as each one had his own spy), that Arthur would come over to attack them and destroy all the islands. No one on earth was his equal when it came to arms, and no one was able to lead such troops. For fear that he would come and attack them and lay waste their lands, freely and of their own volition they went to him in Ireland. They took with them so many of their possessions, and they promised him so much and gave him so much, that they made peace with him and became his vassals. They held their inheritances from him. They promised him a truce and established one, with each one of them providing a hostage. As a result, they would all remain at peace. Arthur returned to his ships. He went back to England and was welcomed with great joy.

THE TWELVE YEARS' PEACE; ARTHUR ESTABLISHES THE ROUND TABLE

(9731–98) AFTER returning home, Arthur reigned in peace for twelve years. No one dared wage war against him, and he did not attack anyone else. On his own, without receiving any other instruction, he set about being trained and conducted himself so nobly, in such fine and courtly fashion, that no one's court was so highly talked about, not even the one presided over by the emperor of Rome. He did not hear of any knight who had performed chivalric acts, or who had done something worthy of esteem, who was not retained as a member of his household, if he could have him, and, if he wanted to be paid in order to serve him, money would never be the reason for his not remaining at court. Because of his noble barons, each one thinking that he was the best and no one knowing who was the worst, Arthur created the Round Table, about which the Britons tell many a tale. The vassals sat there, all holding lands in chief and all equal. They sat at table equally, and they were served equally. None of them could boast of having a seat higher than his peer. They were all seated between two others, and no one was at the end of the tablet. Whether they were Scots, Britons, French, Normans, Angevins, Flemings, Burgundians, or Lorrainers, and from whomsoever they held their fiefs, from the west as far as Montgieu, not one of them could be considered courtly unless he had attended Arthur's court, spent some time with him, and wore the garments, cognizances, and armour according to the fashion of the ones sported by those serving at Arthur's court. Those who were in search of fame and renown came there from many different lands in order to hear about deeds of courtliness, to see Arthur's riches, to become acquainted with his barons and to benefit from his splendid gifts. He was loved by the poor and honoured by the rich. Foreign kings envied him, for they had a great fear that he would conquer the whole world and rob them of their authority. Whether it was for love of his generosity or for fear of his prowess, during this great peace I am describing (I do not know whether you have heard of this), marvels manifested themselves and adventures were encountered, and tales were told so frequently about Arthur that they were turned into fables.* They were neither all lies nor entirely the truth, neither all foolishness nor entirely based on fact. The storytellers told their tales and the raconteurs invented their yarns in order to embellish their accounts in such a way that they made everything appear to have been invented.

ARTHUR GOES TO NORWAY TO MAKE HIS BROTHER-IN-LAW, LOTH, KING

(9799–830) BECAUSE of the excellence of his disposition and of the counsel given by his men, and through the large number of knights he had trained and raised, Arthur said he would cross the sea and conquer the whole of France. But first he would go to Norway and there make his brother-in-law Loth king. Sichelin, the king, who had neither son nor daughter, was dead. He had asked on his deathbed, and he had done the same when he was in good health, that Loth should become king of Norway, and rule over his fief and his kingdom. He was his nephew, and he had no other heir, so by right Loth should have everything. When Sichelin had established this, and expected it to turn out this way, the Norwegians regarded as madness both his command and his decision. When they saw that the king had come to his end, they completely refused to hand over the kingdom to Loth. They did not wish to bring in a foreigner, or to make a foreigner their lord, rather would they all be old with hoary-white hair before they would recognize him in this way. For he would give to people from another land what he ought to be giving to them. One of those they had brought up, and who would love them and their sons, would be made king. In this way, and for this reason, they made Riculf, one of their barons, king.

(9831–62) When Loth saw that, unless he conquered it by force, he would lose what was rightfully his, he sought help from Arthur, who promised him clearly that he would restore the whole of his kingdom to him, and he stated that Riculf had been wrong to take possession of it. Summoning a large fleet of ships and a large number of men, he entered Norway by force. He inflicted great harm on the regions, burning towns and pillaging dwellings. Not wanting to abandon the country, Riculf refused to flee. He thought he could defend himself against Arthur. He assembled his troops in Norway, but he had few of them and few allies. He was defeated and killed. Arthur killed so many of the rest of them that there were very few remaining. When Norway was set free, Arthur gave it to Loth in its entirety, providing that he held it from Arthur and acknowledged him as his overlord. Gawain, who was a brave and renowned knight, had recently come back from the pope, St Soplice (may his soul repose in glory). The pope had bestowed arms on him, and they were very appropriately granted. For Gawain was brave and very prudent, and he had no truck with arrogance or presumption. He wanted to do more than he said he would do, and to give away more than he promised to give.

(9863–86) When Arthur had taken Norway and Loth had full control over it, he chose and gathered together the finest men, and the most valiant and boldest fighters. He also had ships and barges fitted out. When he saw that the weather was fair and the wind favourable, he crossed into Denmark with the other troops he was leading, as he wanted the country for himself. Aschil, who was king of the Danes, saw the Britons and the Norwegians. He saw Arthur, who was conquering everything, and he saw that he could not hold out. He did not want to allow himself to be harmed, or to let his fine land deteriorate. Neither did he wish to spend his gold or his silver, or have his men killed or his towers handed over. He spoke so much, did so much, achieved so much, promised so much, gave so much, and asked and beseeched so much that he came to an agreement with Arthur. He did homage to him and became his vassal, receiving the whole of his kingdom and holding it from Arthur.

MORE FOREIGN CONQUESTS; ARTHUR INVADES FRANCE AND DEFEATS THE ROMAN LEGATE FROLLO

(9887–913) ARTHUR was delighted by his great success and by the conquests he had made. But this was not yet sufficient for him. Selecting I do not know how many hundreds, or how many thousands, of the best knights and the best archers in Denmark, he intended to take them with him to France; this he did without delay. He conquered Flanders and Boulogne, seizing and taking possession of towns and castles. He led his men wisely, not wanting to destroy the land, burn towns, or take booty. He forbade all this, and prevented it, except for food, drink, and provisions. If anyone could be found to sell these things to him, let it be paid for in good coin and not stolen or pillaged. France in those days was called Gaul; it had no king or overlord. The Romans controlled it and held it as their own domain. It had been handed over to Frollo's protection, and he had looked after it for a long time. He received tributes and rents, and at fixed times he passed them on to Rome, to Leo the emperor.

(9914–54) Frollo, who possessed very great prowess, belonged to the Roman nobility. He was afraid of no one. Many messengers informed him of the seizures and of the harm that Arthur and his men were inflicting on his people, thus depriving the Romans of their rights. All the men who were able to bear arms, and who belonged to the fief of Rome, men whose help he thought he could obtain and who were within his jurisdiction he had summoned to come to him, well armed and well equipped. He went into battle with Arthur, but things did not turn out well for him. Discomfited, he fled, losing a large number of his men, some killed, some wounded, some captured. Some returned to their country. This was not a great surprise, for Arthur had a very large number of men. In the lands he had conquered, and in the cities he had taken, there was no one left behind, whether good knight or foot soldier, who was of an age to fight or had the requisite ability, whom he did not take with him, or summon later. He summoned many foreign troops in addition to those in his private household, which was made up of daring knights and proven fighters, and of those of the French who were sufficiently able and daring. As much for his eloquent words, his generous gifts, his personal nobility, or out of fear or pretence, they went to him and made peace, doing homage to him for their fiefs.

(9955–90) After he had been defeated, Frollo came to Paris very quickly. He did not dare stop anywhere else, and he refused to trust anyone else. He was seeking a retreat that he was capable of defending, for he was afraid of Arthur and his men. He had provisions brought from the surrounding towns, and he would await Arthur in Paris and defend himself there. With those who were fugitives, and those who were natives of the place, the city was filled with a large number of men. Each man for his own part strove to bring in corn and provisions and to construct walls and gates. Arthur was aware of what Frollo, who was fortifying himself in Paris, was doing. He came up behind him, set up a siege, and lodged in the surrounding towns. He had the river and the land guarded so that provisions could not get in. The French defended the town successfully, and for nearly a month Arthur stationed himself close by. There were many people in the city and there was soon a dearth of food. Everything they had obtained, brought in, and assembled in a short time had been eaten and used up. You would have seen many people starving. They had very little food, and there were a great many of them. The women and children displayed a great deal of sorrow. If the poor people were to have their way, the city would soon have surrendered. Many of them cried out:

'Frollo, what are you doing? Why do you not seek peace with Arthur?'

(9991–10040) Frollo saw that the people were dejected because of the lack of food. He saw the people who were dying of hunger, and he realized that they wished to surrender. The city, he could see, was destroyed, but he preferred to put himself in danger, and to risk death, rather than abandon Paris completely. He trusted in his own bravery. He let King Arthur know that the two of them should meet in battle, face to face, on the island. Whichever of them would be the winner should have all the other's land and receive the whole of France without their people being destroyed and the town being ruined. Arthur was very pleased with this announcement; it delighted him greatly. Therefore, in connection with the agreement they had reached, they handed over pledges and placed hostages on both sides, those in the host and those in Paris. Lo, the two warriors were armed, and they went into the meadow on the island. Then you would have seen people agitated, with men and women streaming out and climbing up on to the top of walls and dwellings, calling upon God and his names* that the man who wins would maintain peace with them so that no more war would ensue. Arthur's people on the other side were listening, watching, and begging the King in his glory that he would give their lord victory. Then, whoever had seen the two warriors sitting armed on their horses, with their swift mounts ready to dart forward and with their shields raised and brandishing their lances, could have said and spoken the truth that they were seeing two audacious fighters. They had good, swift horses, and fine shields, hauberks, and helmets. It was not easy to know by sight which one was the stronger and which one would win, for each one seemed to be a good fighter.

(10041–78) When they were ready, they drew away from each other on both sides. Spurring their horses and letting their reins go, with their shields raised and their lances lowered, they both went to strike each other with remarkable violence. But Frollo failed with his blow. I do not know whether his horse swerved, but Arthur struck him on top of the boss of his shield, carrying him a whole lance shaft's length away from his horse. He jumped up and rode swiftly towards Arthur, drawing forth his sword. The battle would soon have been over when Frollo stood up on his feet and extended his lance towards Arthur, striking his horse straight in the chest, plunging it right into its heart, and sending horse and rider tumbling to the ground together. Then you would have seen people confused, Britons yelling, and weapons being seized. They would have violated the truce, crossing the water to the island and all causing carnage. When Arthur jumped to his feet, he raised his shield, covered his head, and greeted Frollo with his sword. Frollo was very brave and bold. And he was neither slow nor frightened. He raised his sword on high and struck Arthur in the centre of his forehead. He was strong and the blow was hefty, and his sword blade was tough and sharp. He broke and split Arthur's helmet, and his hauberk was damaged and smashed. Arthur was wounded in the middle of his forehead, and blood ran down his face.

(10079–104) When Arthur felt he was wounded, and saw that he was stained with blood, he was very distressed. His complexion turned wan and it became discoloured by fury. He rode past Frollo and spurred his horse. He was not faint-hearted, and with Caliburn in his hand, as had been the case at many a time of need, he struck Frollo on the top of his head, splitting it right down to his shoulders. He pulled and pushed, and Frollo fell. His brains and his blood were spread all round. His helmet was of no use to him, nor was his hauberk, which he cherished so much. His feet twitched a little and he died there without uttering a word. Those in the town and the host yelled out, some weeping, others laughing. The citizens wept for Frollo, yet they ran to the gate and welcomed Arthur inside, as well as his household knights and his men. Then you would have seen the French coming and offering homage to Arthur, who accepted it and took hostages in order to secure peace. He spent a long time in Paris, where he appointed a bailiff* and ordered that there be peace.

(10105–32) Arthur separated his host into two parts and established two divisions. To his nephew Hoel he gave one half, asking him to conquer with them Anjou, Gascony, Auvergne, and Poitou, and, if he could, he should also conquer Burgundy and Lorraine. Hoel did his bidding. He conquered Berry and then Touraine, Anjou, Auvergne, and Gascony. Guitart, who was duke of Poitiers, was brave and a good knight. In order to maintain his land and his rights, he engaged in battle numerous times. He was often in pursuit and often fled. He often conquered and often lost. Finally, he saw that, if he lost, he would have difficulty in recovering. He agreed to peace, and became reconciled with Hoel, since, except for the tower and the castle, there was nothing left to lay waste, neither vine-stock nor grape harvest to destroy. He swore fealty to Arthur, and Arthur cherished him greatly. He conquered the other parts of France with a great show of power.

(10133–70) When he had created peace in the land, so that there would be no likelihood of war from any quarter, he gave gifts and payments to those who were old, to those who were married, and to those who had been with him for a long time. Then he sent them back to their own regions. The bachelors and the youths, who had their minds set on more conquests, and who had no wives or children, he kept with him in France for nine years. In these nine years he ruled France many marvels happened to him. He overcame many arrogant men and restrained many wicked ones. One Easter, in Paris, he held a great feast for his allies. He compensated his vassals for their losses and recompensed them in accordance with their deserts. He gave each man the reward for his service. To Kay, his master seneschal, a brave and loyal knight, he gave the whole of Anjou and Angers. He received them gladly. To Bedivere, his cup-bearer and one of his private counsellors, he gave as a fief the whole of Normandy, which was then called Neustria. These two were very loyal to him, and they were aware of all his thoughts. Flanders he gave to Holdin, Le Mans he gave to his cousin Borel, Boulogne he gave to Ligier, and to Richier he gave Ponthieu. To a large number of men, according to their status, and to many according to their services, he gave his free domains.* He also gave his own lands to the vavasours.

ARTHUR RETURNS TO ENGLAND AND SUMMONS HIS BARONS TO CAERLEON FOR HIS CROWN-WEARING

(10171–96) WHEN he had given fiefs to his barons, and made all his closest advisers rich, in April, when summer began, he crossed over to England. You would have seen men and women rejoicing at his return. Ladies kissed their husbands, and mothers kissed their sons. Sons and daughters kissed their fathers and women wept for joy. Cousins kissed each other, as did lovers, who, when they had the opportunity, took even more pleasure with each other. Aunts kissed their nephews, and a great deal of joy was experienced amongst them. Through streets and at crossroads you would have seen many people gathering, in order to ask how things were going and what conquests they had made, what they had done and what they had found, and why they had been delayed for so long. They told their stories about tough and harsh battles, about torments they had undergone, and about perils they had encountered.

(10197–236) Arthur honoured all his own men, bestowing his affection on the finest and giving them gifts. To illustrate how wealthy he was, and to make people talk about him, he took advice, and it was recommended that at Pentecost in the summer he should assemble his barons and then have himself crowned. At Caerleon in Glamorgan he sent out a summons to all his barons. Many people took lodging in the city, and many were taking their ease. At that time, people said, it seemed like Rome with its rich palaces. Caerleon is situated on the Usk, a river that runs into the Severn. Those who came from other lands were able to get there by using this river. The river was on one side, and on the other was dense forest. There was plenty of fish and an abundance of venison, and the meadows were fair and the pasture lands splendid. In the city there were two churches of immense gravity. One was dedicated to St Julius, a martyr—there were also nuns there to serve God—and the other to his companion who was called St Aaron. This was the seat of the bishopric and of many wealthy clergy, canons of great learning who were skilled in astronomy. They occupied themselves with the stars, and they often told King Arthur how things he wanted to do would turn out. At that time Caerleon was a good place to be, but since then it has done nothing other than go into decline.

(10237–82) In order to enjoy the splendid lodgings and the great comfort, and because of the fine woods, the beautiful meadows, and the beautiful places you have been told about, Arthur wanted to locate his court there. He had all his barons attend. He summoned his kings, he summoned his counts, he summoned his dukes and his viscounts, he summoned his barons, he summoned his vassals, he summoned his bishops and his abbots. Those who were summoned came, as they should when attending a feast. King Agusel came from Scotland, superbly equipped, Urien, the king, from Moray, and Yvain the courtly, his son. Stater was there, the king of South Wales, and Cadual of North Wales. Cador of Cornwall was there, and also Moruid, count of Gloucester, and Mauron, count of Worcester, whom the king cherished greatly. Guerguint, the count of Hereford, and Boso, the count of Oxford, and Urgent of Bath came. Cursal of Chester and Jonathas of Dorchester came. Anaraud came from Salisbury and Kimmare from Canterbury. Baluc came, the count of Silchester, and Jugein of Leicester, and Argahl from Warwick, a count who had a good number of his own men at court with him. There were many other barons who possessed domains that were not insignificant. Donaud, the son of* Apo, was there, and Regeim, the son of Elaud, Cheneus, the son of Coil, and Cathleus, the son of Catel were there, as were Edelin, son of Cledauc, Kimbelin, and the son of Trunat. Grifu, the son of Nagoid, Run, the son of Neton, and Margoid, Glofaud and Kincar, son of Aingan, and Kimmare and Gorboian, Kinlint, Neton were all there, as was Peredur, who was called the son of Elidur.

(10283–336) Of those who were serving at court, and who were the king's closest advisers and members of the Round Table, I do not wish to make up stories. Of those who possessed smaller amounts of land there were so many that I could not count them. There were many abbots and bishops, and three archbishops from the country, one from London, one from York, and St Dubric from Caerleon. There was a papal delegate from Rome, a man of great piety. Because of his love and his prayers many sick people were cured. London was at that time, and later, the seat of the archbishopric until the English, who ravaged the churches, ruled. At court there were a large number of barons, whose names I do not know. Gillomar was there, king of Ireland, and Malvaisus, the king of Iceland, and Doldani of Gotland, which lacked sufficient food. Aschil, king of the Danes, was there, and Loth, who was king of the Norwegians, and Gonvais, the king of Orkney, who had a large number of pirates under his control. Count Ligier, who ruled over the domain of Boulogne, came from across the sea. Count Holdin from Flanders was there, and Count Gerin of Chartres.

With great splendour he brought with him the twelve peers of France. Guitart came there, count of Poitiers, and Kay, who was count of Angers, and Bedivere of Normandy, which was then called

Neustria. From Le Mans came Count Borel, and from Brittany came Hoel. Hoel, and all those from over towards France, conducted themselves nobly, with fine weapons, fine garments, fine bridles, and well-nourished horses. There was not a single baron from Spain to the Rhine over towards Germany, who did not come to the feast if he had heard the summons, partly for Arthur, partly for his gifts, partly to get to know his barons, partly to see his wealth, partly to hear about his courtly deeds, partly for love, partly because they had been summoned, partly for glory, and partly for power.

COURT FESTIVITIES

(10337–58) WHEN the king's court had gathered together, you would have seen a very fine assembly. You would have also seen a great deal of activity, servants coming and going, lodgings being commandeered and taken over, dwellings being emptied and tapestries hung, marshals allocating lodgings and making attics and bedchambers available. Those who had no accommodation were given the chance to set up camp and erect their tents. You would have seen grooms busily leading palfreys and chargers, building shelters and arranging feedstuff, leading and tethering horses, grooming them and giving them water, carrying oats, hay, and grass. You would have seen squires and chamberlains dashing about in many directions, hanging up and folding cloaks, shaking the dust off cloaks and fastening them, and carrying furs of various colours. It would have seemed just like a fair.

(10359–94) In the morning, on the day of the feast, as we are told in the chronicle, all three of the archbishops came, and also the abbot and the bishops. They crowned the king in the palace and then took him to the church. Two archbishops took him, walking at each side of him. Each of them held on to one of his arms until he reached his throne. There were four swords there that were made of gold, with the pommels, the hilts, and the sections between them also of gold. Four kings carried the four swords, and they walked right in front of the king. When the king held his feast and his court, this was their responsibility. The king of Scotland was one, the second being the king of North Wales, the third being the king of South Wales. It was Cador of Cornwall who held the fourth sword. His authority was no less than if he had been royalty. Dubric, who was the papal legate and the prelate of Caerleon, undertook to perform this task as it was taking place in his church. For her part, the queen was served with great attention. Before the feast she had summoned the noblewomen of the country, and she assembled them at the feast. To join in the celebratory feast, she had come to her the wives of her allies, her female friends and relatives, and beautiful and noble maidens.

(10395–436) She was crowned in her chamber and then taken to the nuns' church. To create a path through the great throng, which would not allow a space to pass through, four ladies in front of her carried four white doves. They were married to the four men who carried the four swords. After the queen there came other ladies, who followed her with great joy, great happiness, and noble splendour. They were very well attired, well arrayed, and well adorned. You could have seen many of them there who thought they were the equal of many another. There were many costly garments there, costly attire, costly mantles, costly brooches, costly rings, many furs of various colours, and garments of many types. At the processions there was a great throng with everyone enthusiastic to move forward. When the mass had begun, which that day was highly exalted, you would have heard organs sounded, clerics singing and playing their instruments, voices falling and rising, and chants going up and down. You would have seen many knights coming and going through the churches. Partly to hear the clerics singing, and partly to gaze at the ladies, they ran from one church to another; there was a lot of toing and froing. They were definitely not aware of the church in which they were spending the most of their time. They could not get their fill of seeing or listening. If this situation had lasted for the whole day, I do not think it would have vexed them.

(10437–82) When the service was over and the 'Go forth, the mass is ended' had been sung,* the king took off his crown, which he had worn in the church. He put on a lighter one, and the queen did the same. They removed the bulkiest items of attire and donned lighter and lesser items. When the king left the church, he went to his palace to eat. The queen went to another palace, taking the ladies with her. The king ate with his men, and the queen ate with the ladies, with great delight and great joy. There used to be a custom in Troy, and the Britons still maintained it, that when they celebrated feasts together the men ate with the men and did not take any women with them. The ladies ate elsewhere with no one other than their servants. While the king sat at the dais, according to the custom of the country, the barons sat round him, each in the order of his status. The seneschal, whose name was Kay, dressed in ermine robes, served the king as he ate. With him were a thousand noblemen, who were all dressed in ermine. In the kitchen the servants thronged, constantly moving to and fro, carrying dishes and plates. On the other side, Bedivere served from the buttery, and he had a thousand youths with him, handsome, noble, and dressed in ermine. They bore wine in cups, ship-shaped bowls of pure gold, and goblets. Not a single one of those serving failed to be dressed in ermine. Bedivere, bearing the king's cup, walked in front of them. The youths came after him, serving wine to the barons.

(10483–520) The queen also had her servants. I do not know who, or how many, there were. She and all her company were served splendidly and finely. You would have seen splendid vessels that were very handsome and beautiful. The food served was sumptuous, and there were many different types of drink. I cannot name everything, and I do not know everything, nor can I account for this wealth. For brave men and for splendour, for abundance and for nobility, for courtliness and for honour, England had the upper hand over the whole of the surrounding kingdoms, and over all those that we now know. Even the poor peasants were more courtly and more valiant than knights in other kingdoms; this was also true of the women. You would never have seen a knight who had done anything worthy of praise who did not sport arms, garments, and equipment that were of the same colour. They designed arms of a single colour, and their garments were of one colour. The ladies were also praised for dressing in one colour. There was never any knight there, of whatever lineage, who was able to experience passionate love or to enjoy having a courtly lady as his beloved, who had not proven himself in knightly deeds on three occasions. As a result, the knights were more worthy, and they performed better in combat, and the ladies were better and lived more chastely.

(10521–60) When the king rose from his meal, they all went in search of entertainment. They left the city and went into the fields. Some went off to play a variety of games, some went to fight with lances and to display their swift-moving horses, whilst others went fencing, stone throwing, or leaping. There were those who threw javelins and those who took part in wrestling. Each one participated in the game at which he was most skilled. The one who overcame his companions and had the prize in some game was straightaway taken to the king and presented to all those present. The king gave him a gift from his own possessions, thus making him very happy. The ladies climbed on to the walls in order to watch those who were playing. Those who had a beloved in the area quickly cast their eyes and faces in his direction. At court there were many jongleurs, singers, and instrumentalists. You could have heard songs being sung, rotrouanges and newly created tunes, music for the viol, lays for tunes, lays for viols, lays for rotes, lays for harps, lays for flutes, lyres, drums, shawms, symphonias, psalteries, monochords, tambourines, chorons. There were many acrobats there, and minstrels, male and female. Some told tales and fables, whereas others asked for dice and backgammon, and there were those who played at hasart, which is a cruel game. Many played at chess or at dice, or at something with higher stakes.

(10521–88) They played in groups of two, with some losing and some winning. Those who threw the highest numbers were envied, and they would tell the others how to make a good move. They borrowed money against pledges, willingly getting eleven for a dozen. They gave pledges and seized pledges, took pledges, and promised pledges, often swearing and often making commitments, often cheating and often tricking, often miscounting and often quarrelling. They threw two by two, often getting a double four, some throwing double ace, a throw of three points and two threes. Sometimes they threw five points, sometimes six points. Six, five, four, three, two, and ace—these led to many taking off a good many of their garments. The person who held the dice had great hopes, and when their companions had it they kept shouting out. Repeatedly they created a din and a commotion, often saying to each other:

'You are cheating me. Throw them out. Shake your hand and play the dice. Before your throw, I am making a higher bid. If you are on the lookout for money, make a bet, as I am doing.' Someone who sat down clothed might be naked when they left.

(10561–620) The feast lasted in this way for three days. When it came to the fourth day, a Wednesday, the king granted fiefs to his young knights, dividing up the domains that were free. He rewarded for their services those who had served him for lands. He gave them townships and castle lordships, and bishoprics and abbeys. To those who came from other lands, who came to the king out of love for him, he gave cups, he gave chargers, he gave some of his own possessions, he gave objects of delight, he gave jewels, he gave furs, he gave garments, he gave cups, he gave goblets, he gave brocades, he gave rings, he gave tunics, he gave cloaks, he gave lances, he gave swords, he gave barbed arrows, he gave copper pots, bows, and very sharp spears, he gave leopards, he gave bears, saddles, bridles, and hunting horses, he gave hauberks and chargers, he gave helmets and coins, he gave silver and he gave gold, he gave the finest parts of his treasury, and there was no one of any worth who came to him from another land to whom the king did not grant a gift that was of such a nature that it honoured a man such as he was.

TWELVE WHITE-HAIRED MEN ARRIVE, DEMANDING TRIBUTE ON BEHALF OF THE ROMAN EMPEROR, LUCIUS

ARTHUR was sitting at a dais, surrounded by counts and kings. Lo, there were twelve men with hoary-white hair, well dressed and well attired. They entered the hall two by two and held hands two by two. There were twelve of them, and they held twelve olive branches. Slowly, in orderly fashion and very finely, very elegantly, and fittingly, they crossed the hall, approaching the king and greeting him. They came, they said, from Rome and were messengers from Rome. They unfolded a charter, and one of them passed it over to Arthur on behalf of the emperor of Rome. Here is the gist of the charter:

(10621–72) 'Lucius, who has Rome within his power, and who has the lordship over the Romans, sends to Arthur, his enemy, what he has deserved. I am very scornful while at the same time marvelling, and I marvel while being scornful, that out of bombast and arrogance you dare to cast your eyes in the direction of Rome. I am very scornful, and I marvel with regard to the person by whom, and where, you are advised concerning conflict with Rome, as long as you know that there is a single Roman still alive. You have acted very stupidly in launching an attack against us, we whose task it is to sit in judgement over the whole world and who control the capital city of the world. You do not yet know, but you will know, and you have not seen, but you will see, what a serious thing it is to anger Rome, whose task it is to govern everything. You have gone further than the natural order permitted, and you have exceeded what was sensible for you to do. Do you know who you are, where you come from, and that you are seizing and holding on to our tributes? Why do you have these, and why are you not giving them back to us? Why do you hold them, and what right do you have to do this? If you continue to hold on to them, you will be acting foolishly. If you can retain them for a long time, without our making you give them up, you will be able to declare, and it will be a marvel, that the lion is forced to flee by the sheep, the wolf by the goat and the hound by the hare.

(10673–710) 'Things cannot work like this, and Nature will not tolerate it. Our ancestor Julius Caesar (but perhaps you have little esteem for him) captured Britain, and he received a tribute that our people have had ever since. For a long time, we have had tributes from the surrounding islands. Out of presumption you have taken each one of them from us, you are acting foolishly, and you have committed an even more shameful act that is worse for us than any loss. You have killed our baron Frollo, and you control France and Flanders wrongfully. Because you have not been afraid of Rome, or of its great power, the Senate summons you, and in so doing it informs you that in mid-August you should present yourself before it, no matter what the cost to yourself, and be prepared to give satisfaction for what you have taken from it, and for what we accuse you. If you delay doing any of this, I shall cross Montgieu by force and take Britain and France from you. I do not think that you intend to wait for me or to defend France against me. Never in my opinion will you dare to show yourself on the other side of the sea. If you were overseas, you would never dare to wait for me to come, and you will never find any hiding place from which I shall not eject you. I shall take you to Rome in chains and hand you over to the Senate.'

(10711–74) These words led to a great uproar, and everyone became very angry. You would have heard the Britons crying out loudly, pledging themselves, and swearing by God that these people who had brought this message would be dishonoured. They would have received much abuse and reproach, but the king got up and cried out to them:

'Keep quiet! Keep quiet! They will not be harmed. They are messengers. They have a lord and are delivering his message. They will be able to say whatever they wish. No one will inflict any harm on them.' When the uproar was over, and the court was at its ease again, the king brought with him his dukes, his counts, and his closest advisers into his stone tower that was called the Giants' Tower. He wanted to hold a council with them there, so that he could respond to the messengers. They were already on the steps, barons and counts side by side, when Cador said, smiling, and within the hearing of the king, who was out in front:

'I have been very fearful,' he said, 'and thought many times, that through idleness and peace the Britons would become cowardly. For idleness attracts cowards; many people have realized this. Idleness makes a man lazy, idleness strips away prowess, idleness inspires a love of pleasure, idleness gives rise to love affairs. Through lengthy repose and idleness youth quickly becomes preoccupied with joking, games, backgammon, and other amusements. Through long delays and repose we can lose our reputations. We have been slumbering for a long time. But the Lord God, in his mercy, has roused us a little in encouraging the Romans to claim our country and the others that we have conquered. If the Romans trust in themselves so much as to do what they say in their letter, the Britons will regain their reputation for audacity and vigour. I never had any affection for a lengthy peace, and I shall never have any.'

'Lord count,' said Gawain, 'upon my word, what troubles you is of no importance. Peace is good after war, and the land is finer and better. Jokes are excellent, and love affairs are also good. For love and for their beloveds, knights perform knightly acts.' At these words that had been spoken they went and took a seat in the tower.

(10775–822) When Arthur saw that they were all seated, with everyone attentive and silent, he was quiet for a moment and thoughtful. Then, raising his head, he spoke:

'Barons,' he said, 'you who have assembled here, my companions and my allies, my companions in prosperity and my companions in adversity. If any great combat has befallen me, you have endured it with me. Whether I have lost or won, you have shared both these outcomes with me. You are partners in my losses and, when I win, in my gains. Through you, and those who assist you, I have known many victories. I have been your leader in many a crisis, on sea and on land, near and far. When actions and advice are needed, I have always found you to be faithful. I have tested you on many occasions and always found you to be brave. Through you I have in my power all the lands that surround us. You have heard the summons and the intent, the bombast and the pride, that the Romans have communicated to us. They have challenged us greatly and threatened us greatly. But if God were to protect you and me, we should easily be freed from the

Romans. They are wealthy and very powerful, and it would be necessary for us to plan, fittingly and reasonably, what we should say and do. When something is planned in advance, it can be sustained more easily at a time of crisis. He who sees the arrow coming can change course or protect himself. We should behave in this very same way. The Romans intend to attack us, and we must make preparations to avoid being harmed by them. They demand a tribute from Britain, and they inform us that they should have it, and from other islands as well, in particular from France.

ARTHUR REFUSES TO PAY THE TRIBUTE AND PREPARES TO MAKE A COUNTERCLAIM

(10823–50) 'FIRSTLY, I shall respond in a fitting way regarding Britain. They say that Caesar conquered it. He was a strong man, and he employed all his strength. The Britons had no means of defence against him. By force he had them hand over a tribute. But strength is not the same as right, rather it is excessive arrogance. People do not consider something to be right when it is taken by force. It is perfectly permissible for us to hold by right something that opponents have taken by force. They have dishonoured us by the harm, the losses, the acts of shame, the torments, and the fear that they meted out to our ancestors. They boasted about having conquered them, and they took tributes and income away from them. We must do them all the more harm, and they have all the more to restore to us. We must hate those who hated them and inflict harm on those who did the same to them. They did wrong by them and reproach us for this. They took tribute from them, and they are asking for it again. They want to inherit our shame as well as what they have stolen from us. They are accustomed to having a tribute from Britain, and therefore they expect to have it from us.

(10851–904) 'For precisely this reason, and for the very same cause, we can make a claim for Rome, and we uphold our claim. Belin, who was king of the British, and Brenne, duke of the Burgundians, two brothers who were born in Britain, valiant and wise knights, went to Rome, besieged it, attacked it, and captured it. They hanged twenty-four hostages in the sight of all their kinsmen. When Belin left there, he entrusted Rome to his brother. I shall let Brenne and Belin be and talk of Constantine. He came from Britain and was the son of Eleine. He ruled Rome and had it as his personal domain. Maximien, the king of Britain, conquered France and Germany, traversing Montgieu and Lombardy, and he had lordship over Rome. These were my kinsmen, and each one of them held Rome in his hands.

'Now you can hear and discover that I should have Rome in the same way as Rome could have Britain, by right, if we take into consideration our ancestors. The Romans received a tribute from us, and my kinsmen had one from them. They claim Britain, and I claim Rome. This is the gist of my advice: may he who can win it from the other have the income and the land. They should not be discussing France and the other regions, which we have taken from them, if they have no intention of defending them. They either do not wish to, or cannot, or perhaps they did not have the right to do so, for by force or through covetousness they retain them in fee. Now may he who can get it all have it all; no other justice is necessary. The emperor threatens us, so may God not permit him to do us any harm. He says he will take away our lands,* then he will take me to Rome as a captive. He has little esteem for us and little fear of us. But, if it pleases God and he comes here, before he returns home he will have no wish to make threats when I make a challenge to him, and he does the same to me. May he who can take everything have everything.'

(10905–54) When Arthur the king had spoken and explained all this to the barons,* there were those who spoke afterwards and those who listened. After the king, Hoel spoke:

'My lord,' he said, 'by my faith, you speak very reasonably. No one could improve on this. Summon your people, call your men and ourselves who are at your court. Cross the sea without delay, go through Burgundy, go through France, go through Montgieu, go through Lombardy. Show the emperor who challenges you that he is wrong and make him afraid that he will not be able to do you any harm. The Romans have incited a situation as a result of which they will be completely destroyed. The Lord God wants you to be exalted, so do not delay or dally. He is placing the empire in your power, and he wishes to do so of his own volition. Remember what the Sibyl said in the prophecies she wrote down: three Britons would emerge from Britain who would conquer Rome by force, two of two have already passed away. The first of these was Belin, and the second Constantine. You are the third to have Rome, and you will conquer it by force. In you will be accomplished the prophecy that the Sibyl made. Why do you delay taking possession of what God wishes to bestow on you? Glorify yourself, glorify us, we who are desirous of it. We can truly say that, as long as we seek your honour, we do not fear blows or wounds, and we have no regard for death or torment. Before the current situation comes to an end, I shall give you for your company ten thousand armed knights. As long as you are lacking in wealth, I shall pledge all my land to you, and hand over gold and silver to you. Whilst you still need it, you would be wrong to let me have any of it back.'

(10955–96) After Hoel had spoken, the king of Scotland, Agusel, the brother of Loth and Hoel, spoke:

'My lord,' he said, 'Hoel speaks well, and when you embark on this undertaking speak to those who are situated within, where the best of your barons, who have heard the message from Rome, are to be found. Be aware of whatever each one of them will do for you, and how much each one will help you. We now need to make plans with respect to help and support. All those who are from your land, and who hold their fiefs and lands from you, should help you and be useful to you; they will act to the best of their ability. I have never heard such fine and eloquent advice concerning war against the Romans. I can never have any love or esteem for them. From the time I was able to understand anything, I hated the Romans and their arrogance. What shame on a wicked people who do not have their minds set on anything honourable, just on amassing wealth so that they experience the need to challenge good people. The emperor, who issued a challenge against you, acted foolishly and committed a very deceitful act. The day will come, I believe, when he will regret doing this, because of this tower that is crammed with silver. The Romans have unleashed such a conflict that they will all be discredited by it. Even if they had never started it, and never been the first to speak of it, we ourselves would have had to set the battle in motion, and to wage war according to our own desires in order to avenge our kinsfolk and to deflate the bombast of those who wish to say, and show, that we ought to render tribute to them.

(10997–1040) 'People say that our ancestors used to pay tribute to them, but I do not believe that they would have given or sent tribute to them. They did not give or render it to them, rather it was taken from them by force. We shall take it from them by force, avenging ourselves and our ancestors. We have won many a battle and been successful in many a great war. But what use are any of our victories if we cannot defeat the Romans? I have never had such a desire for food or drink as I have to see the time when we launch a battle against each other on horseback, gripping our spears, with our shields round our necks and our helmets laced upon us. O God, what riches there are. O God, what treasure will those have who want it, if God protects us from harm. They will never know a day of poverty. There we shall see splendid riches, there we shall see splendid dwellings, there we shall see splendid castles, and strong and swift horses. It seems to me that I am already there and that I am already seeing them defeated. Let us go onwards to conquer Rome, and let us take their land from the Romans. When we have conquered Rome, killed the inhabitants, and taken the city, we shall cross over into Lorraine, conquering it, and Germany as well, with the result that no land is left on this side that is not yours. There will be no one who can escape us, and we shall, rightly or wrongly, take everything. So that what I say matches what I do, I myself shall go with you, taking two thousand knights with me, and there will be such an abundance of foot soldiers that no one will be able to count them.'

(11059–90) When the king of Scotland had spoken, all together they said and called out:

'Shame on anyone who remains behind, and who does not do his best.' When each man had had his say, and Arthur had listened to them all, he had letters composed and sealed, and then they were handed over to the messengers. He made sure the messengers were all honoured and given gifts from his possessions.

'In Rome,' he said, 'you can say that I am lord of Britain, that I rule France, and that I shall rule it, and defend it from the Romans. Be truly aware that I shall shortly be going to Rome, not to take tribute to them, but to demand tribute from them.'

The messengers left Arthur and returned to Rome. They reported how Arthur had been, where he had been, and how they had spoken to him. They said that he was very generous, very courageous, and very wise, and that he was very polite and behaved splendidly. No one, they said, could support the costs he bore. Members of his household were very wealthy and well dressed. They would seek tribute from him in vain, for he said that they were the ones who would be giving it to him. When the lords of Rome had heard the responses of the messengers, and they had listened to the contents of the documents they had brought with them, they understood that the words corresponded with Arthur's refusal to serve them, and with his intention to demand tribute from them. They advised the emperor, giving him counsel that appealed to him: he should summon his whole empire and traverse Montgieu and Burgundy in order to fight with King Arthur and wrest his kingdom and his crown from him. Lucius Hiber did not delay. He summoned kings, counts, and dukes, telling them to come on the tenth day of July, in accordance with how much they loved their honour, let them come to him in Rome, ready to seek out Arthur, wherever he may be.

(11091–124) Those who heard the summons came. Epistrod, the king of Greece, came, and Echion, duke of Boetia. Hirtac came there, the king of the Turks, with strong and dependable knights. Pandras came there, the king of Egypt, and Ypolite. With a hundred cities under his control he was a man of very great power. King Evander came from Syria and Duke Teucer from Phrygia, from Babylon Micipsa, and from Spain Aliphatima. King Boccus came from Media and Sertorius from Libya, Polidetes from Bithynia, and King Xerxes from Iture. Mustensar, who ruled Africa, lived far away, and came from far away, brought Africans, Moors, and also his extensive treasure. From amongst those in the Senate, who had great authority in Rome, came Marcel and Luces Catel, Cocta, and Gaius Metel. There were many other barons whose names I have not discovered. When they had gathered together, they numbered four hundred thousand. One hundred and eight thousand men were mounted, in addition to foot soldiers and men-at-arms.* When they were ready and prepared, they set off from Rome at the beginning of August.

(11125–62) Arthur dissolved his court and asked all his barons for help. He had named them all by their names and summoned each man in order, individually, to help him to the best of his ability, in so far as he wished to have his love. They each stated how many knights they would bring, in accordance with his fief. The Irish, those from Gotland, and from Iceland, the Danes, the Norwegians, also the Orcadians promised a hundred and twenty thousand men, according to the fashion of their country. They were not knights and did not know how to ride a horse. They all bore their arms on foot: axes, darts, javelins, and guisarmes. Those from Normandy and Anjou, from Maine and Poitou, from Flanders and Boulogne promised without delay eighty thousand armed warriors, fully armed. 'They should all', they said, 'provide good service.' Hoel promised ten thousand of them, and Agusel of Scotland two thousand. From Britain, his own land, which is now called England, Arthur counted sixty thousand men with hauberks. The foot soldiers and the crossbowmen, the men-at-arms or the archers, I cannot count, nor could those who saw the massed men of the great host.

ARTHUR HEADS FOR NORMANDY, ON THE WAY TO ROME

(11163–89) ONCE Arthur knew what troops he would have, and how many men each one would bring, he requested and proclaimed that, at the time he appointed each of them, they would come with his fleet to Barfleur in Normandy. When the barons had taken leave of him, they returned to their lands. They had the men they were to take with them make ready. To Mordred, one of his nephews, a remarkable and brave knight, and to Guinevere, his wife, Arthur handed over responsibility for his kingdom. Mordred was of high nobility, but not a man of good faith. He had been in love with the queen, but this had been kept secret. He concealed it very well. Who would have thought that he would love his lord's wife, especially a lord whose men all honoured him? Mordred loved his uncle's wife foully and he acted shamefully. To Mordred and the queen—O God, what a bad transfer of power this was—he entrusted everything except the crown.

(11190–238) Then he made his way to Southampton, where the ships had been brought and the household troops were gathered. You would have seen many a ship being equipped, ships moored and anchored, ships drying out and set afloat, ships secured with plugs and nails, those with their cordage spread out, with masts raised and with gangplanks lowered. Some were loaded up with helmets, shields, and hauberks, and they had lances turned upright. Horses were being led along, knights and men-at-arms were going aboard, and companions were calling out to each other. Those remaining behind, and those setting sail, continued to hail each other. You would have seen anchors raised, head ropes drawn up, shrouds tied down, and sailors dashing about the ships, unfurling sails and yardarms. Some of them struggled with the windlass, while others adjusted the luffs and the tacking spar. Standing in the stern were the pilots, the very finest helmsmen. Each of them strove to navigate with the rudder that controlled the ship. Pushing the tiller forward made the ship veer to port, and pulling it back made it veer to starboard. In order to make the wind fill the sails, they braced the leech rods to the fore and fixed them securely into the leeches. Some of the men pulled on the bunt-lines and brought down the sails a little in order to make the ships run more smoothly. They secured the fore-braces and the sheets and tightened all the ropes. They strengthened the studding sails and the sheets, and they pulled hard on all the ropes, loosening the halyards and bringing down the yards. They tightened the bowlines and the haul, monitoring the wind and the stars, and trimming the sails in accordance with the wind. They bent the brails to the mast so that the wind did not get past it underneath. The ships advanced, taking in two or three reef points. The man who first built a ship was very audacious and noble, setting sail down wind and seeking for land that he could not see, and a shore of which he had no knowledge.*

(11239–78) Arthur's people proceeded joyfully on their way. They had a favourable wind and sailed swiftly. At midnight they were crossing the sea, having set their course for Barfleur, when Arthur began to doze. He fell asleep and could not stay awake. While he was asleep, it appeared to him he could spot a bear high up in the sky, flying down from the direction of the east. It was very ugly, very strong, very big, and very powerful. It was dreadful to behold. From the other direction he saw a dragon flying from the west and with flames shooting from its mouth. From the creature and its radiance the land and the sea shone all round. The dragon launched an attack on the bear, which defended itself steadfastly. They struck marvellous blows against each other, but the dragon clasped the bear and hurled it to the ground. When Arthur had slept for a short time, the dream he had witnessed roused him. He woke up and got to his feet. He told the clerics and the barons about the dream in the order he had seen things happen. Some of them replied that the dragon he had seen was an image of himself and that the huge bear was a sign of some giant he would kill who would come from a foreign land. Others explained it in different ways, but they all interpreted it in a positive fashion.

'This,' he said, 'it seems to me, is the war that must take place between myself and the emperor. But may it all be in the hands of the Creator.'

(11279–318) As he was speaking these words, dawn broke. The weather was fair, and the sun rose. Very early in the morning they arrived at Barfleur in the Cotentin, and they disembarked as soon as they could, dispersing throughout the region. Arthur waited for his people, who had not yet come. He had not been waiting there long when he heard of, and was told of, a massive giant who had come from Spain. He had captured Eleine, Hoel's niece, ravished her and placed her on the mountain that is now called St Michael [Mont Saint-Michel]. There was no altar or chapel there; it was enclosed by the sea's rising tide. Throughout the country there was no one daring enough, no youth or peasant, so proud or so valiant, who dared to fight with the giant or to venture into his domain. When the inhabitants had gathered together and made their way to the mountain in order to fight, often by sea, and often by land, he was not troubled by their hostility. He smashed their ships with rocks, killing and drowning many of them. They had all let him be, as they did not dare to get any closer to him. You would have seen the peasants quitting their houses, carrying their children, taking their wives, and driving along their beasts, climbing the hills, and hiding in the woods. They took flight through woods and deserts, and they were still fearful of dying there. The whole of the land had been abandoned, and all the people had fled. The giant's name was Dinabuc. May he come to a bad end!

(11319–50) When Arthur had heard what was said, he called upon Kay and Bedivere. The former was his seneschal and the latter his cup-bearer. He refused to talk to anyone else. That night, as soon as it was going dark, he had these two knights and their squires take their arms and their horses. He did not want to take the whole army with him, or to make this affair known to everyone. He feared that if they knew about it they would be afraid of the giant, and he was confident that he himself and his prowess were sufficient to destroy it. All night they had ridden so far, travelled so far, and spurred their horses so much that in the morning they came to the shore, where they could make the crossing. They saw a fire burning on the mountain; it was visible from a distance. There was another smaller mountain that was not far away from the larger one. On each one there was a fire burning. This made Arthur doubt which mountain the giant was on, and on which mountain he would find him. There was no one who was able to inform him and no one who had seen the giant that day. He told Bedivere to go and search both of the mountains; he should look for him until he found him. Then he should return and let them know how things were.

(11351–80) Bedivere went on board a small boat and crossed over to the nearer mountain. He could not get there in any other way, for the tide was at its highest. When he had reached this mountain and was climbing up the side of it, he heard great weeping, great lamentation, great sighs, and great cries. He was fearful and began to tremble, for he thought he heard the giant. But very soon he took heart. With his sword drawn, he advanced, and his courage returned to him. It was his intention and his desire to do battle with the giant. He would risk his life to do so. He would not allow his courage to fail for fear of losing his life. But these were vain thoughts, for, when he was up on the plain he saw only a burning fire and a recently created tomb; the tomb was recently constructed. The count came up to it with his sword drawn. He found an old woman there with torn clothes and dishevelled hair, lying beside the tomb, sighing deeply and complaining greatly. She was lamenting for Eleine, displaying great sorrow and letting out loud cries.

(11381–416) When she saw Bedivere, she said:

'Woe is me, who are you? What misfortune brings you here? If the giant finds you, your life must come to an end today in sorrow, grief, and pain. Unhappy one, flee, be on your way before the devil sees you!'

'Good woman,' said Bedivere, 'speak to me and cease crying. Tell me who you are and for whom you are crying, why you are dwelling on this island, and who it is who is lying in this tomb. Tell me all about yourself.'

'I am lost,' she said, 'an unfortunate woman. I cry here for a maiden whom I suckled at my breast. Her name was Eleine, the niece of Hoel, and her body lies in this tomb. I was commanded to suckle her. Alas, why was she handed to me? Alas, why did I suckle her for so long when a devil ravished her? A giant ravished her, and myself as well, and he brought us here. He intended to rape her, but she was delicate and could not tolerate it. He was very large, very big, very ugly, very tall, and very heavy. Eleine could not tolerate this. Enormous and very powerful, he caused the soul to issue from her body. Woe is me, my sweetness, my joy, my pleasure, my love, the giant killed her shamefully, and I have buried her here.'

(11417–58) 'Why', he said, 'do you not escape, now that you have lost your Eleine?'

'Do you want to hear why?' she said. 'I see that you are a noble and a courtly man. Nothing will be hidden from you. Eleine's death made me think I was going out of my mind, for I saw her die in shame. The giant made me remain here to satisfy his lust on me. He has kept me here by force and ravished me by force. I had to give in to his force, for I could not withstand him. As the Lord God is my witness, I do not do this of my own volition. He has only just about avoided killing me, but I am older and stronger, bigger and more resolute, bolder and more confident, than the maiden Eleine. Nevertheless, I have suffered great pain from this, and my whole body is in agony. If he comes here to assuage his lust, you are dead, you cannot prevent it. He is up above, on that smoking mountain. He will soon come down, that is his habit. Quickly, my friend, flee, what have you been seeking here? Do not let yourself be captured. Let me lament and display my sorrow. I would have been dead a long time ago if I had had my way. My love for Eleine was a disaster.' Bedivere took pity on her and comforted her very tenderly. Then he abandoned her and left. He came to the king and told him what he had heard and discovered about the old woman, who was lamenting because of Eleine, who was dead, and because of the giant who lived on the higher mountain that was smoking.

(11459–507) Arthur was very upset about Eleine, but he was not a coward or a laggard. At ebb tide he had his companions mount their horses. They very soon came to the higher mountain as the sea uncovered it. They handed over to their squires their palfreys and their chargers. All three climbed up, Arthur, Bedivere, and Kay.

ARTHUR DEFEATS THE GIANT OF MONT SAINT-MICHEL, BUT MUST BURY ELEINE, HOEL'S NIECE

I SHALL go on ahead,' said Arthur, 'and fight with the giant. You will come after me and make sure that no one strikes a blow there, as long as I can cope on my own and as long as I do not need any help. It would look like cowardice if you saw me in dire straits and came to my assistance.' They granted him his request, then all three of them climbed up the mountain. The giant was seated at the fire, roasting pork by it. Part of it had been cooked on a spit and part on coals. His beard and whiskers were soiled by the flesh cooked on coals. Arthur thought he could surprise him in this way, before he could take hold of his club. But the giant saw Arthur. He was amazed and jumped to his feet, raising to his shoulder his club, which was very large and square. Two peasants could not have carried or lifted it off the ground. Arthur saw him get up and get ready to strike, so he withdrew his sword, raised his shield, and covered his face. He was afraid of receiving a blow, but the giant gave him one such that the whole mountain resounded. Arthur was completely stunned, but he was strong and did not totter. He felt the heavy blow, clung on to his sword, and raised the blade. He lifted his arm, stretched it out, and struck the giant high on the forehead, causing a wound in each of his eyebrows.

(11508–60) Blood ran down from his eyes. Arthur would have dashed his brains out and killed him, and he would never have managed to recover, but the giant had held his club high up in order to withstand Arthur's blow. He moved his head out of the way and stood up tall. Nevertheless, he received a blow that was such that blood ran down his face and his eyesight grew blurred. When he felt that his vision was blurred, then you would have seen the giant go mad. Just as a boar, which has been impaled on a sword's blade and harried for a long time by dogs, hurls himself against the huntsman, in the same way with great anger the giant charged at the king, grabbed him, and refused to let go of him in spite of his sword. Big and strong, he grasped him round the middle and pushed him down on to his knees. But at once he recovered his strength, got back on his feet, and stood up. Arthur was very angry and remarkably skilful. He was furious and fearful. He struggled as best he could, dragging him towards him and thrusting him away. He possessed great strength and was not faint-hearted. With a sudden leap he dodged to one side and squirmed out of his adversary's grasp. As soon as he had escaped and realized that he was free, he was very swift and went round the giant, now on this side of him and now on the other, striking him frequently with his sword. The giant scrambled round, with his eyes filled with blood and unable to tell black from white. Arthur went weaving to and fro, often behind him, often in front, until the blade of Caliburn sank into his brain, he pushed and pulled him, and the giant fell, kicking and yelling. As he fell, the giant made a crashing noise like an oak tree toppled by the wind. Then Arthur began to laugh, for his anger was over. Standing at a distance, he looked at the giant and ordered his cup-bearer to cut off his head and hand it over to his squire. He wanted it to be carried to the host so that it could be exhibited as a marvel.

(11561–608) 'I was afraid of him,' said Arthur, 'with a greater fear than of any other giant than Rithon, who brought sorrow to so many kings.' Rithon had defeated so many kings, and conquered and killed so many, that from the beards of these kings, which had been torn off, he had a cloak of skins made for him to wear. Rithon definitely had to be killed. In his arrogance and pride he had told King Arthur to peel off his beard and be kind enough to send it to him, because he was stronger than him and worth more than any other kings. He would honour his beard and make use of it as a border for his cloak. If Arthur refused to grant him what he requested, they would come together in single combat and fight each other in this way, and whichever of the two killed the other, or could capture him alive, he would have the beard, take the skins, and create from them another border or hem. Arthur fought with him and defeated him on the mountain of Arave. He skinned him and stripped off his beard. After this, Arthur never found any giant with such power or any one of whom he had such fear. When Arthur had killed the monster and Bedivere had taken his beard, they returned from the mountain happily and joyfully. They went back to the host and told them the story of where they had been and why. Then they displayed the head to everyone. Hoel grieved for his niece, and for a long time he felt great sorrow. He was ashamed that she had perished. For Our Lady the Virgin Mary he built a chapel on the mountain. The name derives from the tombstone where Eleine lay, and it now is called Eleine's Tomb [Tombelaine]. From the tomb in which the body was placed it received this name.

THE BATTLE BEGINS TO DETERMINE WHETHER ARTHUR OR THE ROMANS WILL HAVE FRANCE

(11609–46) WHEN the Irish arrived, and also the others who were due to come, Arthur, day after day, travelled through Normandy. He passed by castles and towns, and the number of people grew and got larger. They were all coming to help him at a time of need. He went through France and came to Burgundy. He wanted to go directly to Autun, for he had heard the news that the Romans were making their way there and taking control of the region. They were led by Lucius Hiber, who was the ruler of all Rome. When Arthur had to cross the river you have heard called the Aube, the peasants informed him, as did his spies, that if he wished he could find the emperor nearby, for in close proximity he had fixed his tents and his arbours. He had so many men, was in charge of so many kings, and rode with so many companies of men that anyone who awaited him would be a fool. His men would never cope with them, for it was four against one. He should make peace with him and abandon the combat. But Arthur was not dismayed. He was bold and trusted in God, and he had heard a number of threats. On the Aube, at a secure spot, he built a small castle. He had a good many men put there, and he had soon fortified it. His aim was to leave his equipment there, so that if he found himself in peril he could return to the castle.

(11647–72) Then Arthur called two counts, who were very wise and very eloquent. Each of them was of high birth. One was named Gerin of Chartres and the other Boso of Oxford, who was an expert on what was right and what was wrong. Gawain, who had been in Rome for a long time, was added to these two. Because of the esteem in which they were held, and because they were well known and well educated, the king brought them together and sent them to the emperor. He ordered the emperor to turn back and not to enter France, which belonged to Arthur. If he refused to return, on the first day of his arrival he should test himself in battle in order find out who had the greater right. For as long as he lived, Arthur would defend France against the Romans. He had captured it in battle and taken it in battle. A long time ago the Romans had done the same thing. Now, once more, battle could demonstrate which of the two should have France.

(11673–98) The messengers left Arthur and mounted their finest horses. They wore their hauberks and had their helmets laced upon them. They had their shields round their necks and their spears in their hands. Then you would have seen these knights, and these frivolous youths going to Gawain to give him advice, privately recommending that in the court to which he was going he should, before departing, perform some act that would launch the war that had been threatening for so long. But things would go badly wrong when the two sides got so close to each other without engaging in combat and dispersing so soon. The messengers crossed over a mountain, then a wood, then a plain. They could see the enemy's camp, and they came very close to it. Then you would have seen the Romans coming and knights emerging from the tents in order to meet the three messengers and find out their news. They were asking what they wanted, and if they were coming to make peace.

(11699–740) But the messengers did not come to a stop, or speak with them, until they reached the emperor. They dismounted in front of his tent, and had their horses kept outside. They approached the emperor and related Arthur's message. Each man said what he wished to say and what he considered appropriate. The emperor listened to it all, and when he cared to do so he replied:

'We come from Arthur,' said Gawain, 'and we bear Arthur's message. We are his men, and he is our lord. We must deliver his message in full. Through us he informs you—may all of you be aware of this—that it is forbidden for you to set foot in France or show any concern for it. Arthur rules France, and he will continue to rule it; he will defend it as his own. He informs you that you should take nothing from him, and if you challenge him for it let him be challenged in battle and let the claim be made in battle. The Romans took it in battle and conquered it in battle. He possessed it through battle and ruled it through battle. Let it be shown through battle that he should have power over it. Tomorrow, come without any delay if you wish to claim France, or leave and return home. Leave here, for there is nothing to concern you here. We have won, and you have lost.' The emperor responded that he was not going to retreat. France was his and he would go forward. He would be distressed if he were to lose it, and if he could conquer it he would do so. But it was his opinion that he would conquer and possess France.

(11741–64) Quintilien was sitting next to him and he spoke after him. He was his nephew and a very arrogant and very quarrelsome man.

'Britons', he said, 'are very boastful and they make very good threats. They issue boasts and threats, but they threaten much and do little.' I believe he would have said more, and he would have abused the messengers, but Gawain drew forth his sword, advanced, and made his head fly off his body. He said to the counts:

'Go and get on your horses!' Both the counts mounted, Gawain with them and they with him. Each one took his horse, and they left immediately with their shields round their necks and lances in their hands. They did not take their leave of the Romans. Lo, the court was in an uproar. The emperor shouted out:

'What are you doing? They have dishonoured us. Capture them for me, for it will be wrong if they depart.'

(11765–802) Then you would have heard men shouting:

'Arms, arms! Horses, horses! Come now, come now, on your horses, on your horses, spur, spur, quick, quick!' You would have very clearly seen the host quivering, putting on saddles, seizing horses, taking up lances, girding on swords, and spurring on to catch them up quickly. The counts took flight, looking round from time to time, and the Romans followed them in great haste, some taking the road, others the moorland, here two, here three, here five, here six, here seven, here eight, here nine, here ten. There was one who spurred on ahead, with his fine and swift-moving horse. He overtook his companions and repeatedly yelled:

'Stop here, knights, stop here! Not to turn round would be shameful.' But Gerin of Chartres did turn round. He took his shield and stretched out his arm, carrying it beyond his horse, as far as the lance would go. Then he said to him:

'Now things are worse. Your horse has leapt too far forward. You would have been better staying back at the tents rather than remaining here.' Boso took note of Gerin's action and heard his offensive remarks. He wished to do something similar. He turned his horse's head and went dashing off to do battle with a knight, and he with him without fear. Boso struck him through the throat right up to the marrow in his neck. He fell, with his throat gaping open, as Boso's lance had been thrust into his mouth.

(11803–22) The count cried out to him:

'Lord master, I know how to feed you with such morsels. Be in peace, lie here, and wait for those who are following you. Tell those who are to come here that the messengers went this way.' There was one man, born in Rome of a good Roman family. The Romans called him Marcel, and he had a very swift horse. He was one of the last to mount, but then he soon rode past those who were out in front. He did not carry a lance, for in his haste to depart he had left it behind. He went to attack Gawain, spurring his horse and loosening his reins. He had already managed to come up beside him, so that Gawain could not get away from them. Having promised to hand him over alive, he stretched out his hand to capture him.

(11803–56) Gawain saw how quickly he was coming up and that he was able to make such swift progress. He held on to his rein and came to a stop. Marcel was so close to him that he overran him. As he passed him by, Gawain drew his sword and plunged it straight into his head.

He split his body right down to his shoulders. His helmet failed to protect him, and he fell down and ended his life. Gawain said to him in courtly fashion:

'Marcel, you will inform Quintilien in hell, which is where you are going, that through you I tell him that the Britons are very bold. They wish to challenge for their rights, and they do more than threaten.' Then Gawain summoned his companions Gerin and Boso by name, saying that each of them should turn round and do battle with one of the pursuers. Gawain told them to do this, and they did so. Then they immediately killed three Romans. The messengers departed swiftly, and their horses carried them quickly, with the Romans, who did not spare them in any way, chasing after them. They successfully caught up with them, repeatedly striking with their lances and dealing heavy blows against them, sometimes with their lances, sometimes with their spears. But they never managed to strike hard enough to be able to hold on to them, wound them, unhorse them, or do them any harm.

(11857–80) There was one man there, a cousin of Marcel, who was riding an extremely swift horse. He grieved for his cousin, whom he saw lying beside the road. The pursuers were spurring through the meadows. They were coming up beside the three messengers and attempting to strike lateral blows. But Gawain saw this clearly and dashed forward to attack him. His opponent did not have the opportunity to turn round. He let his lance drop so that it was of no use to him. He drew his sword, and, intending to strike, raised his arm. Gawain completely cut off the arm he had raised. He made his sword, arm, and hand fly off over the meadow. He would have given him another blow, but the Romans were harrying him. They continued to pursue them until they fled into a wood that lay between them and the castle that Arthur had just built.

(11881–926) Arthur had sent six thousand knights after the messengers to search the woods and the valleys, and to scout round the region. They would have met up with the messengers, and, if need be, they would have come to their aid. They had made their way through a wood and come to a standstill close to it, sitting armed on their horses and watching out for the messengers. They saw all the plains covered with armed men in large divisions, and they recognized their messengers and saw the pursuers. They burst forward to face them with one voice and one cry. Immediately, the Romans pulled back and spread out amongst the meadows. Some of them were upset that they had gone so far in pursuit, for the Britons, who dealt them many a blow, launched a spirited attack on them as they turned. They attacked many of them and captured many. Petreius, a wealthy man, who had no equal for arms in Rome, had ten thousand armed men under his control; he commanded so many men. He heard about the attack that the Britons had launched. With ten thousand knights he immediately went to the help of the Romans. Using outright force and power, he caused the Britons to retreat into the wood with the armed men he was leading; they could not withstand him. The chase lasted as far as the wood because they were unable to stand firm against them. In the wood they defended themselves, but they could not resist. Petreius attacked them, but he lost many of his men, for the Britons knocked them down and dragged them into the wood. From the wood to the heath the slaughter was extremely intense.

(11927–64) When Arthur saw that his messengers were delayed, and that those he had sent out after them were not returning, he called to Yder son of Nu, and handed over to him five thousand knights. He sent them after the others and requested that they should keep a look-out for them. Gawain and Boso were doing battle and the others were dealing harsh blows. There was a great noise and a great uproar. Then Yder, the son of Nu, arrived. He thus invigorated the Britons, who recovered the ground that lay in front of them. Yder spurred his horse, shouting out his battle-cry, as did the men he brought with him. The combat was successfully accomplished, and many a saddle was emptied. Many a horse was captured and seized, and many a knight was sent tumbling. Petreius kept the battle going, holding his men back and retreating. He was skilled at fleeing, at turning, at pursuing, and at coming to a halt. You would have repeatedly seen fine chases with men turning in many places. He who was bold found someone else who was bold, he who wanted to joust soon jousted, he who wished to strike blows struck blows, and he who could not resist fell to the ground. The Britons spurred impetuously, not wishing to be arranged into companies. Their desire was to joust and to bear arms, and they desired to perform acts of chivalry, for which reason they did not move out of line. They were not concerned about how things turned out; they just wanted the war to start.

(11965–98) Petreius, a very savage man, kept his brave warriors close to him. He was skilled in battle, skilled in war, and also skilled in delaying tactics and in attacking. He often turned about and often spurred his horse. He rescued those who fell from their horses. Boso of Oxford, who could judge the state of a battle, realized that they would never escape without losses unless they killed Petreius, either killing him or capturing him. For through him the Romans resisted, and the Britons very rashly penetrated their men. He summoned a number of the boldest and the finest men to advise him.

'Barons,' he said, 'you who love Arthur loyally, speak to me. We have begun this battle without our lord knowing about it. If it works out well for us, all will be well, but if it is bad for us he will hate us. If we end up losing and gaining no glory from this field, we shall experience shame and loss, and incur Arthur's hatred. For this reason, we ought to strive to confound Petreius so that we can capture him dead or alive. Otherwise, we shall not manage to get away without suffering great losses. You must all do what I do, and follow me wherever I spur my horse.'

(11999–2040) They said that they would do this: wherever Boso went they would go. When he was accompanied by the men he required, and had seen and witnessed what sort of man was Petreius, who supported all the others, he hastened over in that direction ferociously, as did all the others. They never stopped or ceased riding until they came to the throng in which Petreius was riding and organizing his troops. Recognizing him, Boso charged over towards him and brought their horses into contact. He stretched out his arms and grasped him. He trusted his companions, and of his own volition he let him fall to the ground. Then you would have seen something wondrous: he fell down amidst the great throng. With Petreius in his arms Boso held his grip on him, and Petreius dragged himself along. He strove to make Boso let him go. The Romans raced to his rescue, and those bearing lances soon shattered them. When the lances were no longer of any use, they fought with their polished swords. They wanted to rescue Petreius, and the Britons wanted to provide help to Boso. You would have seen a fierce combat, a dense battle, and a harsh fight, with helmets bending, shields being pierced, hauberks torn, shafts breaking, saddles emptied, saddles turned, men falling to the ground, and men being wounded. The Britons shouted out their battle-cry, and the Romans did the same with theirs. Some of the men struggled to get hold of Petreius, and the others were constantly pulling him back. So dense was the fighting that it was scarcely possible to distinguish between Roman and Briton, except from their speech and their cries.

(12041–82) Gawain passed through the great throng, creating a way through with his sword. He struck and thrust, slashed and pushed, knocking down many of his opponents and scattering them. No Roman who saw the blows he struck failed to give way to him. Yder turned the other way, clearing a path through the Romans. Gerin of Chartres came to his assistance, and each of them fought for the other. They overtook Petreius and knocked both him and Boso down on to their backs. The Britons raised Boso and put him back on his horse. They held on to Petreius, who had received many a blow. In order to provide him with the protection of their troops, they led him to safety through the throng. Leaving him in the care of excellent custodians, they started the battle again. The Romans had no one to protect them, and they were like a ship without a helmsman that is driven by the wind whichever way it wishes, when there is no one to steer it properly. It was the same with the company of men that had lost its leader. Having lost its constable, it could no longer be protected. The Britons continued to scatter them, and they knocked down large numbers of them. They overtook the fallen and caught up with those fleeing, capturing some and killing some, stripping some and putting some in chains. Then they went about pulling their companions back and returning to their prisoners in the wood. They brought Petreius and presented him to their lord, along with a large number of other prisoners with him. Arthur thanked them, saying to them that if he were victorious he would increase the size of each man's fief.

(12083–126) Arthur had the prisoners watched over, and he handed them over to the guards. After discussion, and having taken advice, he decided to send them to Paris. He would keep them in prison until he could do with them what he wanted, for if he kept them with his men in the host he feared losing them somehow or other. Then he provided equipment for those who would take them, and he established who would lead them: Cador, Borel, Richier, and Bedivere the cupbearer, four counts of very high lineage. The king asked them to rise early and escort the prisoners, accompanying them until those leading them were safe and the fear had passed. The emperor had soon heard the news through his spies that those taking the prisoners away would be setting off early in the morning. He had ten thousand knights mount their horses, and he ordered them to travel all night until they outstripped the prisoners and, if possible, rescued them. Sertorius, lord of Libya, and Evander, king of Syria, and Caricius of Rome and Catellus Walerteius. Each of the four was a great landowner, and each was trained in war. These men were chosen and summoned to go and rescue the prisoners and to be in charge of the others. That evening ten thousand armed men set off. They were led by those who lived in the country, who were familiar with the straight paths. They rode all night and made such good progress that they reached the road to Paris, where they found a suitable spot to set up their ambush. There they silently came to a stop.

(12127–72) Next morning, Arthur's men were there, riding along with a goodly degree of confidence, but nevertheless fearing a trap. They rode in two groups. Cador and Borel with their men were upfront, and the counts Richier and Bedivere, whose task it was to look after the prisoners, followed by five thousand men. They were escorting the prisoners, whose arms were tied behind their backs and their feet tied underneath their horses. Suddenly, they came across the ambush set up by the Romans. The Romans jumped out, all at once. The whole area quivered and trembled. They attacked them boldly, and their opponents defended themselves well. Bedivere and Richier heard the great uproar and they saw the blows. They brought the prisoners to a halt and moved into a secure spot. They handed them over to their squires and ordered them to look after them. Then they let the horses go, and they did not cease spurring them until they joined forces with their own men. Then they did battle with great vigour. The Romans rushed here and there, spurring on their horses and intending to devote their energy into rescuing the prisoners, rather than into harrying the Britons. The Britons surged forward together and withdrew together, and they went to and fro together and defended themselves together. The Romans dashed up and down, seeking out the prisoners here and there. They strove so hard to find the prisoners that they lost a good number of men. The Britons divided themselves into groups and established four squadrons. Cador had the Cornishmen, Bedivere the Herupeis.* Richier had a company of his own men, and Borel had with him the men from Maine.

(12173–98) King Evander saw that their own strength and the number of their men were decreasing. He had them hold back, since they were unable to get to the prisoners. Then he had them stay together and strike in orderly fashion. The Romans had the upper hand and things turned worse for the Britons. They harried them and captured many of them. Four of the best men were killed: Er, Yder's son, a valiant and strong knight, was killed there, and Hyrelgas of Periron, no one was bolder than he was, Aliduc of Tintagel, whose kinsmen mourned him greatly, and Mauric Chadorkeneneis;* I do not know whether he was Breton or Welsh. Borel of Le Mans, a noble count, who gave great assistance to his men, conducted himself boldly and offered great encouragement to his men. But Evander charged towards him and caused the iron of his lance to pass right through his throat. Borel fell to the ground and was unable to stand up again.

(12199–232) The Britons continued to be dismayed, for they were losing so many of their men. Against one of their men there were seven Romans. They wanted to get their hands on them soon, so that they would soon be killed, captured, and discomfited, and they would soon have lost their prisoners. But Guitart, the count of Poitiers, who that day was in charge of the foragers, was soon to hear the news that a contingent of Romans was on the point of rescuing the prisoners. He gave the horses full rein in that direction with the three thousand knights, the foragers, and the archers. The Romans, who were discomfiting the Britons, were making every effort to strike, when Guitart arrived with his household knights, spurring on with their lances lowered. They unhorsed more than a hundred men, who never rose again. Lo, the Romans were alarmed, and they all regarded themselves as shamed. They thought that Arthur would be coming, with all his men following him. When they saw so many of their men falling, they had no hope of rescue. Those from Poitou attacked them violently, and the Britons were not faint-hearted. Men on both sides grew in strength, and they did their very best to unhorse the Romans, who turned round and fled, completely exposed and unprotected. Not knowing anywhere else that would be safe, they wanted to return to their camp.

ARTHUR IS VICTORIOUS, BUT AT GREAT COST

(12233–62) THE Britons pursued them for a long time and avenged their dead well. They followed them and caught up with them, not sparing any effort to knock them down. King Evander and King Catellus, and five hundred or more of those left, were struck and knocked down, some being killed and some captured. They captured as many of them as they liked, and as many as they could take away with them. Then they got back on the road, where the battle had taken place. Throughout the fields they looked for Borel, the brave count of Le Mans, and their dead. They discovered the count lying covered in blood, giving up the ghost. They carried away the wounded and buried the dead. They entrusted the first batch of prisoners to those to whom Arthur had given the order, and just as he had commanded, and sent them to Paris. The others, who had been recently captured, they had tightly bound. They took them to the castle with them and presented them to their lord. They told him what had happened and about the ambush, and with one voice they promised them that if he did battle with the Romans he would without doubt defeat them.

(12263–86) The emperor heard the news about the great defeat, about Evander, who was killed, and about the other men, who had been taken prisoner. He saw how dismayed his men were, and he witnessed the start of the war. He saw how badly things were going for him and that he would not make any gains. He was disconsolate and dismayed. Going over things in his mind, he was afraid. He was uncertain about what he should do, whether he should fight with Arthur or wait for the remainder of his men, who should be following him. He was terrified of fighting because it would not be to his advantage. He made the decision to go to Autun, via Langres. He summoned his men and sent them on their way. Late in the evening they reached Langres, where they took lodgings in the city and set up camp throughout the valleys. Langres is situated on the top of a hill with valleys surrounding it.

(12287–320) Arthur soon found out what they were intending to do, and which way they were heading. He was aware that the emperor would not do battle until he had more men, and he did not want to allow them to settle and take comfort so close to where he was. In so far as he could, he secretly summoned his men and gave orders to them. He went past Langres on the left, turning right beyond it. His aim was to outstrip the emperor and deny him access to Autun. With his army he travelled all night until morning, whether it was through woods or on plains, until he reached a valley that was called Soeïse.*

Anyone wishing to travel from Autun to Langres had to pass through this valley. Arthur had his men arm themselves and organized his squadrons so that whenever the Romans arrived they would be prepared to deal with them immediately. The equipment, and the camp followers, who would be of no use in battle, he placed beside a mountain, to look like an armed company, so that the Romans, if they saw them, would be frightened by how many of them there were. He arranged six thousand six hundred and sixty-six first-rate men in a wood at the top of a hill. I do not know whether it was to the right or to the left. Morid, count of Gloucester, would be the leader of this company.

(12321–57) The king said to them:

'Stop here, and, whatever happens, do not stir. If necessary, I shall come here and direct the others towards you, and if the Romans by chance flee in defeat chase after them and overtake them, killing them and not sparing any of them!' They replied: 'We shall do this.' Then Arthur chose another troop made up of noblemen, vassals, and those with helmets laced upon them, who were on horseback. He placed them in a more visible location with no one else as their leader other than himself. This was his own household, men whom he had nurtured and raised. As his own banner he had his dragon held in their midst. From the remaining men he created eight companies with two leaders in each one. One half of the companies was on horseback and the other half was on foot. He issued commands to all of them together, telling and begging those on horseback that when the foot soldiers were doing battle they should strike the Romans laterally and launch a lateral attack on them. Each squadron numbered five thousand five hundred and fifty-five knights, all of high quality. The divisions each had eight sections, four behind and five in front. In the middle were the other troops in very large numbers, each armed in his own fashion.

(12358–92) The front part of the first squadron was under the command of Agusel of Scotland, and the other part was under the leadership of Cador of Cornwall. Boso and Count Gerin of Chartres were in charge of the other company. The third squadron was handed over, well equipped and well armed, to Aschil, the king of the Danes and to Loth, the king of the Norwegians. Hoel took charge of the fourth one, along with Gawain, who was no coward. After these four there were four others, all ready to do battle. Kay the justiciar and

Bedivere the cup-bearer had control of these. Bedivere was the leader of the Herupeis and Kay led the Angevins and those from Chinon. Another of the squadrons was commanded by Holdin, count of Flanders, and Guitart from Poitou; they were glad to take charge of them. When Count Jugein of Leicester and Jonathas of Dorchester received the seventh company, they were lord and constable over them. Corsalen, count of Chester, and Urgent, count of Bath, had the eighth squadron under their control; Arthur had complete trust in them. The good men-at-arms, the good archers, and the valiant cross-bowmen were positioned on either side, outside the thick of battle, in order that they could shoot from the flank. They were all in front of the king, and he was behind them with his own squadron.

(12393–450) When Arthur had arranged his troops and established his squadrons, hear what he said to his retainers, his barons, and their sons:

'Barons,' he said, 'I am very comforted when I hear of your great qualities, your great virtues, and your great conquests. At all times I find you bold and well prepared. No matter who is upset by this, your prowess is constantly increasing and becoming all the greater. When I recall and consider that during your time Britain is, through you and your companions, mistress of thirty lands, I am delighted and filled with pride. I trust in God and in yourselves to conquer yet more lands, to capture more and to possess more. Your prowess and your skilful hands have conquered the Romans twice. Know that my heart gives me to understand, and everything points this way, that you will win another victory today. You have defeated the Norwegians, and you have defeated the Danes. You have defeated the French, and you rule France against their will. Since you have been able to defeat the best, you will definitely be able to defeat the worst. Their desire is to impose tax on you and to exact a tribute from you. They want to recover France. They expect to find here the sort of people they are bringing in from the east. One of us is worth a hundred of them. Do not spend any time fearing them, for women are worth just as much as they are. We must trust in God, and we must not give up hope that with a modicum of audacity we shall easily win. You will never fail me because of anyone else, and never take flight because of anyone else. I shall certainly find out how each man is performing and which one is the most successful. I shall be everywhere, see everything, and attend every critical situation.' When the king had spoken and set forth his views, they replied to him with one voice that they much prefer to die there and to leave the battlefield without a victory. Then you would have heard many solemn promises, many oaths being sworn, and many pledges being made. They swore that they would not fail him for fear of death, and that they would come to the same end as he did.

(12451–72) Lucius was born in Spain of a very good Roman family. Younger than forty and older than thirty, he still enjoyed the life of a young man. He was bold and possessed great courage, and he had already performed many acts of bravery. Because of his strength and his valour he had been made emperor. Early in the morning he left Langres, and he thought he could go straight to Autun. His numerous forces had all been set in motion, and the road was very broad and extensive. When he heard about, and was aware of, the trap that Arthur had created ahead of him, he saw that either he had to do battle or that he would have to withdraw. He was reluctant to return, for that would seem to be cowardice. If these enemies caught up with him, they would do him a great deal of harm, for joining battle and taking flight at the same time could not possibly be achieved.

(12473–518) He summoned his kings, his princes, and his dukes, of which he had two hundred and more, and also the senators. He addressed them:

'Fathers,' he said, 'noble lords, brave vassals, fine conquerors, you were the offspring of fine ancestors, who conquered great domains. Through them Rome is the capital of the world, as it still will be as long as Romans are alive. They conquered the mighty empire. It will be shameful if it deteriorates in our era. They were noble and you are noble, a valiant son of a valiant father. Each of you had a valiant father, and today their valour shines forth in you. Each man must make the very best effort to resemble his brave father. Shame will fall on anyone who deserves to lose his father's inheritance, and who because of cowardice abandons what his father conquered for him. I do not say, you must know, that I consider you to have declined. You were brave and you still are brave, and I regard you all as valiant. My lords, I can see and you can see. I know, and you know it well, that the way that leads directly to Autun has been cut off. We cannot pass that way unless it is by fighting. I do not know what new robber—either a robber or a thief—has closed off the way in front of us that I was going to take you. They thought that I was fleeing and abandoning the land to them, but I made a complete turn in order to force them into the open. Now they have launched an attack on us. So take up your arms and arm yourselves. If they wait for us, we shall strike them, and if they flee we shall pursue them. Let us contain their wickedness and destroy their power.'

(12519–62) Then they all dashed to pick up their arms, not wanting to wait any longer. They got ready to fight, created their squadrons, and organized their troops. There were many pagan kings and dukes mingling with the Christians, who held their fiefs from Rome, and they served the Romans because of their fiefs. In groups of thirty, forty, sixty, and hundreds, in legions and in thousands, the knights departed, many on foot and many on horseback, some on the mountains, and some in the valleys. Having all been ordered and arranged, they set off to do battle with Arthur's men. On one side, the Roman host, armed, entered the valley. On the other side, the Britons entered in front of them, having taken possession of the battlefield. Then you would have heard a great blowing of horns and a loud noise made by the bugles. In serried ranks and with quiet movements they approached and clashed with each other. As they got close, you would have seen arrows shot and darts hurled. No man there dared open his eyes or reveal his face. Arrows flew like hail, and the air became dark and gloomy. They started to shatter lances and to break and pierce shields. Then there was a mighty cracking of lances, and bits of broken shafts flew about. They started to use their swords and to deal great blows with their shining blades. A marvellous combat took place. I have never seen one that was more perilous, nor one more dense and more hostile. Anyone desiring to strike soon had the chance to do so. There was no place for those who were foolish or frightened, and cowards could not protect themselves. The mighty throng and the crowd hindered them from striking one another.

(12563–98) You would have seen the ground shaking greatly, one squadron attacking another, one troop colliding with another, some men striking each other, others shoving each other, some coming one way and some the other, some falling and others standing, shafts breaking with bits flying off them, swords drawn, shields raised, the strong overcoming the weak, the living trampling on the dead, saddle-girths and breastplates smashed, saddles emptied, and horses taking flight. They fought for a long time and dealt blows for a long time, as the Romans did not retreat or make gains over the Britons.

It was not easy to know who would win the day, until the squadron approached that was led by Bedivere and Kay. They saw that they were not making any gains and that the Romans were standing firm. With anger and outright hatred, they hurled themselves against the Romans with closely arrayed troops, right into the thick of the fighting. Bedivere struck well, as did Kay. God! What members of a king's court, what a seneschal, and what a cup-bearer they were! They conducted themselves so well with their steel blades. What a couple of warriors they would have been if they had lived for any length of time. They had accomplished a great deal and would have accomplished more. They went about breaking up the throng and striking down many of their opponents. They were followed by their large company of men, harrying the enemy greatly and striking immediately.

(12599–634) They received and dealt many a blow, killing and wounding many men. Bedivere, who did not rest or stop what he was doing, dashed into the throng. For his part, Kay never came to a standstill, for he knocked down many opponents and laid many men face down on the ground. If they had held back and retreated a little, until the Britons who were following them had caught up with them, they would have had great glory, great advantage, and protection against death. But they were too keen and too determined to keep pushing forward. They did not know how to spare themselves, and they wanted to pierce enemy ranks, trusting in their own great valour and in the large number of men they had under their control. But they encountered a troop of men being led by the king of Media. His name was Boccus and he was a pagan. He was a very courageous man, and he had a large number of men with him. Not fearing the size of their army, the counts fought with them. There was a very fierce battle and a well-sustained combat between pagans and Saracens, and Herupeis and Angevins. King Boccus had a sword in his hand. What a catastrophe it was that he came! He defeated the two counts. He struck Bedivere in the chest, causing the iron tip of his lance to pass right through his body. Bedivere fell, his heart broke, and his soul departed. May Christ protect him!

(12635–54) Kay found Bedivere dead and he wanted to carry him away. He held him very dear and loved him deeply. With as many men as he had he caused those from Media to disperse and to abandon the battlefield. But, as they tarried and waited whilst they took possession of Bedivere's body, the king of Libya arrived. His name was Sertorius and he was highly thought of. He had a very large number of pagan troops, whom he had brought from his own domain. They mortally wounded Kay and killed many of his men, wounding many and striking many. But he held on to the body. The remainder of his men rallied to defend it, and they carried it to the golden dragon, whether the Romans agreed to this or not.

(12655–78) Hyrelgas was Bedivere's nephew and he always loved his uncle dearly. From his men and his kinsmen he took as many as three hundred, with helmets, hauberks, and swords. They were mounted on fine, strong, and swift-moving horses. He gathered these men together in one division, then said to them:

'Come with me. I wish to avenge the death of my uncle.' Then he began to approach the Romans. He caught sight of the king of Media, whom he recognized from his banner. So he launched an attack on this division, continuing to shout out Arthur's battle-cry, like a madman who cannot be brought under control. He did not fear anyone or anything he encountered, intent as he was on being able to avenge his uncle. His companions darted forth with him. They took up their shields and lowered their lances, killing many of them and overthrowing them. They trampled over the fallen, and clashed with the troops who had killed Bedivere.

(12679–721) Using the strength of fine horses and the anger of fine warriors, they darted to the right and to the left under the leadership of Hyrelgas, not ceasing until they reached the banner, where they found King Boccus. Hyrelgas stared at him and turned his horse towards him, charging ahead through the throng and striking him on the top of his head. Hyrelgas was strong, and the blow was mighty; the blade was tough and sharp. The helmet was split and shattered and the coif of his hauberk was torn. He sliced through his body down to his shoulders. His heart burst and his soul departed. Hyrelgas stretched out his arm and grabbed hold of the body before it fell, dragging it across his horse in front of him and holding him face upwards on his horse. He dragged the body across the horse in front of him, uttering no sound or cry. The knight was enraged, and the horse was powerful. He retreated to where his men were in order to avoid blows from pagan or Roman. He dispersed the throng and broke through it, with his companions opening up the way for him. He carried the body as far as his uncle and hacked it to pieces. Then he said to his companions:

'Come, sons of barons. Let us go and kill these Romans, these scoundrels, these sons of whores. People who do not believe in God, or have any faith in him, have been brought to this country in order to kill us and our allies. Let us go, let us kill the pagans and also the Christians who have joined forces with the pagans with the intention of destroying Christianity. Come and put your strength to the test.'

(12722–62) Lo, they returned to the battlefield, and then you would have heard noises and shouting, and seen intense fighting with helmets and swords gleaming and sparks flying from the steel. Guitart, the brave duke of Poitiers, did not act like a coward, rather did he sustain the fighting on the battlefield all round him. He clashed with the king of Africa and they struck violent blows against each other. But the king of Africa fell to the ground, and the count passed in front of him, killing Africans and Moors. Holdin, who was duke of the Flemings and ruler of Bruges and Lens, swung round in the direction of the division of Aliphatima, a Spanish king. Count Holdin was also killed. Ligier, who was count of Boulogne, did battle with the king of Babylon. I cannot say who was the better striker, but each of them knocked the other down off his horse. The count died, and so did the king. Three other counts were killed there: Balluc, Cursal, and Urgent. All three of them were in charge of a large number of men. Urgent was lord of Bath and Balluc was count of Wiltshire. Cursal was count of Chester, which bordered on Welsh territory. These three were swiftly killed, having been attacked on both sides. The men whom they were supposed to lead, and who followed their banners, retreated to the division that Gawain, together with his companion Hoel, controlled. Never have there been two such vassals.

(12763–94) Never in times gone by have there been two such warriors for bravery and courtliness, nor with such a reputation for chivalry. The Bretons followed their lord Hoel. Their division was ferocious and bold, to such an extent that they were not afraid of any press or crowd. They darted here and there and broke through their opponents' ranks. Those who earlier had been pursuing their men and striking them down in heaps, were soon made to turn their backs. They caused many a man to thrash about helplessly. With the hefty blows they struck, and the large number of men they brought with them, they came right up as far as the banner that bore a golden eagle at its summit. There they found the emperor and the flower of his army. With him were noblemen and fine knights from Rome. There you would have seen mortal combat. Never, I believe, would you have seen one such. Kymar, who was count of Triguel, was in Hoel's division. He was a man of great courage, and he did much harm to Romans. But a Roman, who was on foot, struck him down dead with his lance. Two thousand Britons were killed with him, including three companions who were of noble birth.

(12795–812) One of these three was called Jaguz and he was from Bodloan. The second one was Richomarcus and the third Boclovius. In the squadron there were not six men of their valour and their reputation. If they had been counts or kings, there would, I believe, have been forever talk of their prowess. Men of immense vigour, they massacred the Romans. No one fell into their hands without losing his life, whether it be by lance or by sword. They launched an attack on the emperor's squadron in front of their own men, and the Romans caught up with them and killed all three of them at the same time.

(12813–52) Hoel and his cousin Gawain were filled with rage when they saw the great slaughter that the Romans had inflicted on them. In order to harm their enemies and avenge their companions, they charged at them like lions, and like beasts that had been let loose from captivity. They destroyed and massacred the Romans, striking them and raining blows down on them. The Romans held on very well and were met with good resistance. They received many blows and dealt many. They struck well and were well struck. They shoved well and were well shoved. Gawain was filled with great fury, and his desire to strike was not sated. His valour was always fresh and his hand was never weary. He went in pursuit of the Romans with vigour, and he made a vigorous effort to reach the emperor and do battle with him. He made such progress and performed so well, charging backwards and forwards, that he came up against the emperor, and each cast eyes on the other. The emperor saw Gawain and recognized him. They struck each other with great force, but both were strong, and neither of them fell to the ground. The emperor was tall and strong, and he was young, bold, and powerful, skilful, and of great power. He was filled with joy and delighted to be able to fight with Gawain, whose fame was so great. If he were able to escape with his life, he thought that in Rome he could boast of his exploits.

(12853–85) Raising their arms and lifting their shields, they attacked each other with remarkable blows. They did great damage to one another and pressed each other hard. They struck each other in many ways, and each one of them dealt blows against the other. Splinters flew off their shields and sparks flew off their steel blades. They were both very brave men. If they had had the entire battlefield to themselves, one of them would have come to his end. But the Romans recovered and gathered at the golden eagle, bringing help to the emperor, whom they had almost lost. They pushed back the Britons and took charge of the battlefield. Arthur saw that his men were withdrawing and that to his detriment the Romans were gaining in strength and taking over the battlefield. He was not able to wait, and he did not wish to do so. He moved forward with his division, shouting out:

'What are you doing? Advance. See me here, your protector. Do not let a single one of them get away. I am Arthur, your leader, and I do not flee the battlefield. Follow me. I shall lead the way and make sure that no one is faint-hearted. Remember your own bravery, you who have conquered so many kingdoms. I shall never leave this battlefield alive. I shall either conquer here or die here.'

(12886–911) Then you would have seen Arthur fighting, killing men and knocking them down, breaking hauberks, shattering helmets, cutting off heads, arms, and hands. He held Caliburn, which was smeared in blood. Anyone he caught up with he knocked down dead. I cannot describe his blows. With each blow he killed a man. Like a lion driven by hunger, he killed each beast he encountered. The king did exactly the same, leaving neither horse nor man alive. Whoever received a blow from him, or was wounded by him, had no use for a doctor, for he would never recover from the blow that Arthur had struck, however slight it may have been. They all fled from Arthur's path, like the sheep that flees before the wolf. He pursued the king of Libya. Sertorius was his name and he was a powerful man. Arthur sliced the head off his body, saying to him:

'A curse on you who came here bearing arms in order to cover Caliburn with blood.' The man who lay there dead said nothing.

(12912–42) Polidetes stood next to him. He was a powerful king of Bithynia, a pagan land. Arthur found him in front of him and dealt him a remarkable blow, slicing the head from his shoulders. His head fell to the ground and his trunk remained upright. As Arthur struck his blows and spoke his words, the Britons attacked the Romans, and the Romans responded ferociously. They drew their swords and shattered their lances. They inflicted great harm on the Britons, returning force with force. Arthur saw them and this gave him a great deal of strength. He struck great blows with Caliburn, but the emperor did not tarry. He killed Arthur's men one after the other, yet they could not come into direct contact with each other and attack each other, so dense was the throng and so intense was the battle. The two sides fought well, and you would soon have seen many thousands of men dead. They fought ferociously and killed each other ferociously. It was not clear who would win, who would be defeated or who would be killed, when Moruid arrived with his company, which was in the wood on the mountain, where Arthur intended to rally his troops if things turned out badly for his men. Six thousand six hundred and sixty-six knights with their horses and, with shining helmets, bright hauberks, and upright lances, their blades raised, came down the mountainside without the Romans catching sight of them.

(12943–76) They came up behind them and struck them, splitting their army into two and dispersing all its members. They separated them from each other and laid them low. Their horses trampled on them, and they killed them with their swords. The Romans could not stay on their feet and could not carry on. Great throngs of them fled, and they trampled over each other. The emperor was struck down. He was hit in the body by a lance. I cannot say who knocked him down, and I cannot say who struck him. He was caught in the throng and killed in the throng. He was discovered dead amongst the dead, wounded in the body by a lance. Those from Rome, those from the east and all the others at the same time, fled the battlefield. The Britons pursued them and destroyed them, killing so many of them that they were all wearied by the whole process. They passed over the dead bodies. You would have seen blood running in rivers and the dead lying in mountains. Fine palfreys and fine warhorses ran loose over the fields.

(12977–3009) Arthur was happy and joyful because he had overcome the arrogance of Rome. He gave thanks to the King of Glory through whom he had gained his victory. He had all the dead men searched for, and his own men and his allies removed. He had some of them buried in that spot and some taken to their own lands. He had a great many of the men buried in the abbeys throughout the region. The emperor's body was removed and guarded with great honour. He sent him to Rome on a bier, and he informed the Romans that from Britain, which he ruled, there was to be no further tribute, and anyone seeking a tribute from him would be sent back to him in the same way. Kay, who had been mortally wounded, was taken to his castle at Chinon. He created and built Chinon, and from Kay it received its name Kynon. He did not live long and died very quickly. He was buried in a hermitage in a wood near Chinon. In Bayeux in Normandy, which he ruled, they buried Bedivere near the gate, south of the city. Holdin was taken to Flanders and buried in Thérouanne, and Ligier was taken to Boulogne.

ARTHUR VOWS TO TAKE REVENGE ON MORDRED, WHO HAD STOLEN HIS WIFE AND HIS KINGDOM

(13010–52) ARTHUR, who remained in Burgundy, spent the whole winter there. He captured the cities and made peace with them. In summer he wanted to cross Montgieu and to travel to Rome, but Mordred caused him to turn back. O God, what shame, O God, what wickedness! He was his nephew, son of his sister, and he was in complete charge of his kingdom. He had handed over the entire kingdom to him. Mordred wanted to take it all from him and retain it for his own purpose. He took homage from all the barons and hostages from all the castles. After this great wickedness Mordred committed another act of villainy, for contrary to the Christian religion he took the king's wife to his own bed. The wife of his uncle and his lord he took to bed as a traitor would do. Arthur heard of this, and he knew in truth that Mordred had not maintained faith with him. He had ruled his land, but had taken his wife. Arthur was not grateful to him for such a service. He passed over all his troops to Hoel, and he handed over France and Burgundy to him, asking him to take care of everything and bring peace everywhere. He would return to Britain, taking with him those from the islands, and he would take revenge on Mordred, who had his wife and his domain. He would have no esteem for all his conquests if Britain, his fief, were to be lost. He would prefer to leave Rome unconquered than to lose his own land. He would return very soon, he said, and go to Rome. Thus, Arthur made his way to Wissant, complaining of the perjury of Mordred, who had forced him to leave behind him a great conquest. At Wissant he made his fleet ready.

(13053–76) Mordred found out that Arthur was coming back. He did not want to, or deign to, make peace with him. He informed

Cheldric from Saxony, a duke who had brought him eight hundred well-provisioned ships, all filled with knights. In order to gain their assistance and their might, Mordred gave them, and granted them as an inheritance, the land from the Humber as far as Scotland, and the domains that Hengist had in Kent when Vortigern married his daughter. When Mordred had organized his men, they were a fine and powerful group. Between the pagan and the Christian troops there were sixty thousand knights with hauberks and warhorses, and Mordred thought he could wait for Arthur with confidence, since he expected to be able to defend the ports against him. In order to seek peace or to repent, he had no wish to pass over to him what was rightfully his. In order to seek peace, or to repent, he knew himself to be so guilty that to seek peace would be foolish.

(13077–102) Arthur had his ships readied. He had so many men with him that I could not count them. He wanted to reach Romenel [Richborough]* and he set his ships in that direction. But before he had landed there, Mordred swiftly attacked him with his men, who had sworn an oath to him. Those in the ships did their best to dock, and those on land prevented them from doing so. On both sides they strove, shooting arrows and hurling darts, piercing bellies, breasts, and heads, and, when they could get close enough, putting out eyes. Those in the ships had to devote so much attention to steering them and to the effort to reach land that they had no opportunity to strike or protect themselves. A great number of men lay dead in the water. They repeatedly fell and toppled, calling those on land traitors. As he tried to unload the ships on shore, Arthur suffered a great loss of men, as many heads were sliced off bodies. His nephew Gawain was killed there. Arthur suffered immense sorrow because of him, for he loved no man so much.

(13103–42) Agusel, the powerful king of Scotland, was killed, along with Gawain, and also many others, whom the king mourned and lamented greatly. As long as they were on the shore, Arthur could do nothing but lose men. But once they were on level terrain and equal footing, neither Mordred, nor the great army he had with him, could survive for long. Mordred's men came from many places; they had been brought up in peace and repose. They did not know how to protect themselves, how to turn about, or how to strike as did Arthur's troops, who were brought up on war. Arthur and his men struck them there, and with their swords they provided them with excellent service. They killed them in their twenties and their hundreds, and they slaughtered many of them and captured many. The massacre was great, and it would have been greater if evening had not prevented it. Daylight failed and night came. Arthur stood up and held his men back. Mordred's men took flight. Do you think that they acted as guide for each other? No one cared for anyone else, for each man's thoughts were for himself. Mordred fled all night long in search of refuge, wherever he could find it. He thought he would be able to stay in London, but he was not welcomed by those who were there. He crossed the Thames and London, not stopping until he reached Winchester, where he lodged in the city. He summoned his men and his allies. Against their will, he took oaths of fealty and homage from the citizens that they would do their best to maintain the city in peace and to remain loyal to him.

(13143–200) Arthur, who had a great hatred for Mordred, had no intention of remaining idle. He was filled with sorrow because of Agusel and Gawain, whom he had lost. His sorrow for his nephew was immense, and I do not know where he put the body. He turned his anger and rage against Mordred, if only he could kill him. He followed him to Winchester, summoning men from all parts. He wanted to besiege the city and surround it with troops. When Mordred saw Arthur and the host, he gave the impression that he would fight, and that he wished to fight, for if he were besieged for long he would not escape without being captured. If it were possible for him to be captured, he would never escape from Arthur alive. He made all his men gather together, take up their arms, and arm themselves. He arranged them into divisions and sent them out to do battle. As soon as they had departed, all the members of the host rushed over in that direction. Many blows were struck immediately, many men were killed and many wounded. Things began to go badly wrong for Mordred, as his men proved to be of no use to him. But he gave thought to protecting himself. He had committed a large number of misdeeds and was afraid of the king. He gathered together secretly all his closest advisers, the men he had raised and those who hated Arthur most. He let the remainder of his men fight, while he took a path to Southampton. He did not stop until he reached the shore. With him he took helmsmen and mariners, to whom he made promises and gave bribes. He made them take to the sea so that Arthur could not catch them. They took him to Cornwall. He was afraid of

Arthur and was keen to flee. King Arthur besieged Winchester, defeated the people, and captured the city. To Yvain, the son of Urien, who was a prominent member of the court, he gave Scotland as his heritage, and Yvain did homage to him for it. He had been the nephew of Agusel, and he claimed it as his rightful heritage, for Agusel had no son or wife, who could take the kingdom from Yvain. Yvain was a man of great valour, and he enjoyed immense fame and honour from the battle and the war that Mordred had launched in England.

(13201–22) The queen heard and found out that Mordred had been forced to flee so often. He could not defend himself against Arthur, and he did not dare to wait for him on the battlefield. The queen was staying in York and she was deeply concerned and saddened. She recalled the wickedness she had perpetrated in committing shameful acts because of Mordred. She had dishonoured the good king and given her love to his nephew Mordred. He had married her in contravention of religion, and as a result she had shamed herself. She would rather be dead than alive, and she was deeply sad and downcast. She fled to Caerleon and entered an abbey there, becoming a veiled nun. She was hidden away in the abbey and not heard of, or seen. She was not found, or known about, because of her shameful behaviour and the sin she had committed.

BOTH ARTHUR AND MORDRED ARE MORTALLY WOUNDED AT THE BATTLE OF CAMLANN; ARTHUR IS TAKEN TO AVALON TO HAVE HIS WOUNDS TENDED, GIVING THE KINGDOM TO CONSTANTINE, CADOR'S SON, UNTIL HIS RETURN—THE 'BRETON HOPE'

(13223–74) MORDRED held on to Cornwall, but he had lost all his other land. By land and by sea he sent for, and summoned, pagans and Christians, He summoned the Irish and the Norwegians, and he summoned the Saxons and the Danes, and all those who hated and feared Arthur, those who had no land and those who were willing to serve in order to hold land. He summoned those who had no land, but who wished to give service for it. He gave, promised, and begged, like a man who was in great need. Arthur was sorrowful and upset that he had not avenged himself on Mordred. It troubled him greatly that Mordred had even a small amount of land. He had gathered men there and was making every effort to have more. It was his intention to hold on to his land and to capture more. Arthur found out about this, and it upset him. He summoned his whole host as far as the Humber. The number of men involved was great; I do not know how many there were. The king had a large number of men, and he went looking for Mordred where he knew him to be. He wanted to kill and destroy this traitor and this perjurer. Mordred had no desire to flee. He preferred to take a risk and expose himself to danger, rather than to keep on fleeing. The battle took place near the river Camble* in the region of Cornwall. The troops gathered in great fury, clashed with each other in great fury, and the battle was joined in great fury. Great was the number of men and great was the slaughter. I do not know who performed best, who lost or who conquered, who fell or who remained upright, who did the killing or who died. The loss was great on both sides, and the plain was covered in corpses and in the blood of the dying. At that time the fine young knights raised by Arthur perished, youths he had assembled from a large number of lands and from the Round Table, and who were famous throughout the world. Mordred was killed in the battle, as were most of his men, and also the flower of Arthur's troops, the strongest and the finest.

(13275–98) Arthur, if the account does not lie, was mortally wounded. He had himself taken to Avalon so that his wounds could be treated. He is still there. The Britons are waiting for him,* as they say and understand. From there he will come, and he will go on living. Master Wace, who composed this book, does not wish to say any more about his end than the prophet Merlin does. Merlin says about Arthur, and he is right, that his death would remain in doubt. The prophet told the truth. Since then, it has always been doubted, and will be doubted, I believe, for all time, whether he is dead or alive. In truth, he had himself taken to Avalon five hundred and forty-two years after the Incarnation. It is a great shame that he did not have children. He bequeathed his kingdom to Constantine, the son of Cador of Cornwall, his cousin, telling him that he would be king until he returned.

(13299–330) Mordred had two fully grown sons. They were very arrogant and very presumptuous. They saw all the barons who were dead, as well as the large number of troops who were destroyed. They saw that Arthur was long gone, and they saw the man who had just been appointed king. The Saxons, who were with Mordred and had escaped from the battle, joined forces with them. They flattered and beseeched them until they retained them as mercenary soldiers; they granted them extensive lands. They took possession of the best lands in the country. One of them launched an attack on London and the other wanted to keep hold of Winchester. They thought they would be lords there. But Constantine, who made a great effort to defeat them, came after them. He found one brother in Winchester and decapitated him before the altar of St Amphibal. Pay heed to whether or not this was an act of sin and wickedness. Then he followed the other brother. The latter was aware of this, and he had heard that he had come, so he went and hid in a church. But this was no help to him, for the king decapitated him there; he made his head fly off his trunk. He reigned for three years and was then killed. This caused great sorrow to his friends. He was carried to Stonehenge and buried with great honour.

(13331–55) Cunan, his nephew, reigned after him. He was arrogant and had a very high opinion of himself. He was not skilled in making or maintaining peace, and he allowed his men to join battle. They fought throughout the cities. The barons were at war, and there was often great discord between himself and his men. He made war against his uncle and captured him, and he killed his uncle's two sons because they were his rightful heirs and ought to have ruled his kingdom after him. He was king for five years and a little more, and after him Vortyporus reigned. During his reign the Saxons, who thought they could take the land, rebelled. They caused a great deal of trouble to his men. May God destroy their whole lineage! They got off to a good start, causing serious damage to the king. In the end he made a huge effort, assembling soldiers and gathering men together. He did not spare a single one of the Saxon dwellings without taking a good hostage from it. Then he maintained peace until his death.

(13356–84) Malgo, his nephew, who loved chivalry very much and practised it all his life, was king after him. He conquered the islands in the vicinity and took homage from their kings. In beauty and in fine manners he outdid all his ancestors. He was very handsome and very elegant, and he loved all his kinsmen. He was exceedingly generous, and he never held on to money. He considered himself as scorned, dishonoured, and shamed if on a particular day he had not given away a goodly amount of money, for whoever it might be would have been grateful to him. He had only the one bad trait that marks out those called Sodomites. No one knew of any other vice of his, and he did not commit any other act of wickedness. Then Cariz was king of the land, but in war he lost the whole of it. He was grief-stricken and ill-fated, and he was filled with hatred for other people. In his time there was a great invasion by pagans and foreigners, whom Gormund brought over the sea. You have definitely heard of them, as they created the destruction leading to the loss of the name Britain.

GORMUND, THE AFRICAN, CONQUERS IRELAND, AND DESTROYS MUCH OF BRITAIN

(13385–428) GORMUND was rich and powerful, and he was a man of very great valour. He was bold and of noble disposition, and he came from a very important family. He was from Africa, the son of a king who followed the pagan religion. He would have had the kingdom after his father and been king if he had wanted to be. But he did not wish to, or deign to, be king. He gave the kingdom to one of his brothers. He granted his land and his domain to one of his younger brothers, saying that he would never be king unless he was victorious over a kingdom. Across the sea he would go, he said, making conquests so that he would be king in another land. With regard to him, Merlin prophesied that he would become a pirate. He sought sailors, helmsmen, and various types of ships. Gormund took with him in his ship a hundred and sixty thousand armed men, all well known and famous, in addition to helmsmen and to sailors, and to men-at-arms and to archers. I do not know how many ships there were; there were many ships and a great many men. He sailed across many great seas, capturing many islands and many kings. He seized and took possession of many lands. He went sailing so far over the seas, conquering kings and lands, that he arrived safely in Ireland. He captured it quickly and called himself king of Ireland. Then he wanted to go to England. In England there were Saxons, who were waging war on the Britons. They had made frequent challenges and engaged in battle, in order to make conquests over Thongcastre in Lindsey, which had initially been held by Hengist, and Kent, which had at first been ruled by Octa, his son, who dwelt over towards Scotland.

(13429–62) The Saxons had often had everything and often lost everything, often given hostages and often paid homage, so that the

Britons would recognize them and agree to their homage and offer them both peace and a truce. When they had made a variety of promises, done homage, and provided hostages, their loyalty was so suspect that as soon as they saw the place and the opportunity, and as soon as some new king died or became enfeebled, they immediately turned to rebellion, theft, and robbery. They dwelt in Northumbria. That was where they came from, and that is the place to which they returned. They heard about Gormund, who was so powerful and brave. They agreed to peace and a truce with the British, and they sent messengers to Gormund. They gave him many gifts and made many promises to him. Then they beseeched him and requested that he should come over to them in Britain and hand the land over to them. They would gladly hold it from him and gladly serve him in respect of it. They would give him an annual tribute, and they would recognize him as their lord. He was a pagan, and so were they, but the Britons were Christians. They should assist each one another and destroy Christianity. As they had just one religion, they should have just one king.

(13463–514) When Gormund heard their request, he made his way to Northumbria with the fleet he had ready. He went to talk with the Saxons, and with hostages and oaths of fealty he confirmed their agreement to free the land and to hand it over to the Saxons. The Saxons would keep faith with them and give him an annual tribute. Then they began to destroy the land. O God, what pain and what harm for a fair and noble land to suffer that has fallen into such utter ruin! The Saxons led the way for the Africans, burning houses and destroying towns. They beat, chased away, and killed knights, peasants, clerics, monks, and nuns. They contravened the law of the Lord God. You would have seen a large amount of land destroyed, women shamed, men impaled, children disembowelled in their cradles, money seized, booty carried off, towers knocked down, and towns burnt down. The king was lacking in power, and he was unable to muster enough men to be able to dare to stand in Gormund's way. He did not dare to wait for him in open country, for he could not defend himself to his advantage. The pagans went about seizing everything; no cleric or priest was safe. The good bishops and canons, the good abbots or good monks, had no guarantee of safety. Disheartened, they all left their cells and their abbeys, taking with them holy bodies and relics. They were fearful and filled with sorrow. Those who could flee the fastest did so. The poor fled and the rich fled, the townsmen fled and the peasants, the villeins fled and the vavasours, and also a large number of barons. They had little faith in tall towers, since they had no hope of finding assistance. Bedchambers were emptied, halls were abandoned, and some fled to Wales. Those who could do so, and who had ships, went to Brittany. Those who had no access to ships remained in Cornwall.

(13515–58) Gormund went in search of Cariz, and he fled until he was seized in Cirencester, where Gormund besieged him. Ysembard was present at the siege, as he could not find refuge elsewhere. He was the nephew of King Louis, who had driven him out of France. He had cast him out of France and dispossessed him of his fief. Ysembard spoke to Gormund. He became his vassal and renounced God. He renounced God and his belief in him in order to take revenge on the king of France. This wretched man was so deceived, so deranged, and so faithless that he abandoned the Creator's love and received the pagan religion. The pagans besieged Cirencester. None of those inside wanted to be there. The pagans surrounded them with their pavilions, erected their tents, and set up their encampment. They had laid waste the whole region, seized provisions, and taken them away. They enclosed the city so tightly that no one inside dared to leave it. They built slings and watchtowers, and they attacked them repeatedly. They had their devices brought up to the walls, but they could not construct anything that the inhabitants could not withstand. They interlaced timber and wattle, rebuilt the battlements, and prepared the gates. In the daytime they opened them, and at night they kept watch. They prepared parapets and also walls. As some slept, others remained awake. They drew up stones to defend themselves, and yet they were intensely perturbed, for they did not know, and could not see, any device through which they could defend themselves. Those outside attacked them frequently, but they did their very best to defend themselves. Gormund could not take them by force.

(13559–91) When Gormund saw that he could not capture them, and that he had to take a rest, all round the city he built castles with brattices and battlements. He handed one over to Ysembard, so that in his direction he could watch the city. Another he gave to his barons and another to the Saxon princes. In the area where he was able to rest he built a tower for his own use. He was there and he lay there. He amused himself there and he slept. The people inside were not cowardly. When they saw an opportunity, they launched an attack on those who were on the outside. There were often violent battles and skirmishes, and men were often captured, wounded, and killed. But those outside, who were very numerous, made their opponents withdraw into the city. They pushed and shoved them but had little success when it came to capturing the walls. Those inside defended themselves for a long time. They withstood the attack for a long time, and they would have continued to do so and been impossible to take by force, if the town had not been engulfed by flames. This caused great damage and great harm. Those outside, using great trickery such as had never been heard of before or since, set the city on fire.

(13592–624) Hear how they set the city alight. Using snares and birdlime, they captured sparrows and set fire to nutshells. Inside the nutshells they concealed fire and flammable material made out of flax and tinder. They attached them to the sparrows' feet, thus committing an act of great cunning. In the evening, when eventide came, they released the sparrows. The birds flew to the nests where they were accustomed to spend the night, in piles of corn and hay and in the eaves of dwellings. The fire took hold and heated up, setting fire to, and burning, the town. The Britons saw the town burning, flames dancing off it and dwellings collapsing. They made ready to do battle, but they were defeated, as they were so small in number. King Cariz withdrew, and so did all the others, one after the other. He made his way straight to Wales. I cannot say what happened to him. In this way the famous city was completely destroyed and laid waste. Because it was captured due to sparrows, and conquered due to sparrows, some people used to call it, and some still do, the City of Sparrows, in order to record the marvel that the city, which held on for so long, was lost due to these birds.

HOW GORMUND'S 'DONATION' ENABLES THE SAXON TAKEOVER OF BRITAIN

(13625–62) GORMUND destroyed many a city, many an ancient castle, many churches, many clerics, many bishops, and many abbeys that were not subsequently rebuilt or occupied. The ruins are still visible, as are the deserted spaces and the wasteland that Gormund created in many places in order to rob the Britons of their fiefs. When he had laid waste the country, burnt the towns, and stolen everything they had, he gave the kingdom to the Saxons. He had promised to give it to them if he conquered it, and he did so, truly doing right by them. Having had a great desire for the land, they welcomed it. Because of the lineage they came from, which was the first to have the land, they called themselves English in order to have a memory of their origins, and the land that was given to them they called England.* One says Engleterre in French, just as one says England in English. It is the land of the English, according to the name; that is how it should be interpreted. As soon as Brutus came from Troy, the name that it always had was Britain, right up to the time I am telling you about when, because of Gormund, it lost its name and acquired new inhabitants, new kings, and new lords. They wished to maintain their customs and did not wish to take on any other language. They changed the names of the towns and named them in their language.

AUGUSTINE'S MISSION TO CONVERT THE ENGLISH (STRUGGLES AGAINST THE BRITONS, WHO WERE ALREADY CHRISTIANS)

(13663–92) THE English wished to choose a king, but they were unable to decide on whether they should have just a single king, with everyone being subject to only one monarch. But they could not agree on a single king, so with common consent they appointed a number of kings in a number of regions and divided up the lands. On many occasions they fought each other and on many occasions they made peace. As each one became stronger, he would defeat the weakest. Thus, over a long period of time they had no crowned king, nor were any churches rebuilt, and the Christian religion was not adhered to. No altars were consecrated or dedicated, and no child was raised to the font or baptized. More than a hundred years passed without the existence of any religion or faith. St Gregory, who was pope at that time, heard of this. He sent St Augustine there. He was a fine cleric and the pope loved him deeply. Forty highly regarded clerics accompanied him. He first arrived at Thanet, and from there he went on into Kent. He approached Canterbury, and the people honoured him greatly.

(13693–747) King Aldebert, who ruled Kent, came from Hengist's lineage. He heard of St Augustine and was baptized, believing in

God. After the king, his whole household was born again and baptized. Augustine derived great joy at the people he converted. In the name of the Holy Trinity he built a church in the city. He went round the land giving sermons, creating churches, and ordaining clerics. In some places he came across people who were wicked and who did good only with reluctance. Augustine strove very hard, and he worked for a long time before he could cause them to serve God and to love God. When he had covered the whole of the country and travelled round it extensively, his journeying brought him to Dorset, proclaiming the law of the Lord God. Close to Dorset, over towards the south, there were people to whom Augustine gave sermons and proclaimed the law of God. These were people of evil disposition, and they had no interest in his sermons. In places where the saint gave sermons and said things that were to their advantage, they hung rays' tails on the back of his clothing. With these tails they sent him away and chased him for a very long time. He prayed to Our Lord that, because of this great act of dishonour and this terrible degradation, a sign and reminder should be sent to them. Indeed, they received them, and would do so for all time, for all those who shamed him and who hung the tails on him were given tails of which they were never able to get rid. Then all of those who came from this lineage had tails. They were, and still are, equipped with tails. They have tails behind them in remembrance of the shame they inflicted on the friend of God by humiliating him with tails.

(13748–82) When St Augustine had escaped from them, he went into a valley that was five leagues away from Dorset, between two valleys towards the north-west. He came to a stop at the foot of the mountain along with his companions, who were all weary. They stopped there to get some rest. They were hot, thirsty, and tired, and Augustine began to think about how he could go on tolerating the shame that was being inflicted on him. He started to wonder whether he should leave. Then God appeared to him and said to him clearly:

'Keep to your plan,' he said, 'and act with confidence. You are my servant, and you are pleasing to me. What you do pleases me. You will receive help from me, for I am with you. Whatever you require I shall grant you. The entrance to heaven is open to you, and you are permitted to come inside. You will find heaven open at the point where those people enter who serve me well.' Augustine had seen God and heard his words of comfort. He gazed at him for as long as he could, and that was for as long as it pleased God. He approached the place where God had been, and weeping he said a prayer there. He bent down, kissed the ground, and fell to his knees repeatedly. Then he fixed a staff in the very spot where he had seen God. A spring burst forth from it that covered the whole area. The water spurted out and the stream increased, creating its own channel and running down.

(13783–812) Before that time the region had not been occupied or cultivated, because there was no source of water there, and no spring water spouted forth. Augustine thanked God and comforted his companions. The place where he saw God he called Cernel. The meaning in the vernacular of this place I have mentioned is 'he sees God', or 'he saw God'. Clerics know this well: the meaning of *cerno*, *cernis* is 'to see', and in Hebrew God's name is El.* These two words make up Cernel. *Cerno* and El are put together, but one letter has been removed from the end of *cerno* so that the combination, from Hebrew and Latin, is formed via an excision. This is what Augustine saw, and this is what he wanted, when he gave the place its name. It should act as a reminder for us that the Lord God was in this place, and that he had seen him there. When we hear this name Cernel, we are to be aware and recall that the Lord God showed himself there, spending time there and speaking there.

(13813–64) When the English and the Saxons, first the kings then the barons, had received baptism, been raised at the font and anointed with holy oil, Augustine, who had a great desire for their salvation, was filled with joy. In the lands ruled by the Britons, who defended themselves against the English, he found monks, abbots, seven bishops, and an archbishop, whose see was Caerleon. In Bangor there was an ancient abbey. Dionot was its abbot, and it had almost two thousand monks, divided into seven groups. In each of the seven sections there were around three hundred monks. Thus, there were seven monasteries. They lived off their own manual labour. Augustine asked to see the seven bishops, telling them that he was a legate from Rome and that he was primate of England. They should receive his blessing and be subject to him. They replied, saying:

'We have no need to do this, for we have our own archbishop, whose see is at Caerleon, and who has been ratified by Rome. This will never be altered by anyone. We must not do so, especially because the English are our opponents. They have thrown us out of our lands and dispossessed us of our fiefs. We are, and have been, Christians who were born of Christians. They are of pagan stock and have recently been converted. To us it seems to be humiliation and great shame, and not one of us would be bold enough to recommend that we should be subject to him, who strives to provide salvation for those who have driven us out of our lands, and who have taken up residence there. All these people are our enemies. They have converted the English and are on good terms with them. They are friendly with them and have a good association with them.'

(13865–904) Augustine could not make any more progress, nor could he make them change their minds. He discussed this with King Aldebert, who became very annoyed. Aldebert was king of Kent. He summoned Elfrid, who was a kinsman of his, and king of Northumbria. They gathered the English together, their allies and all their vassals, the strongest and the bravest. They intended to destroy Bangor and put Abbot Dionot to death, together with all the monks and the other clerics in the city. They had no respect for them, and they were unwilling to submit to them or to make a profession of faith, except to the prelate in Caerleon. They had rejected Augustine in vile and shameful fashion. They summoned their knights and their foot soldiers, gathering them together in Leicester. That way they wanted to cross over and enter Wales. Brochinal ruled the city. He was a British count, and he summoned as many men as he could, intending to do battle with the English. But the English held firm, and because he had so few men he was defeated. He lost a great many of his men and fled into a wood. The good hermits, the good monks, the God-fearing canons, as well as the inhabitants of Bangor, all came to Leicester to beseech Elfrid, and those who were to rule over them, to show mercy and pity to the people and the clergy.

(13905–44) Those who belonged to the religious orders, clerics who only wanted what was good, hermits, monks, peasants, the poor, and citizens who had gone into hiding, emerged from many places, many barefoot, many in rags; they all went to seek mercy from these foreigners. But these men were cruel, wicked, and as proud as lions. Being in the ascendancy, they did the worst they could. God, what grief! O God, what wickedness! They did not show any more mercy than a famished wolf shows to sheep. They slaughtered them in great numbers, capturing two thousand two hundred of them, beheading them, and killing them. No monk or cleric was spared. They turned those who confessed their faith into martyrs. Then they wanted to go to Bangor, to destroy the city, and to kill people. The Britons and the Welsh who heard this gathered many men together to oppose them. In the land there were three barons, who were lords over the British. The reason they were lords was that they were stronger and better warriors. Bledric of Cornwall was a lord, and he ruled Devonshire. Just as the water from the river Exe flows from the spring from which it surges forth as far as the sea, where it descends into the sea, they ruled the Britons for a long time. But when Adelstan reigned, he drove them across the Tamar. Chatwan was king of North Wales, and Margadud was king of South Wales. The whole of the land was theirs as far as the Severn, which runs from Malvern close to the mountain.

(13945–82) But Adelstan pressed them so much that he pushed them beyond the Wye. The three men who were lords over their opponents took with them knights and foot soldiers, and angrily and violently they attacked the English and the Saxons, who withstood them with great vigour and great power. But Elfrid was soon wounded, and he fled the battlefield. But a remarkable number of his men and allies were killed there. Bledric, count of Cornwall, was killed in this battle. Then the Britons gathered together and went to Leicester. They made Chatwan, who was a learned and brave man, king by general agreement. He summoned and called upon all his men-at-arms, and also his knights and barons. The English, who controlled the earldoms and had themselves called kings, all came seeking his mercy. They became his vassals and then he said he would cross the Humber, unless he were obstructed by a more ferocious people. He would destroy Northumbria and drive all the people out of it. If King Elfrid waited for him and did not defend himself forcibly, he would be captured while still alive, or killed on the battlefield, or dispossessed of his lands. Elfrid heard that he was coming and that he was making threats. He summoned his vassals and his kinsmen, and the English and the Saxons, who were making war on the Britons.

(13983–4010) On both sides, there was a very large number of people, some bold and some cowardly. The noblemen in the country, who had allies on both sides, saw the evil that would result from this, and the loss that would be huge if the two kings, who hated one another so grievously, did battle with each other. They went backwards and forwards so often between the kings, and took so much advice, that they caused the kings to make peace and to confirm this peace through hostages. They came to a decision about lands, such that each one of them would have his own share of it, and that each one should bear faith to the other. Elfrid's land would be to the north of the Humber and Chatwan's to the south of it. In this way they had peace between them, and there was such love between them that it could not be greater. They shared their possession, for everything belonging to the two of them belonged to each one of them. They could not have greater love. They took wives and had children. They had two sons at the same time: Elfrid's son was called Edwin and Chatwan's son was called Chadwalein. They were both born in the same year.

(14011–50) In order to retain the love of their fathers and to make their sons love each other, the sons were placed together, raised together, and instructed together. The boots and the garments they were given were similar. When they were able to ride well, carry shields, wield lances, spur horses, hold tight to the saddle, draw swords, and strike blows, they were knighted at the same time. Chatwan, I believe, had them taken to Armorica, where weapons were given to them, for his kinsmen who lived there were Breton and born of Bretons. When their fathers were dead, and they had passed away from this world, each of the sons ruled the lands he had inherited. Henceforth, they were friends for two years, and for two years they retained their fathers' affection for each other. Edwin ruled the far side of the Humber and Chadwalein this side of it. Chadwalein received a lot more castles, town, and cities than King Edwin. When it pleased him, he had himself crowned. He held great feasts and great court celebrations, and he conducted himself very nobly. Edwin beseeched him and asked him to grant and agree that he should be consecrated, blessed, and crowned, from the far side of the Humber, where he lived, just as Chadwalein was on this side of it. Chadwalein said he would consult with his people, discuss the matter with them, and let him know shortly what they said.

STRIFE BETWEEN THE BRITON CHADWALEIN AND THE NORTHUMBRIAN EDWIN

(14051–88) THEY met at a ford alongside the river Douglas to debate this matter and see how it could work out. They were on either side of the two banks of the river and had to communicate through messengers. Whilst the messengers, the oldest and wisest men, passed from one king to the other, carrying recommendations between them, King Chadwalein dismounted. He was tired and fell asleep. His nephew Brien held his head for him. He was angry and upset that Edwin was asking to be something he had never been. He sighed very deeply with wrath and displeasure. He sighed greatly and swelled with anger. Tears ran down his face thick and fast. The king's head was moistened by them in such a way that he woke up. He raised his hand up to his head and found that his face was damp. Then he began to look at Brien, who burst into tears.

'Brien,' said the king, 'what is the matter? Why are you crying, what is wrong?'

'My lord,' he replied, 'I shall tell you. I am angry and feel great sorrow that in our time and through us—this causes me sorrow and anger—our land has suffered a loss of esteem. Great shame has befallen us. You want to create two crowned kings, and you could thereby come to an unfortunate end, because it is normal for one king to rule and thus for just one king to be served.'

(14089–120) Because of what Brien said the king retracted what he had commanded should be done. He announced strongly to King Edwin that he would do nothing of the sort, for the barons had gainsaid it. They said it would be contrary to what is reasonable, contrary to what is right, and contrary to religion that what should belong to one king should be divided and handed over to two kings, so that each of the two is crowned. He did not want to divide up his kingdom and diminish its jurisdiction. Edwin, who was an arrogant man, replied angrily that he would never seek permission for this, and that he would have himself crowned without obtaining permission, and he would have just as much freedom within his kingdom as he had where he was. Chadwalein stated that, if he were to do this, he would take his crown from him and remove his head along with it. Edwin replied that he was not afraid of his threats. In this fashion they parted in anger, and each of them hated the other. There was ill will on both sides, and each issued a challenge to the other. Edwin was wicked and pitiless, and he was also haughty and swollen with anger. Because he was doing the asking now, he said, he would shortly be the one who was being asked. Lo, the war between them was launched and the land was ravaged.

(14121–50) The vast majority of the inhabitants fought each other, seizing lands and plundering towns. Chadwalein assembled a large host, came to the Humber, and crossed the river. He wanted to lay waste Northumbria and deny Edwin his inheritance. Edwin was very brave, and no losses he might incur would make him want to flee. It was his intention to defend himself and his land, and he did not deign to seek peace or a truce. He launched a mounted attack against Chadwalein, defeating him, and routing him. Chadwalein tried to depart and to return to his own land, but Edwin positioned himself in front of him, blocking and controlling the road. Chadwalein fled by a different route. Through woods and by means of detours, he fled to Scotland with Edwin pursuing him. He incurred increasing pain and hardship and had to flee to Ireland. The king of Ireland welcomed him and honoured him as he should. Edwin remained behind, since he could not reach the ships, and he seized Chadwalein's kingdom, destroying castles, demolishing towers, taking control of lands, laying waste cities, ransoming people, and ravaging towns.

(14151–204) Brien's sister was pointed out to him. He found her in Worcester and took her to York, where he had her guarded in her bedchamber. I do not know who brought Pellit to him, a cleric born in Spain. He was very learned and very knowledgeable about astronomy. By the course of the shining stars, and the flight of the birds, he was aware of events that were of concern to them. Chadwalein was unable to do anything, to bring ships together or to gather people without Edwin knowing about it. He repeatedly prepared his ships and established a large division of men. He repeatedly sailed over the sea and tried to dock at the ports. But Edwin, who defended the land against him, managed to get there before him, for the soothsayer foresaw everything, where and when he expected to arrive. Chadwalein was deeply perturbed that he had turned back so often. He had been followed from his land by men-at-arms, kinsmen, and allies. Many of them had abandoned their inheritances for love of him. He told them he would go to Brittany and speak to King Salomon; they were both from one family. Salomon possessed great power, and he had often summoned him. Whether it was by night or by day, in the morning or in the evening, they travelled and sailed until they reached Guernsey, an island over towards the west. In my view, from that point onwards there is no other inhabited island between Cornwall and Brittany. They had scarcely been on the island when the king became ill. He was suffering from an acute fever that could only be cured by intense sweats. He had a longing for venison; he was unable to eat any other kind of meat. The king called upon Brien, begging and commanding him to go in search of venison, no matter what method he used to get it. For the king would never be cured unless he ate some.

(14205–51) Brien was very upset because of the king, and he greatly desired to make him well. He called serving boys and youths, and he had hounds and brachets brought. They searched valleys and plains, cliffs and mountains, going over the whole land without finding any stag or hind, nor fallow deer, hare, or roebuck. At that time Brien grieved deeply. When he saw that his uncle would die because there was no venison, and that he did not know where to find any, he cut a piece of the fleshy part of his own thigh, cooked it, and roasted it well. Then he had it offered to his uncle. I do not know whether the king tasted it, but he got better and survived, and as soon as he was able to get up he had his ships launched, making straight for Kidalet, which at that time was a city between Dinan and the coast. To this day one can still see its ruins. One king welcomes the other, honouring him more than was necessary. With great honour he provided him with lodgings and a place to stay. If he wanted to go and attack Edwin, he would help him out generously with money and men. They were together all winter and they stayed there all winter. Meanwhile, they got hold of some ships, sought help, and acquired troops. They sent Brien to England in disguise in order to kill the soothsayer, who could give a full account of what was happening. They discussed the matter and came to the conclusion that they would not go to England as long as the soothsayer was still alive, nor would they dock in that country. If he wanted to put his mind to it, he was perfectly capable of saying at which port and at what time those in the ships would turn up.

(14252–308) Brien took a great risk. He set sail at Barfleur and landed at Southampton. He changed his clothes for some that were much worse and put them on. He had an iron staff made in the fashion of a pilgrim's staff, with a long and sharp tip made of iron and with a pointed edge. He changed his appearance to make himself look like a pilgrim going on a long journey. In disguise he went about in full view of other people, looking like a poor penitent. He leant on the staff and had a constant limp. He sought and hunted for the king's court until it was found at York. He joined the ranks of the poor and hid himself among them. Among the wretched he was wretched, like a needy beggar. Brien's sister emerged from a bedchamber to fetch water for the queen. Brien went and stood in her path so that she would recognize him and see who he was. She knew him and recognized him, but he said to her with a wink that she should give no sign that in any way she was connected to him. He kissed her and she kissed him, and both of them burst into tears. They moved away from the throng so that no one, man or woman, would spot who they were. She told him the whole story and pointed out to him the soothsayer Pellit, who was present. By chance he had come outside and was going up and down, moving amongst the poor. Brien left his sister, who was very fearful for him. He stood in the way of the soothsayer, who was moving amongst the beggars. Brien waited and watched until he passed by him, then with the large iron staff he was carrying he delivered such a shove that he drove it right through his body. He thrust it deeply, and the soothsayer fell to the ground without a yea or a nay. He left the staff behind him and cleverly walked off through the poor without being detected, recognized, or suspected.

(14309–45) That day Brien hid amongst the poor and mingled with them. At night he left the city, and quietly and secretly he left the region far behind him. By night and by day, he achieved so much that he came to Exeter on the Exe. Suddenly, all round him there was a great throng of Britons and of Cornish, of knights and of townspeople. They kept on asking about where he came from and where he was going, what he wanted, what he was seeking, what he was saying, and what he was doing. They asked him about Chadwalein, where he was, why he was taking so long, and if he would tell them whether he would ever come back and rule the land again.

'Yes,' said Brien, 'you will very soon see him returning with such a host that Edwin will never be able to get to him, nor will he be able to remain here in the kingdom. For the love of the king, he has harmed us and oppressed us many times. Build castles and provision towers, for very soon you will have assistance.' Brien talked to the Britons. He was aware of what many of them desired. He captured and took possession of Exeter. He wanted to rule over it, so he fortified it. He sent word to his uncle by letter concerning what he had achieved, and how he had done it. He gave him all his news, and the king sought ships and skiffs. King Salomun, his cousin, sent him some men, some of his own and some from amongst his neighbours, two hundred knights, in addition to helmsmen and sailors. They sailed up to Totnes, and this filled the peasants with joy.

(14346–97) King Edwin was distressed by the loss of his good soothsayer and of Exeter, which Brien had captured and occupied. With a large number of troops he sent Peanda, the king of Mercia, which was part of England, in order to protect the land and the ports, and to besiege Exeter, if he could not take it in any other way. Peanda besieged Exeter, his aim being to get inside the city, but he failed to do so. Brien, who ruled it, was inside until King Chadwalein came. He had come to Totnes and disembarked from the ships. He asked for news, and it was given to him: Brien, his nephew, was besieging it and he would be hanged if he were caught. The king, upset by what Brien was doing and keen to provide assistance, rode along with his vassals, passing woods, plains, mountains, and valleys, reaching the siege as soon as he could. O God, what joy this brought to Brien! Chadwalein had powerful companies of men with splendid equipment. He established four divisions, then he attacked the besiegers, capturing or killing many men, the most powerful and the strongest. Peanda himself was captured, but he was not wounded or killed. He was held securely and well guarded. He could not be rescued until he had paid homage to the king and been deprived of his inheritance. He swore an oath of allegiance for his fief, and to create a secure alliance and a secure affection between them Chadwalein took in marriage one of Peanda's sisters, a very beautiful, noble, and courtly maiden. Chadwalein summons the Britons. He said kind words to them and thanked them for their hardship and the hatred they had suffered for love of him. He laid waste the land in the country, where he knew Peanda's enemies would be.

(14398–424) He crossed the river Humber, destroying castles and pillaging towns. Edwin summoned all the kings who were Saxons and English (a number of them were called kings, but in reality they only ruled counties). Edwin had them all with him, whether on the basis of homage or of fealty. He rode against Chadwalein, but he did not fear him. On a battlefield called Heavenfield the battle and the dispute between Chadwalein and Edwin took place. Between them there was an intense and mortal hatred. Edwin was killed, and also his son, who was called Osfriz. Also killed was the king of Orkney, who had come to their aid. There were also many others captured, many slain, and many wounded. The slaughter was great, as was the capture of men, whom Chadwalein punished severely. They defeated them, and their kinsfolk who had been fighting against them. He had the women and children killed, even those who were still suckling. Age was of no use to them, nor was reputation, beauty, or family.

(14425–58) Edwin left an heir, who ruled the kingdom and the manors. When he was baptized, his name was Osriz. But Chadwalein had his empire. He launched a war and an attack against him, killing him and two of his nephews because they ruled part of the kingdom and were to inherit his lands. No one he could find was left to claim the inheritance. Then Oswald, a noble baron in the way he preserved the Christian religion, and a noble and open-hearted man, inherited the kingdom. But Chadwalein waged war against him and drove him towards Scotland. When he saw that he had fled such a distance away that he could not catch up with him, he did not want to drive him further away, nor harass all his men. He handed over to Peanda part of his men, asking him to drive out Oswald and pursue him until he had captured him and killed him. When Oswald found out about the preparations being made, he was very pleased and accepted advice that he would not flee from Peanda, rather he should wait for him if he were to follow him. He came to a standstill in the middle of a field called Heavenfield. This name is Heavenfield in English, and in French it is Champ Celestiel. He had a cross erected in the field and had it worshipped by his people.

(14441–72) 'Worship the holy cross,' he said, 'confess your sins, beg for mercy. Repent of your sins and seek pardon for your misdeeds. Whatever happens later, confess humbly. Those who live, or those who die, can have greater confidence.' They did what he commanded, and on their knees they worshipped God and the Cross humbly, with a humble heart and a sweet voice. They asked God for mercy, scourging themselves and seeking pardon.

(14459–94) Then they got ready to fight, in case there was anyone who wanted to attack them. Peanda arrived and launched an assault against them. But things turned out badly for him, for he lost the finest of his men, and he himself took flight. Arrogant and filled with anger, he went to make his complaint to Chadwalein. Never, he said, would he be at peace with him or hold any land from him if he did not gain vengeance for Oswald, who had caused him so much grief. When it pleased them, they gathered their armies together and travelled to Northumbria, where they did battle against Oswald. Both sides lost a large number of men. Peanda encountered Oswald and, filled with an intense hatred for him, he decapitated him. The sorrow and the loss were great. Men were killed, land ravaged, women made widows, towns laid waste, and dwellings deserted.

(14495–534) Oswi, one of Oswald's brothers, took possession of his brother's kingdom. The barons, who had lost their lord, accepted him. He saw a body of people very much weakened and the land much impoverished. He saw Chadwalein's great strength and how strong and powerful he was. He saw that he could not hold out against him if Chadwalein attacked him. He thought it was better to abandon his jurisdiction, and to humble himself willingly, rather than to wage war with such a man, against whom he could not defend himself. He spoke to Chadwalein, gave him a large amount of gold and silver, and submitted to his power. He became his vassal, swore fealty to him, and did homage to him. Chadwalein trusted him with his fief. In this way was peace granted and in this way it was maintained for a long time. Oswi had kinsfolk and nephews, highly esteemed and very brave. In order to have a section of the lands, they became involved in war and conflict. But Oswi defended himself well, with the result that no one managed to take his land from him. He drove them over to this side of the Humber. They came to Peanda, who was a strong man, promising to give him goods and lands, and beseeching him to provide them with support and advice and to wage war on Oswi on their behalf. Peanda said that he did not dare to do this, unless he had Chadwalein's acceptance. He would not dare to launch a war, or be the first one to break the peace. But he would find out, if he could, whether Chadwalein would permit him to do this.

(14535–68) It happened one Pentecost that Chadwalein held a feast at court. He had himself crowned in London and summoned all his barons. There was no sign of Oswi. He had not come. I do not know whether he did not want to come, or was not able to do so, or whether or not Chadwalein had summoned him. Peanda rose to his feet and asked Chadwalein how it could be, or what the reason was, that Oswi had not come to the court. All the barons were there, and the English and the Britons as well. Oswi alone had not deigned to offer service, or to attend court.

'Some obstacle', said the king, 'must have held him back. Perhaps he is lying on his sickbed.'

Peanda replied: 'That is not the case. You do not know Oswi. From Saxony he has summoned men on horseback and on foot. He is hiring men and seeking mercenaries. As soon as he is able and has the opportunity, he thinks he can launch a great war. He cannot, and does not want to, have peace. But, if it does not trouble you, I wish to go and destroy his arrogance. If I have your leave, I shall hand him over to you, dead or alive, and drive him out of the land.' Chadwalein said: 'I shall talk of this.'

(14569–602) Then he had Peanda depart, and he sent all the English away. He retained the oldest of the Britons, the most powerful and the wisest, and he explained the request that Peanda had made. Margadud, who was the lord of South Wales, was sitting next to Chadwalein:

'The mortal anger and the hatred between us Britons and the English', he said, 'began a long while ago and, whatever happens in the end, I believe it will last for a long time to come. They are always ready to harm us. Never will they have any affection for us, nor will they maintain loyalty or peace with us. Remember their acts of wickedness, remember their treachery, remember their cruelty, remember that they have harmed you. You have often said and sworn, but you have completely forgotten, that if you could just rid yourself of them you would not let them enter this kingdom. Since you do not dare to destroy them, either through a lack of desire or a lack of ability, let them bring shame on each other and leave them to work things out between themselves. Peanda is English by birth and all the members of his family are English. Oswi is also English. Do not be upset at all if one mastiff skins another, or if one evil-doer takes out his spite on another. Let one animal strangle the other, and one trample on the other.'

(14603–56) All the Britons supported Margadud's arguments. Then Peanda was recalled, and he was given complete freedom to do harm to Oswi, if he could. Cadwalein would never object. Prenda left court, very arrogant and haughty. He attacked Oswi violently, and repeatedly he caused him harm. Osriz often sent word to him, fervently beseeching him to agree to peace and a truce with him and not to do him any more harm. If he wished, he would give him gold, silver, and other possessions. Peanda refused to do this, or ever to make peace with him. Oswi was not a cowardly man. When he saw it was impossible to have peace, concord, or a truce, he strove to defend himself. His anger grew and became more intense, and they joined battle angrily. Oswi had great faith in God, and his belief in him was steadfast. Peanda was filled with arrogance, and he trusted in his large number of household knights. But he was defeated and killed, along with many of his allies. Osfriz, his eldest son, was raised at court.

He sought and received his inheritance and did homage for it to Chadwalein, who was a fine justiciar. He was a loyal and upright king. He ruled the land for forty-eight years, and he was often at peace and often at war. In London he fell ill and took to his bed. There he came to his end and there he died. The Britons grieved for him. But there is no escape from death. So that he would be remembered for a long time, they had cast in copper a knight on horseback with royal apparel. The king's body was placed inside it, then it was positioned above one of the gates in London, towards the west. It remained there for a very long time. Close by, a chapel was built that was dedicated to St Martin; it was splendid and handsome.

AFTER CHADWALEIN'S LARGELY PEACEFUL FORTY-EIGHT-YEAR REIGN, HIS SON CADWALLADER WAS THE LAST BRITON TO RULE BRITAIN

(14657–706) AFTER him reigned Cadwallader, who was the son of Chadwalein, nephew of Peanda. He was the nephew of Peanda, the son of his sister and a well-loved king. In his time there was a scarcity of grain, and as a result of this there was shortage, which led to famine. It was expensive in the towns and expensive in the cities. You could easily have travelled for three days without finding any bread, grain, or other provisions to buy, so great was the scarcity everywhere. They lived off fish and game, venison and roots, and off leaves and herbs. They had no other provisions. Along with this misfortune came another that was just as harsh. It cost the lives of many people because of contaminated air and wind. In the dwellings, the fields, the streets, the markets, and the carts, people fell down while eating, walking up and down, or speaking. They died suddenly without lingering. Fathers died and children died, lords died and wives died, peasants died and knights died. Sons had no need to mourn their fathers. You would have seen very few people remaining on the isolated and empty paths. You could never have seen such sorrow. There were too few people to bury all the dead. Those who were supposed to be seeing to the burial had themselves to be buried with the dead. Those who could flee took flight. They abandoned their fiefs and their dwellings, as much for the great scarcity of corn as for the great loss of life. Anyone who sees their neighbour's house burn down has little hope. Cadwallader, who was king and had responsibility for protecting the land, crossed over to Rennes in Brittany to King Alain, who loved him greatly. He had been the nephew of Salomun, who had loved his father very much. He welcomed him very joyfully and looked after him splendidly.

(14707–74) England was impoverished. The corn had failed, people had perished, and the land was laid waste so that no one was working it. For eleven years and more it was deserted and devoid of peasants. In so far as there were any Britons left, they lived in the mountains and the forests, as did any English inhabitants who had remained there and escaped the famine; those who were born later lived as well as they could. In order to restore the towns and work the land, they sent news to Saxony, where their ancestors had been born, so that with women and children, accompanied by their household knights and servants, they would come in force and have lands as they wished. They would have fine land to work. They would lack nothing, apart from men to work it. They came frequently, in abundance, and with large companies of men. They made camp throughout the lands, greatly increasing in numbers and multiplying. They found no one to hinder them, or who could deny them lands. They came frequently and in abundance, and they upheld the customs and laws as their ancestors had earlier done in the lands from which they came. They wanted to keep within their lineage the names, the laws and the language. For *kaer* they said *chester*, and they said *shire* for *suiz*, and *tref* they had called *tune*. *Map* is a Welsh word and in English it is *son*. *Kaer* means 'city' in Welsh, *map* means 'son', and *tref* means 'town', and *suiz* 'county'. It is said by some that in Welsh a district is called *suiz*, and *shire* in English is the same as *suiz* in Welsh. The British language is still spoken correctly in Wales. In this way the earldoms and baronages, and the regions and lordships, were ruled in the way the Britons had created them. At that time Adelstan was king. He was the first of the English to have the whole of England under his control, except for Wales and Cornwall. He was the first to be anointed and consecrated, and the first to be crowned. Many people said he was a bastard. King Edward was his father and he went to worship in Rome. To St Peter he granted on the altar a present of a silver penny every year from each person occupying a dwelling and living under his authority. The first to make this gift was one of his ancestors, named Yne. His ancestors kept to this steadfastly, and they continued to give this gift to the pope.

FOLLOWING THE FAMINE, CADWALLADER SEEKS KING ALAIN'S HELP IN BRITTANY, BUT A DIVINE VOICE TELLS HIM TO GO TO ROME, RATHER THAN RETURNING TO RULE BRITAIN

(14775–824) CADWALLADER wished to come back and rule his land. Once he discovered it was populated, and that the plague was over, he wished to return to his land. He made preparations for his journey, and then he prayed to God fervently that he would give him some sign that it pleased him that he should return, for he wanted to do what pleased him. A divine voice told him that he should abandon this journey and embark on another. He should give up his intention of going to England and go to the pope in Rome. Then, with his sins forgiven, he should go on his way with the blessed. It is the English who would have Britain, and it would never be recovered by the Britons until Merlin's prophecy* had been fulfilled. Nor could this ever happen until the time came when his remains were taken from his tomb and transported from Rome, so that they could be presented in Britain. Cadwallader marvelled at this, and at the same time he was troubled by the divine announcement that he had heard so clearly. He told his good friend King Alain what he had heard. He opened up his repositories and summoned clerics who were good grammarians.* The history books were brought out, and information was sought to show that what Cadwallader said of the vision was in harmony with the pronouncements of Merlin and Aquile, the good soothsayer, and also with what was written by the Sibyl. What Cadwallader did was not different from this, and he abandoned his ships and his men. He called Yvor and Yni. Yvor was his son by his wife, and Yni was his nephew, his sister's son.

CADWALLADER SUMMONS YVOR AND YNI TO RETURN TO BRITAIN TO RULE THE BRITONS, WHO ARE NOW CALLED THE WELSH

YOU will go into Wales,' he said, 'and be lords of the Britons, so that through the lack of a lord they do not descend into ignominy.'

(14825–66) They did what he ordered and prepared his journey. He went to St Sergius, the pope, who cherished him and honoured him. He confessed his sins and then undertook penance. He had not been in Rome for long when he fell sick. The illness was severe, and death could not be avoided. He died eleven days before May, on the nineteenth day of April down here in earthly exile and seven hundred and one years after Christ and the incarnation of Christ in the Virgin Mary. The holy body was carefully prepared and placed in the ground. His soul rose to Paradise. May we take our place with him there. Yvor and Yni sailed across the sea, with a large number of ships and men. The remainder of the Britons, whom we now call Welsh, and who live over towards the north, became their subjects. They were never to acquire sufficient power to possess Logres. They all changed so much, and they were all so altered. They are all so different now, and they have degenerated when compared with the nobility, honour, customs, and way of life of their ancestors. The name has become Wales, either from Duke Gualo, who ruled Wales, or from Galeas the queen, who controlled the land.*

Here ends the history of the Britons, and of the line of barons who came from the lineage of Brutus and ruled England for a long time. Master Wace composed this narrative* in French one thousand five hundred and fifty-five years after God became flesh for our redemption.

EXPLANATORY NOTES

REFERENCES to other editions of the *Roman de Brut* are to the name of the editor and/or translator (Arnold, Weiss); the same applies to references to editions of Geoffrey of Monmouth's *Historia Regum Britanniae* (*HRB*) or its First Variant (FV) (Thorpe, Wright, Reeve and Wright). In each case, full details for each reference are given in the Primary Sources sections of the Select Bibliography.

Full details of the MSS which are referred to, for example MS H, are given in the List of Manuscripts.

3 *WHOEVER wishes to hear about . . . kings and heirs . . . Master Wace . . . has translated this*: Weiss is correct in pointing out that, for some reason, Wace has omitted the Description of Britain (largely geographical, but also political) that is found at the beginning of Gildas, *The Ruin of Britain*; Bede, *Ecclesiastical History*; 'Nennius', the *Historia Brittonum*; Henry of Huntingdon, *History of the English People*; Geoffrey of Monmouth, *HRB*, and the FV (Weiss, p. 3 n. 1).

the book: 'Li livres' ('the book') cannot be identified as a specific text (though we know that Wace used at least the *HRB* and FV). In Old French texts, this expression is a frequently used convention to refer to written sources collectively.

Paris . . . had abducted Helen from Greece: Wace says this perhaps because in Greek legend Helen was the most beautiful of Greek women and her capture was the cause of the Trojan War.

6 *law*: the Old French term *lei* (or *loi*). In line 199, for example, it can have a number of overlapping meanings: 'law, faith, religion, custom, justice, oath, pledge', etc.

13 *Straits of Gibraltar*: in the Old French text, 'porz d'Africe' ('ports of Africa').

16 *lo*: the first of a number of occasions in this work where Wace uses the expression 'ez vus'/'ez les vus' ('lo'/'lo and behold!'/'here comes . . . !') to draw attention to a sudden dramatic event.

18 *Totnes in the port of Dartmouth*: Dartmouth itself is a town. The reference may be to the port of Dartmouth or the estuary of the river Dart. See Arnold, II, p. 794, and Weiss, p. 29 n. 1.

21 *Firth of Forth*: in the Old French text, 'Escoce Watre' ('Scottish Water').

24 *Castle of Maidens*: 'Whatever the historical and literary genesis of Geoffrey's "Castellum Puellarum" on "Mons Agned", and however vague Geoffrey's own apprehension of the two epithets may have been, in a translation of his *Historia*, where *something* would have to be written, the passage might

be rendered "*Edinburgh Castle* on *Edinburgh Rock*"' (R. Blenner-Hassett, 'Geoffrey of Monmouth's *Mons Agned* and *Castellum Puellarum*', *Speculum*, 17/2 (1942), 254).

25 *courtly*: the terms 'courtly' and 'courtliness' are used in this translation to convey the Old French terms *cortois(e)* and *cortoisie*. A man or woman who is courtly, or who behaves according to the principles of courtliness, shows a thorough understanding of all matters relating to life at court, including politeness, kindness, common sense, eloquence, and the ability to dress well.

34 *five*: Weiss restores the MS P reading 'quatre' ('four') here.

37 *Moriane*: homeland of Ceoflo. According to Louis-Fernand Flutre (*Table des noms propres avec toutes leurs variantes figurant dans les écrits en français ou en provençal et actuellement publiés* (Poitiers: Centre d'études supérieures de civilisation médiévale, 1962), 274), the location is unknown. For Moriane Wright has Flanders, with Ceoflo as king of Moriane (*HRB*, §35.16, Chelfus, Ceulfus), translating 'Cheulfo duci Morianorum' as 'duke of the Flemings'. The duke's identity is ultimately uncertain ('duke of the Flemings' meaning those of Flanders).

41 *swiftly*: Arnold's reading 'oituant' here, which is difficult to understand, appears in Weiss's text as 'trutenant', found in MS P, which she translates as 'hastened'.

42 *possessions*: translation of Arnold's 'aveirs'; Weiss's text has 'aneus' ('rings').

46 *stone-throwers, catapults, battering-rams*: the terms 'troies' and 'multons' here refer to machines used for hurling stones and shattering walls (see Hans-Erich Keller, *Étude descriptive sur le vocabulaire de Wace* (Berlin: Akademie-Verlag, 1953), 284–5).

In no way were they shown any pity: Arnold has 'ne s'esmaient' ('were not afraid') here, whereas Weiss's text has 'nes manaient' ('showed them no pity').

48 *Karelion [Caerleon]*: (Kaer-, Kaerlegion, Kaerlion, Kaerusc, Karlion), a town on the river Usk, was the headquarters of the Second Augustan Legion (*c.*74–287/296) (Roman fortress of Isca, 'city/fortress of the Legion' in Old Welsh). It was the legendary site of Arthur's court and at the 'forefront of kingship of Wales' in the twelfth century (see Raymond Howell, 'The Demolition of the Roman Tetrapylon in Caerleon: An Erasure of Memory?', *Oxford Journal of Archaeology*, 19/4 (2000), 394, and John Gillingham, 'The Contexts and Purposes of Geoffrey of Monmouth's *History of the Kings of Britain*', *Anglo-Norman Studies*, 13 (1990), 99–118).

55 *notes*: when used in a musical context, the Old French term *note* can mean 'note, sound, melody, tune, song, or an instrumentalist piece' (meanings from the Anglo-Norman Dictionary under 'note').

56 *Angles*: Wace's use of the term 'Engleis' is very complex and is in large part linguistic and geographical, not political. At times, however, Wace uses it to distinguish the Germanic peoples from the Britons; in this line, it has been translated as 'Angles', the early people who came before the Saxons

(though Wace does not specify who came first). As noted in the Introduction, Wace does have difficulty reconciling the two versions of the Galfridian material (the vulgate and FV)—the former as pro-Briton and the latter as pro-English (Anglocentric), particularly at the end of his *Brut*, where he needs to explain how England was named after the Saxons. Wace tries to finesse the circumstances with an etymological reasoning that the Saxons were descended from the Angles (rather than there having been two separate groups). Thus, the Angles became the 'English' ('les Engleis'), saying why the English were called *Angleis* and not *Sednes* or *Saissuns* (or other variations of Old French terms for 'Saxons'; see also note to p. 202). He also uses this etymological explanation to justify why, after Gormund's 'Donation', Britain became 'Engleterre'.

57 *When those from Rome had conquered*: the Old French text here is 'Quant cil de Rome ourent conquis'—Wace has used the phrase 'cil de Rome' perhaps for purposes of syllable count or other poetic reasons obscure to us. In our translation, the phrase 'cil de Rome' and its numerous variants have been translated as 'those from Rome' or 'the Romans' since the latter is ultimately the meaning. This line (and those similar) will be listed under 'Rome' in the Index of Geographical Names, and also in the Index of Personal Names, under 'Romans', to indicate how very often Wace refers either to Rome or to the Romans—who are certainly not minor players—in the *Brut*.

78 *Sever . . . rebuilds Hadrian's Wall*: in AD 205–8 Sever (Septimius Severus), Roman senator and emperor, rebuilt the wall 'between Deira and Albany' (*HRB* §74.20), most likely referring to the reinforcing of Hadrian's Wall, dating from AD *c.*122; see also Weiss, p. 135 n. 3.

82 *Choel*: (Coel) is count of Colchester in MSS C, S, and F, but count of Gloucester in the remaining MSS; see Weiss, p. 141 n. 5. He becomes king of England in the majority of Wace MSS, though in the vulgate (§78.128) he is 'rex Britonum' ('king of the Britons'; in the FV his kingdom is not specified). Wace MSS C and J read 'de Bretaigne' and in MS F the location of the kingdom is not specified.

85 *sheriffs*: the term 'viscuntes' in the text is best translated as here as 'sheriffs' rather than 'viscounts'.

86 *Cunan*: Wace uses this form, which refers to Conan Meriadoc (*HRB*, §81.199), Conanus Meriadocus, supposedly Octavius' nephew, the figure from Welsh legend credited with founding Brittany; see also Thorpe, pp. 158–9.

88 *a very beautiful daughter, who was called Ursula*: Wace appears to identify the legend of St Ursula with the story of the Ursula who was sent by her father, King Dionot, from Britain to Brittany with eleven thousand companions (to become wives of the Bretons), but who on the way were subsequently shipwrecked, raped, drowned, and martyred by the Huns; see Weiss, p. 153 n. 3.

91 *a wall on a bank of soil*: the Antonine Wall, which was built in AD 140–2, stretching from the Firth of Forth to the Clyde. See Weiss, p. 157 and n. 1.

99 *a port in Kent*: on the basis of MS P, Weiss emends this line in Arnold ('A un port a Kent arriverent') to read 'A Sanwiz un port arriverent' (four MSS—P, C, K, and N—have this reading); thus, Weiss's translation specifies that the boats landed in the port of Sandwich in Kent. For the landing, *HRB* (§98.248) and FV (§98) each give Kent as the location but nothing more specific. See also Arnold's variants for v. 6706, which contain a reference to 'Sanviz' (MS S), to 'sandwiz' (MS F), and include MS J's addition of 'Cist port est tot droit en Tanet [Thanet] | Prés de Sancwic en.i. islet'.

106 *the Kalends of May*: the first day of May.

109 *provost*: see Glossary; Weiss translates this as 'town governor'.

110 *'incubi'*: the full expression in the text is 'incubi demones'; Weiss translates as 'incubus demons'.

112 *he will defeat all his enemies*: in place of vv. 7333–582, MS D substitutes a 172-decasyllabic preamble to a version of Merlin's Prophecies inserted into the MS D version of Wace's *Brut*, followed by an epilogue attributed to a certain Helias. Wace's work resumes at v. 7583 in MS D. For indications of which MSS contain insertions of Merlin's Prophecies, see Jean Blacker, '"But That's Another Story": Wace, Laȝamon, and the Early Anonymous Old French Verse *Bruts*', *Arthuriana*, 31/4 (2021), 47–102, at 83–92 (App. I), and Blacker, 'Anglo-Norman Verse Prophecies of Merlin', critical edn and trans., *Arthuriana*, 15/1 (2005), 1–125.

on top of a mountain named Cloart: Weiss has a location named Doare, which does not occur in Arnold's text. She has emended with MS P (but see Arnold's note to v. 7328, II, p. 805). Arnold's 'Cloart' is the majority reading from the MSS. Blenner-Hassett has suggested that Wace is referring to Great and Little Doward Hill in Herefordshire (*A Study of the Place-Names in Lawman's Brut* (Stanford, CA: Stanford University Press, 1950), 29–30) since forms resulting from 'Cl' were often confused with 'D' by scribes.

119 *the Dance that the giants created*: the Giants' Dance ('carole as gaianz'), discussed in vv. 8042–61, were stones set in a circle; according to Geoffrey of Monmouth (*HRB*, §128.230–7; §130.269–77), the stones, which supposedly had curative properties, were brought to Mount Killaraus in Ireland from Africa by giants, and Merlin engineered their transfer (from Mount Killomar, as it is called in Wace) for Aurelius (with the help of Uther Pendragon and 15,000 armed men) to the fields near Amesbury to create Stonehenge (see under 'Giants Dance' and 'Stonehenge' in the Index of Geographical Names; Pierres Pendues, i.e., 'Hanging Stones' French name for this structure).

130 *Octa . . . Eosa*: Octa was Hengist's son, and Eosa was Octa's cousin (v. 8416), though he is alternatively referred to as Octa's companion (v. 8834), which he literally was in the battle in which the Britons defeated the Saxons (*HRB*, §141.584–5) (vv. 8909–11). A cousin can, of course, also be a companion. He also appears to have been referred to earlier as Ebissa (v. 7042).

134 *the river Douglas*: the river Duglas/Douglas, allegedly in Lindsey, is the site of four of Arthur's twelve battles in Nennius' *Historia Brittonum* (ed. and trans. Morris, ch. 56, English, p. 35, and Latin, p. 76), but it has not yet been identified and may ultimately be unlocatable. We have translated it as 'Douglas' but wish to disambiguate between it and the river Douglas in the north-west. For the possible location of the river, see Andrew Breeze, who argues for Douglas Water in Scotland ('The Historical Arthur and Sixth-Century Scotland', *Northern History*, 52/2 (2015), 174); for various perspectives on these battles, their possible locations and historical plausibility or otherwise, see David N. Dumville 'The Historical Value of the *Historia Brittonum*', *Arthurian Literature VI* (1986), 1–26, and Peter J. Field, 'Arthur's Battles', *Arthuriana*, 18/4 (2008), 3–32.

lecher/scoundrel: the Old French term *lecheor* has a variety or meanings: 'glutton, debauched person, a married woman's lover, trickster', etc. In Wace's usage of the term, however, it seems to be a term of general abuse, 'scoundrel, wretch'.

139 *Moray . . . the city*: while Arnold is correct in stating that Moray is a region in the vulgate (§149) and that 'Geoffroy ne mentionne pas une "cité de Mureif"' (II, p. 808), Weiss is also correct (p. 237 n. 2) that Wace follows the FV as well, which reads in addition 'Mireif civitatem Albanie' (§149), i.e. implying that Moray was a town as well as a region. The 'cité' in Wace's mind may have referred to a walled city within the region of Moray.

the lake of Lumonoi [Loch Lomond]: Wace has followed either the form in the vulgate or in the FV (§149), *stagnum Lumonoi* (or *Lumonoy*), to refer to Loch Lomond in Scotland.

145 *fables*: in Old French a *fable* (see also vv. 9798, 9896) can be not only a fable but also 'a story, fiction, tale, lie, falsehood'.

148 *God and his names*: in certain forms of Judaism, it is believed that God possesses various names, each one representing, because of their holiness, a unique attribute of the divine.

149 *bailiff*: the term *baillis* here could also be translated as 'steward' or 'governor'.

150 *free domains*: described in the text here as 'delivres', this signifies lands that were available to the lord untrammelled and unencumbered. Those mentioned here had fallen to Arthur, as their owners had died without an heir.

152 *son of*: Erik Kooper ('Guests of the Court: An Unnoticed List of Arthurian Names (British Library, Add. 6113)', in Catherine M. Jones and Logan Whalen (eds), *Li premerains vers: Essays in Honor of Keith Busby* (Amsterdam: Rodopi, 2011), 223–34) proposes that Wace, like the FV, 'de-Welshed' the guest list, but actually Wace uses the French 'fiz' rather than *map/mab*, retaining the original meaning of the Welsh sons in the vulgate though with the French word for 'son' (see Weiss, p. 259 n. 2).

154 *'Go forth, the mass is ended' had been sung*: Wace retains here the Latin terminology: 'E Ite missa est chantez'. See Weiss, p. 263 n. 1 (she translates as 'and the last words of the mass sung').

161 *our lands*: Wace is referring here to land granted by the overlord to a knight or a vassal in exchange for loyalty or service.

barons: where Arnold's text has 'barons', Weiss has 'Bretuns'.

164 *men-at-arms*: the term translated here is 'servanz'. Weiss is correct to say that the figures of men in Lucius' army are confusing (p. 281 n. 1). However, it would appear that Geoffrey gives the figure of 460,100 troops (§163.10–11). Wace has 400,000, plus 180,000 mounted (180,000 is found alone in FV §163, MSS R and a; FV MSS D, E, and S all have the figure of 280,000). Thus, we have not found a direct origin of Wace's troop count.

166 *Then he made his way to Southampton . . . a shore of which he had no knowledge*: we are indebted for the translation of this paragraph (vv. 11190–238) to William Sayers, 'Arthur's Embarkation for Gaul in a Fresh Translation of Wace's *Roman de Brut*', *Romance Notes*, 46/2 (2006), 143–56.

179 *the Herupeis*: inhabitants of La Hérupe, an old term for Neustria. See Margaret Houck, *Sources of the Roman de Brut of Wace* (Berkeley and Los Angeles: University of California Press, 1941), 197–200, who states that Wace apparently thought this group of people were the Normans, since Arthur had given Normandy to Bedivere (vv. 10415–18). For Wace, following Geoffrey and possibly contemporary Norman usage, Normandy and Neustria may have been considered synonymous (rather than Neustria retaining its older meaning of all the territory between the Seine and the Loire).

180 *Chadorkeneneis*: as here in 'Mauric Chadorkeneneis', this seems to mean 'from Cahors' and is a very obscure Arthurian name. Wace states that he does not know if this personage was Breton (rather than 'Briton') or Welsh.

181 *Soeïse*: this form, which occurs in the majority of Wace MSS, is Wace's name for the valley on the way from Autun to Langres (*HRB*, Siesia, §168.242, and FV, Siesia). Many localities have been proposed for this site, where Arthur fought his (legendary) battle against the Romans. This is an excellent example of the difficulties of Geoffrey of Monmouth's geography, much of which was invented. For proposed sites, see Thorpe, p. 247 n. 1; William Matthews ('Where was Siesia-Sessoyne?', *Speculum*, 49 (1974), 680–6); Hans-Erich Keller ('Two Toponymical Problems in Geoffrey of Monmouth and Wace: Eustreia and Siesia', *Speculum*, 49 (1974), 687–98); and Weiss, p. 309 n. 2.

193 *Romenel [Richborough]*: this is Wace's version of 'Rutupi Portu' as in *HRB*/FV (Richborough in English). Weiss emends, on the basis of MS D, to 'Sandwiz'. Arthur wanted to land at Sandwich to fight Mordred (according to Arnold's variants, seven major *Brut* MSS have 'Sanwiz' or a variation); see the note to p. 99.

196 *Camble*: this is the name Wace uses for the river that is referred to in the *HRB* (§178.46) as the river Camblan, supposedly in Cornwall. It is most frequently referred to in Arthurian legend as the site of Arthur's last battle—against Mordred—at Camlann.

The Britons are waiting for him: for the 'Breton hope', see the Introduction, n. 30, p. xix.

202 *they called themselves English . . . the land they called England*: it is very likely that Wace uses a term equivalent of the term 'Angles' not as a political or social reference to one of the early Germanic groups thought to have arrived in Britain, perhaps as the ancestors of the Saxons (which would have been an error on Wace's part). Wace appears to use the term equivalent of 'Angles' ('Engleis' as in v. 13645) primarily for lexical or linguistic reasons, to explain why the English were called *Engleis* and not *Sednes* or *Saissuns* (or other variations of Old French terms for 'Saxons'; see also the note to p. 56).

204 *The place where he saw God he called Cernel*: Wace follows William of Malmesbury and Goscelin in providing a Latin and a Hebrew etymology for Cernel—'cerno' (Latin 'I see') and 'el' (Hebrew for 'God')—to commemorate the site where St Augustine saw God, and where a spring flowed forth, the future site of Cerne Abbey. The abbey is not mentioned by name (on Hebrew etymology in Wace's *Brut*, see Michelle Warren, 'Memory Out of Line: Hebrew Etymology in the *Roman de Brut* and *Merlin*', *Modern Language Notes*, 118/4 (2003), 989–1014). As is typical of Wace, even more so than either of his primary sources for the *Brut* (the vulgate and FV), he places an etymological passage at a crucial moment, as if initiation and commemoration cannot be accomplished without performing the ceremony of naming and explicating the name, rather like a sort of linguistic baptism.

218 *Merlin's prophecy*: on this particular prophecy uttered by Merlin, the *HRB* (§205.564–6) states: 'God did not want the Britons to rule over the island of Britain any longer, until the time came which Merlin had foretold to Arthur' (ed. Reeve and trans. Wright, 2007). The FV omits 'Arthur' from some of the MSS (Weiss, p. 371 n. 5).

grammarians: the term 'gramairien' (here 'gramaire') can refer in Old French to someone who knows Latin, to a magician, or in general just to a wise man.

219 *Their name has become 'Welsh' . . . controlled the land*: Wace's sources read: 'As their culture ebbed, they were no longer called Britons, but Welsh, a name which owes its origin to their leader Gualo, or to queen Galaes or to their decline' (trans. Wright, *HRB*, §207.592–4, with variations in MSS, and FV MSS). The phrase 'siue a barbarie trahentes' (*HRB*, §207.594) refers to the common view in the twelfth century that the Welsh were barbarians, having slipped into 'barbarism' (not that Geoffrey or Wace were arguing in favour of this opinion; see esp. Gillingham, 'The Contexts and Purposes of Geoffrey of Monmouth's *History of the Kings of Britain*', *Anglo-Norman Studies*, 13 (1990), 99–118). In Wace, Gualon is a Welsh duke (vv. 1280–1) and Galaes a Welsh queen (v. 1278), but he furnishes no more details than those given by Geoffrey or the FV.

narrative: the term *romanz* here (also spelled *roman, romans*), which normally at this time refers to something written in French or in the vernacular, is often seen by scholars as referring to a certain type of fictional narrative, i.e. what will later be called a romance.

LIST OF MANUSCRIPTS

Complete or nearly complete MSS (with Arnold's sigla, or, if not given sigla by Arnold, by location *):

A London, College of Arms, Arundel XIV, Anglo-Norman, 14th cent.

C London, British Library, Cotton Vitellius A. X, Anglo-Norman, late 13th cent.

D Durham, Durham Cathedral Library, C. IV. 27, Anglo-Norman, late 12th–early 13th cent.

E London, British Library, Harley 6508, Continental, 14th cent.

F London, British Library, Additional 32125 (vv. 10527–2772 missing), Anglo-Norman, late 13th cent.

G Paris, Bibliothèque Sainte-Geneviève 2447, Continental, 14th cent.

*Paris, Bibliothèque de l'Arsenal 2982, Continental, 18th cent. (copy of G, but without 'Dits et proverbes des philosophes')

H Paris, Bibliothèque nationale de France, fr. 1450, Continental, 13th cent.

J Paris, Bibliothèque nationale de France, fr. 1416, Continental, late 13th cent.

K Paris, Bibliothèque nationale de France, fr. 794, the so-called 'Guiot' MS, Continental, 13th cent.

L Lincoln, Lincoln Cathedral Library 104, Anglo-Norman, 13th cent.

N Paris, Bibliothèque nationale de France, fr. 1454, Continental, 15th cent. (identical to O and V)

O Paris, Bibliothèque nationale de France, fr. 12556, Continental, 15th cent. (identical to N and V)

P London, British Library, Additional 45103, Anglo-Norman, late 13th cent.

R Paris, Bibliothèque de l'Arsenal 2981 (vv. 13944–14013 and 14064 to end [14866] missing), Continental, 14th cent.

S Paris, Bibliothèque nationale de France, nouv. acq. fr. 1415, Anglo-Norman, 14th cent.

T Cambridge, Corpus Christi College 50, Anglo-Norman, second half 13th cent.

V Vienna, National Library 2603, Continental, 15th cent. (identical to O and N)

*Vatican City, Biblioteca Apostolica Vaticana, Ottoboniani latini 1869 (first item extant in this MS, fos. 96–183), Anglo-Norman, 13th cent.

Fragments or Extracts (with Arnold's sigla, or if not given a siglum, by location *; if unknown to Arnold **, also by location)

B London, British Library, Royal 13. A. XXI (begins at l. 8729), Anglo-Norman, late 13th–early14th cent.

M Montpellier, Bibliothèque Interuniversitaire Section Médecine 251 (ends v. 5664), Continental, late 13th cent.

X Oxford, Bodleian Library, Rawlinson D. 913, four fragments from two MSS, Anglo-Norman, late 12th–early 13th, 14th cent.

Y Paris, Bibliothèque nationale de France, fr. 12603 (vv. 67–1950), Continental, late 13th–early 14th cent.

Z New Haven, Yale University, Beinecke Library 395 (vv. 1–7141), Anglo-Norman, late 13th–early 14th cent.

**Berkeley, University of California, Bancroft Library 165 (ll. 387–580 and 1769–954), Continental, late 13th cent. (discovered by John Levy)

*Cologny, Geneva, Biblioteca Bodmeriana 67 (ll. 13642–end [14866]), Anglo-Norman, second half 13th cent.

**Durham, University Library, Additional 1950.A.8 (vv. 1287–8, 1324–6, 1364–7, 1405–7, 2453–5, 2493–5, 2533–5, 2575–7), Anglo-Norman, early–mid 13th cent.

**The Hague, Royal Library, 73.1.53 (scattered 7,348 lines out of 14,866), Continental, 13th cent.

**London, College of Arms, 12/45A (roll, dorse, vv. 9059–13680, with many lacunae), Anglo-Norman, late 13th–early 14th cent. (discovered by Olivier de Laborderie)

**London, University Library 574 (vv. 6680–710, 6782–812), Anglo-Norman 14th, 15th cent.

*Vatican City, Biblioteca Apostolica Vaticana, Palatina latina 1971 (vv. 1219–2421, 3613–4752), Anglo-Norman, 13th cent.

**London, Westminster Abbey, Muniments Room, C.5.22, 2 fragments (vv. 9065–74, 9077–98, 9101–8, 9212–16, 9219–32, 9235–40, 9245–8, 9253–62, 10329–30, 10359–80, 10385–400, 10523–32, 10589–98, 10621–30, 10633–42, with lacunae; 11407–12, 11447–52, 11487–92, 11529–34, with lacunae), Anglo-Norman, early 13th cent. (discovered by Judith Weiss)

**Zadar, Croatia, Public Library (vv. 13485–629 with lacunae; 14287–443, with lacunae), Continental, 13th cent.

GLOSSARY

bachelor a young man or young knight, rather than specifically an unmarried man
bailiff an administrator of justice in the name of a lord or a king
belfry the place in a tower where bells are located
boss a projecting knob in the centre of a shield
bourg a town or village usually close to a castle
brachet a hunting dog
brattice a wooden parapet or platform on a fortress
castellan title of a governor of a castle
cognizances heraldic device or badge identifying its wearer
coif the hood of a hauberk
coron/charon an instrument with strings for plucking
crenel an indentation in the battlements of a castle
constable a warden of a castle, a local official charged with keeping the peace, or a military commander
dais platform or table raised one or two steps above the floor
fief/fee land held in return for feudal service
guisarme long-handled weapon with curved blade and spike
hasart a game of chance played with dice
hauberk a piece of armour consisting of a full-length coat of mail
jongleur minstrel, itinerant player, juggler
lands in chief lands held directly from the crown with no other tenants or subtenants intervening
lay a short musical or narrative composition, melody
mangonel a catapult used as a siege engine
marshal officer in charge of a household
monochord musical instrument involving one stretched string
provost a steward, magistrate, or official
psalterion a stringed instrument of the zither family
rote stringed musical instrument
rotrouanges a musical melody accompanied by the rote
shawm a double-reed woodwind instrument also known as the chalemel
symphonia a stringed instrument
seneschal a high administrative court officer or steward
sheriff officer representing the monarch in a county
vassal a holder of land by feudal tenure in return for homage and allegiance, or just a brave man

vavasour a nobleman of minor rank, literarily a vassal of vassals ('vassus vassorum')
villein a feudal tenant who owed services to a lord in return for a piece of land on which to grow crops
viol a bowed and fretted stringed instrument
wattle material for making walls or fences

INDEX OF PERSONAL NAMES

References in these indexes are given according to the forms used in the translation, which is based on Ivor Arnold's text. Some personal names have been standardized to follow more widely recognized tradition: for example, Walwein is rendered as Gawain (also known as Gauvain), Artur as Arthur, and Ganhumare as Guinevere. Also included here are the better-known Latin equivalents, which are often, but not always, created by Geoffrey of Monmouth. Alternative forms occurring in the text, but not used in the translation, are given in brackets. For further information on the names in these indexes, see the indexes and notes to other published editions and translations of Wace's *Brut* which are cited in the first section of the Select Bibliography, and also Roland Blenner-Hassett, *A Study of the Place-Names in Lawman's Brut* (Stanford, CA: Stanford University Press, 1950), and Louis-Fernand Flutre, *Table des noms propres avec toutes leurs variantes figurant dans les écrits en français ou en provençal et actuellement publiés* (Poitiers: Centre d'études supérieures de civilisation médiévale, 1962).

INDEX OF GEOGRAPHICAL NAMES

The Oxford World's Classics Website

www.oxfordworldsclassics.com

- Browse the full range of Oxford World's Classics online
- Sign up for our monthly e-alert to receive information on new titles
- Read extracts from the Introductions
- Listen to our editors and translators talk about the world's greatest literature with our Oxford World's Classics audio guides
- Join the conversation, follow us on Twitter at OWC_Oxford
- Teachers and lecturers can order inspection copies quickly and simply via our website

www.oxfordworldsclassics.com

A SELECTION OF **OXFORD WORLD'S CLASSICS**

	Bhagavad Gita
	The Bible Authorized King James Version *With Apocrypha*
	The Book of Common Prayer
	Dhammapada
	The Gospels
	The Koran
	The Pañcatantra
	The Sauptikaparvan (from the Mahabharata)
	The Tale of Sinuhe and Other Ancient Egyptian Poems
	The Qur'an
	Upanisads
Anselm of Canterbury	**The Major Works**
Thomas Aquinas	**Selected Philosophical Writings**
Augustine	**The Confessions** **On Christian Teaching**
Bede	**The Ecclesiastical History**
Kālidāsa	**The Recognition of Śakuntalā**
Laozi	**Daodejing**
Rumi	**The Masnavi**
Śāntideva	**The Bodhicaryāvatāra**

A SELECTION OF **OXFORD WORLD'S CLASSICS**

	Classical Literary Criticism
	The First Philosophers: The Presocratics and the Sophists
	Greek Lyric Poetry
	Myths from Mesopotamia
APOLLODORUS	**The Library of Greek Mythology**
APOLLONIUS OF RHODES	**Jason and the Golden Fleece**
APULEIUS	**The Golden Ass**
ARISTOPHANES	**Birds and Other Plays**
ARISTOTLE	**The Nicomachean Ethics**
	Politics
ARRIAN	**Alexander the Great**
BOETHIUS	**The Consolation of Philosophy**
CAESAR	**The Civil War**
	The Gallic War
CATULLUS	**The Poems of Catullus**
CICERO	**Defence Speeches**
	The Nature of the Gods
	On Obligations
	Political Speeches
	The Republic and The Laws
EURIPIDES	**Bacchae and Other Plays**
	Heracles and Other Plays
	Medea and Other Plays
	Orestes and Other Plays
	The Trojan Women and Other Plays
HERODOTUS	**The Histories**
HOMER	**The Iliad**
	The Odyssey

A SELECTION OF OXFORD WORLD'S CLASSICS

HORACE	The Complete Odes and Epodes
JUVENAL	The Satires
LIVY	The Dawn of the Roman Empire Hannibal's War The Rise of Rome
MARCUS AURELIUS	The Meditations
OVID	The Love Poems Metamorphoses
PETRONIUS	The Satyricon
PLATO	Defence of Socrates, Euthyphro, and Crito Gorgias Meno and Other Dialogues Phaedo Republic Symposium
PLAUTUS	Four Comedies
PLUTARCH	Greek Lives Roman Lives Selected Essays and Dialogues
PROPERTIUS	The Poems
SOPHOCLES	Antigone, Oedipus the King, and Electra
SUETONIUS	Lives of the Caesars
TACITUS	The Annals The Histories
THUCYDIDES	The Peloponnesian War
VIRGIL	The Aeneid The Eclogues and Georgics
XENOPHON	The Expedition of Cyrus

A SELECTION OF **OXFORD WORLD'S CLASSICS**

	An Anthology of Elizabethan Prose Fiction
	Early Modern Women's Writing
	Three Early Modern Utopias (Utopia; New Atlantis; The Isle of Pines)
FRANCIS BACON	**Essays** **The Major Works**
APHRA BEHN	**Oroonoko and Other Writings** **The Rover and Other Plays**
JOHN BUNYAN	**Grace Abounding** **The Pilgrim's Progress**
JOHN DONNE	**The Major Works** **Selected Poetry**
JOHN FOXE	**Book of Martyrs**
BEN JONSON	**The Alchemist and Other Plays** **The Devil is an Ass and Other Plays** **Five Plays**
JOHN MILTON	**The Major Works** **Paradise Lost** **Selected Poetry**
EARL OF ROCHESTER	**Selected Poems**
SIR PHILIP SIDNEY	**The Old Arcadia** **The Major Works**
SIR PHILIP and MARY SIDNEY	**The Sidney Psalter**
IZAAK WALTON	**The Compleat Angler**